THE RISE OF PORTUGUESE POWER IN INDIA 1497-1550

THE RISE OF PORTUGUESE POWER IN INDIA
1497-1550

R. S. WHITEWAY

GYAN

Published by

GYAN

Gyan Publishing House
5, Ansari Road
Daryaganj, New Delhi-110002
Phone: 011-47034999, 9811692060
E-mail: books@gyanbooks.com

Distribution Network
gyanbooks.com
India, USA, Canada, UK, Australia, France

ISBN : 978-81-212-3963-9 (PB)
First Published, 1899

2nd Impression 2020

Printed at: Gyan Press, Delhi.

The Rise of Portuguese Power in India
1497-1550
Author: R. S. Whiteway

PREFACE

I KNOW of no English book which quite covers the ground that I have attempted to explore. The nearest approach to the subject was made in "The History of the Portuguese in India," published a few years since, but I have been unable to avail myself of the undoubted erudition of the author as he has not connected his narrative in any way with the general history of India.

In the study of Oriental history the absence of surnames is a great drawback, each individual stands alone, and his name awakens no chord of sympathy as when we read of the Cecil under Elizabeth and of the Cecil under Victoria. The Portuguese occupy an intermediate position between the East and West; the son, as a rule, takes his father's name, but not always: it requires some research to discover that Pero da Silva, Alvaro d'Ataide and Estavâo da Gama were all three sons of Vasco da Gama, and meanwhile our interest is dulled.

In the matter of Oriental names the Portuguese transliteration presents some difficulties—Çarcamdacâo for Sikandar Khan, Codavascâo for Khuda Bakhsh Khan, and Xacoez for Shaikh Iwaz are soluble, but some have defied indentification. Where possible the name has been taken from the "Taháfatu-l-Mujáhidín", from Elliot's "History of India" or from Bayley's "Gujarat." Before leaving the subject of names it may be noted that the different systems of cataloguing the Portuguese writers throws some difficulty in the way of enquirers. One of the early historians is

Fernâo Lopez de Castanheda; he is usually quoted as Castanheda and the custom has been followed here, but in the British Museum catalogue he will be found under Lopez, and, worse than all, under Fernâo in that monumental work, the Bibliotheca Lusitana of Diogo Barbosa Machado.

I have endeavoured to give a history of the rise of the Portuguese power in India derived from the best available sources, and to give, not merely a record of military expeditions and of the change of governors, but also the details which throw light on the social life and on the idiosyncrasies of the chief men of the time. I hope I may have succeeded. The Portuguese connection with Ceylon has been so fully dealt with by Sir Emerson Tennant, and its connection with the Malay States by Crawfurd, that only a summary has been added to give completeness to this book. If the subject prove of sufficient interest the work will be concluded with a volume on the decline of the Portuguese power in India.

In the first four chapters authorities have been freely quoted; in the remaining ones they are only given where the narrative is not based on the following historians:

Castanheda to	1538
Correa to	1550
Barros to	1526
Couto from 1526 to	1550

I have to thank Sir Alfred Lyall and Mr. E. White for valuable suggestions and advice.

CONTENTS

BIBLIOGRAPHY

Except where specially stated below, the quotations in the Notes give the reference to the page of the edition mentioned here.

ALBUQUERQUE, AFONSO D', *Cartas*, quoted as Cartas.

Vol. I, published by the Royal Academy of Lisbon in 1884.
Vol. II, promised, but not yet published.

Where they are contemporaneous the Letters supersede the Commentaries, but they do not cover so long a period.

ALBUQUERQUE, AFONSO D', *Commentaries.*

Translation. Hakluyt Society. 4 volumes. 1875—1884.

ALVAREZ, FATHER FRANCISCO, *Narrative of the Portuguese Embassy to Abyssinia, 1520—1527.*

Translation. Hakluyt Society. 1881.

ANDRADE, J. F. D', *Vida de D. João de Castro*, quoted in the text as Vida.

The Edition used is that edited by Fr. Francisco de S. Luiz and published by the Royal Lisbon Academy in 1835. It is a bombastic and untrustworthy work.

ANNAES MARITIMOS E COLONIAES, quoted as An. Mar. e Col.

A periodical in 6 volumes or series, 1840—46. The reprints of original papers are contained in the non-official part. They unfortunately follow no order of any kind, alphabetical or chronological. The documents appear to have been literally transcribed and are very important.

ARCHIVO PORTUGUEZ ORIENTAL, quoted as Ar. Port. Or

Most of the quotations give the number of the Fasciculus and of the document, a few, when the fact is noted, give the page of the volume. These are publications of State papers from the Goa Archives. They commence from 1515 and are of the greatest interest.

Fasciculo 1. Letters from the King of Portugal to the City of Goa.—2nd Edition, One Volume. 1877.

Fasciculo 2. Privileges of the City of Goa, including copies of complaints made to the King by the City.—One Volume. 1857.

Fasciculo 3. Letters and Orders of the King of Portugal to Viceroys and Governors.—Two Volumes. 1861.

Fasciculo 4. Ecclesiastical Councils of Goa and the Synod of Diamper.—One Volume. 1862.

Fasciculo 5. Miscellaneous Documents.—Three Volumes. 1863.

Fasciculo 6. Miscellaneous orders of the King and Viceroy, commencing with the 17th century.—One Volume. 1875.

BAYLEY, Sir E. C., *Gujarat*, 1886.

A collection of the local histories of Guzerat, translated on the principle of Elliot's "History of India." Unfortunately only Vol. I was ever published.

BARBOSA, DUARTE, *The Coasts of East Africa and Malabar.*

Translation from the Spanish. Hakluyt Society. 1866.

Barbosa went to India as early as 1500. Correa frequently praises his learning and his knowledge of the Indian languages.

BARBOSA, DUARTE, Same work in Portuguese.

Published by the Royal Lisbon Academy in 1867.

BARROS, JOÃO DE,
COUTO, DIOGO DE, } *Decadas.* 24 Volumes. 1778—1788.

The quotations are given by Decades, Books and Chapters.

Barros is an official historian: he is rhetorical and was never in India. His facts are well arranged, but as an authority he ranks below those who knew the country. His statements sometimes clash with those of the original documents and occasionally show extreme ignorance of India. Three Decades, ending with the death of Henrique de Menezes, were published between 1552 and 1563, in the author's lifetime. The fourth Decade, which purports to have been made up from notes, was published in 1615; its value is small. Couto, who continued the work from the end of the third decade, was also an official historian, but he spent almost all, if not all, his life in India after 1556. His 4th, 5th, 6th and 7th Decades alone were printed during the author's lifetime; the 6th Decade was burned after printing, before publication, and we learn from Barbosa Machado in his work, Bibliotheca Lusitana, *s.v.* Adeodato da Trinidade, that Adeodato, who was Couto's brother-in-law, touched up the sixth Decade previous to reprinting into the form we now have it, to please certain persons who did not like the unvarnished narrative of Couto. The remainder of Couto's papers came also into the possession of this brother-in-law. The 8th and 9th Decades were stolen in Couto's lifetime from his house while still in manuscript—what we have now is an abstract prepared by him. The 11th, though it was written, has never been found; its place has been supplied by a compilation of the Editor in the edition used here. The 8th Decade was published in 1673 the 9th in 1736; 5 Books of the 12th (all that exist), to the end of the term of D. Francisco da Gama, in 1645. The 10th Decade, which was the first composed, was not printed in full until 1788. Couto died in 1616. Where his history is untouched it is of great value.

BERMUDEZ, D. JOÂO DE, *Breve relaçâo da embaixada.*

Published in 1565 and reissued by the Royal Lisbon Academy in 1875.

BOCARRO, ANTONIO DE, *Decada XIII.* Written in 1635.

First published in two volumes by the Royal Lisbon Academy in 1872.

BOTELHO, SIMÂO, *O Tombo do Estado da India.* Written in 1554.

First published in *Subsidios* by the Royal Academy of Lisbon in 1868.

BOTELHO, SIMÂO, *Cartas*. Letters dated from 1547—1552.

Contained in the same volume as the *Tombo* with separate paging.

CABRAL, PEDRO ALVAREZ, *Navegaçâo*. A Contemporary account of his voyage written by an anonymous pilot.

Published first in Ramusio, Vol I, and translated from Italian into Portuguese and Published by the Royal Lisbon Academy in 1867.

CALCOEN.

A Dutch narrative of the second voyage of Vasco da Gama, translated into English by J. Ph. Berjean and published in 1874—very valuable, but wants editing.

CAMOENS, LUIZ DE, *Os Lusiadas*.

CASTANHEDA, FERNÂO LOPEZ DE, *Historia do descobrimento e Conquista da India*.

A history in 8 books, ending with the term of Nuno da Cunha. Quoted in the text with the number of the book and chapter from the reprint of 1833. Couto (IV. 5. 1.) tells us that there were originally 10 books, but 2 were destroyed by order of the King on the complaint of certain persons that the truth was told too plainly. Castanheda went to India in 1528 and stayed there about ten years. All his history is very valuable indeed, more especially the first six books. Where his work can be compared with original documents it stands the test well. Books 1 to 6 were printed partly in 1552 and partly in 1554, the last two in 1561 after the author's death.

CASTANHOSO, MIGUEL, *Historia das cousas que o muy esforçado capitâo D. Christovâo da Gama fez nos Reynos do Preste João*.

A history of the Abyssinian expedition under Christovâo da Gama in 1541, by a member of it. Printed in 1564 and republished by the Royal Lisbon Academy in 1855. A most noteworthy narrative.

CASTRO, D. JOÂO, *Roteiro no anno de 1541*.

Published in 1833.

CASTRO, D. JOÂO, *Primeiro roteiro da Costa da India.* (1538—1539.)

Published 1843.

Both the above logs contain passages of considerable value; that of his voyage out as Governor in 1545 is of little use. His letters are scattered over several periodicals. See Investigador Portuguez—Instituto—Revista Universal.

COLERIDGE, Father H. J., *Life of St. Francis Xavier.*

2 Vols. 1890.

CORREA, GASPAR, *Lendas da India.*

First published bv the Royal Lisbon Academy in 4 Volumes. 1858—61. Correa went out first in 1512, part of his history was written as late as 1566; the date of his death is unknown. It would be easy to prove from the work that he had Castanheda's history before him when he wrote. Vol. I is legendary, the atmosphere is oriental and the facts are very dubious. The other volumes beginning with the term of Albuquerque, whose secretary Correa was, are of the very highest interest. A translation of the three voyages of Vasco da Gama from the Lendas was published by the Hakluyt Society in 1869.

COUTO, DIOGO DE, *Decadas.* See BARROS.

COUTO, DIOGO DE, *Soldado Pratico.*

Published in 1790. A diffuse work on the evils that afflicted the Portuguese Government of India at the end of the 16th century, written with much parade of learning. The author died in 1616.

DELLA VALLE, PIETRO, *Travels.*

Translation. Hakluyt Society. 2 Vols. 1892.

ELLIOT, Sir H., *History of India.* 8 Vols. 1867—77.

EMPOLI JOÂO DE, *Viagem.* (1503.)

Published in Ramusio Vol. I, translated into Portuguese and published by the Royal Lisbon Academy in 1867.

FALCÂO, LUIZ DE FIGUEIREDO, *Livro em que se contem toda a fazenda e real patrimonio* (1612) 1859.

A monument of the industry of the Secretary to Philip III of Spain and II of Portugal, first published in 1859.

FARIA Y SOUSA, MANOEL, *Asia Portugueza.*

A late writer in Spanish. 3 Volumes. 1674. Vols. I and II are little more than compilations from Barros and Couto. An English translation by Captain J. Stevens in 3 Vols. published in 1695 is incomplete. It omits whole passages.

FONSECA, JOSÉ NICOLAU DE, *Goa*, 1878.

Published in English in connection with the Indian Gazetteer.

FRYER, DR. JOHN, *New account of the East Indies and Persia.* 1698.

GALVANO, A., *Discoveries of the World.*

Translation. Hakluyt Society. 1862.

HAKLUYT, RICHARD, *Principal Navigations of the English Navigators.*

5 Volumes. 1809—1812.

IBN BATUTA, *Travels.*

Translated by Lee. (O. T. F.) 1829.

INSTITUTO, O, COIMBRA. 2 Vols. 1854.

Some of D. Joâo de Castro's letters were published in this periodical.

INVESTIGADOR PORTUGUEZ. Vol. XVI. 1811.

In this volume of this periodical were published some of D. Joâo de Castro's letters.

LEGUAT, FRANÇOIS, *Voyage.*

Translation. Hakluyt Society. 2 Vols. 1891.

LEMBRANÇA DAS COUSAS DA INDIA. (1525.)

Published in *Subsidios* by the Royal Lisbon Academy, 1868.

LINSCHOTEN, *Voyages.*

Translation. Hakluyt Society. 2 Vols. 1885.

LIVROS DOS MONCÔES, 4 Volumes.

Published by the Royal Academy of Lisbon, 1880—1893. The records reprinted run from 1568 to 1618.

LOGAN, W., *Malabar.* 2 Vols. 1887.

LOPES THOMÉ, *Navegaçâo.* (1502.)

First published in Ramusio Vol. 1, this was translated back into Portuguese and published by the Royal Academy of Lisbon in 1867. The author has considerable literary ability.

MAGALHAENS, FERNÂO, *Roteiro da Viagem.*

Published by the Royal Lisbon Academy, 1826.

MAGALHAENS, FERNÂO, *The First Voyage round the World.*

Hakluyt Society. 1874.

MAJOR, R. H., *India in the XVth Century.*

Hakluyt Society. 1857.

MAJOR, R. H., *Life of Prince Henry of Portugal.* 1868.

MIDDLETON, Sir H., *Voyage to Bantam and Maluco.*

Hakluyt Society. 1855.

MOCQUET, JEAN, *Voyages.* 1830.

This is a reprint of the earlier edition. The voyage to Goa was in 1608.

NAZARETH, JOSÉ MARIA DO CARMO, *Numismatica da India Portugueza.* 1890.

NUNES, ANTONIO, *O Livro dos pesos medidas e moedas.*

Published in *Subsidios* by the Royal Academy of Lisbon, 1868. Written in 1554.

ORTA, GARCIA DE, *Colloquios dos simples e drogas e cousas medicinaes da India.* 1872.

First published in 1563. It covers far more ground than its title promises.

PINTO, FERNÂO MENDEZ, *Perigranaçôes.* 4 Vols. 1829.

A romance with some traditions embedded. First published in 1614, it professes to relate events for some years from 1538.

PURCHAS, SAMUEL, *His Pilgrimes.* 1625—26.

PYRARD, FRANÇOIS, *Voyage.*

Translation. Hakluyt Society. 2 Vols. 1887—90.

RAE, GEORGE MILNES, *The Syrian Church in India.* 1892.

REBELLO, GABRIEL, *Informação das Cousas de Maluco.*

Published by the Royal Academy of Lisbon, 1856. A valuable book written in 1569.

REVISTA UNIVERSAL. 2nd series. Vol. I. 1849.

Contains one letter of D. João de Castro.

ROTEIRO DA VIAGEM DE VASCO DA GAMA. 2nd edition. 1861.

A translation has been published by the Hakluyt Society.

ROWLANDSON, *Taháfat ul Majáhidín.* (O. T. F.) 1833.

STEPHENS, H. MORSE, *Portugal* in "Story of the Nations" Series. 1891.

STEPHENS, H. MORSE, *Albuquerque* in the "Rulers of India" Series. 1892.

SUBSIDIOS, see BOTELHO, LEMBRANÇA, NUNES.

TENREYRO, ANTONIO, *Itinerario.* 1829.

A reprint of an interesting account of an overland journey in 1528.

VARTHEMA, LUDOVICO DI, *Travels.*

Translation. Hakluyt Society. 1863.

YULE, Sir H., *Marvels described by Fr. Jordanus.*

Hakluyt Society. 1863.

YULE, Sir H., *Cathay and the Way Thither.* 2 Vols.

Hakluyt Society. 1866.

YULE, Sir H., *Glossary.* 1886.

CHAPTER I

INTRODUCTORY

BEFORE the last quarter of the 15th century the Indian Ocean was to the Christian nations of the West a closed sea, penetrated only by a few daring explorers. The Cape of Good Hope was unknown, and the routes overland from the Red Sea and the Persian Gulf had been barred to Christians by the advance of the followers of the Muhamedan faith. Africa, which bounds that ocean on the west, has changed but little during the last four centuries. Then, as now, it exported raw material only; and among its indigenous population there were no seafaring races. India, which bounds it on the east, had advanced far on the road of civilization, but the majority of its inhabitants were of the Hindu religion and were debarred by its tenets from crossing the sea. In the 5th century Chinese ships were seen as far north as the banks of the Euphrates; the length of their voyages, however, gradually lessened, and by the beginning of the 15th century they came no further than the Malabar Coast. About the middle of that century they ceased to visit India altogether; but when the Portuguese reached Calicut, their memory was quite fresh in the minds of the people.[1]

At the time when this history opens, the whole of the carrying trade of the Indian Ocean, both to the east and to the

[1] The Arabs visited China from a very early date. In the 15th century the Calicut people were called *Chini bachagan*.—India in the 15th Century: Abdu-r-razak, p. 19.

west, was in the hands of those who dwelt on its northern littoral. The wealth that the monopoly of this carrying trade poured through those two gates, the mouth of the Red Sea and the mouth of the Persian Gulf, into the marts of Arabia and Persia, has tinged the dreams of the Arabian Nights and given a definite bent to the popular conception of the East. But it did more—it supplied the sinews of war without which the fanaticism of the Muhamedan armies would in vain have attempted a footing in Europe. The chief importance to the world at large of the discovery of the route to India by the Cape of Good Hope lay in the blow that this discovery struck at the Muhamedan power. It is true that Spain and Portugal had freed themselves before Vasco da Gama sailed from the Tagus, and it is true that for many years after the Portuguese fleets had temporarily cleared the Indian Ocean of the Red Sea traders, the Turkish advance hung like a nightmare over Venice and Hungary, nevertheless the main artery had been cut when the Portuguese took up the challenge of the Muhamedan merchants of Calicut and swept their ships from the ocean. I propose to trace the events—often gloomy and even repulsive—that accompanied the intrusion of this Western power into the alien civilization of the East,—an intrusion which that East has resented by absorbing and degrading the intruder. Disastrous though the results have been to the nation that opened the new route, the effect on the history of the world of its action has been imperishable, and Portugal can look back with pride to the strenuous efforts of a century that culminated in the discovery of the Cape of Good Hope by Bartholomew Dias, and to the pages of its history that are illuminated by the names of Albuquerque, Duarte Pacheco, Magalhaens,[1] and of the uncle Paulo and his nephews, Estavâo and Christovâo da Gama.

[1] Better known in England as Magellan.

From before the dawn of history the Arabs had been the carriers of the merchandize of the East across the Indian Ocean, and after the discovery, in the first century of our era, of the succession of the seasons which enabled ships to cross and recross with regularity, they monopolized this carrying trade.[1] They had a large admixture of Semitic blood in their veins, and had at least one peculiarity of that race very strongly marked—they were not producers, but traders. Not only did they monopolize the sea-borne traffic, but they also, in Southern India, distributed the merchandize thus brought, to the consumer on land. For instance, when Duarte Pacheco had, in 1504, to defend Cochin from the attacks of the Samuri and the Muhamedan traders whom he patronized, one of his first difficulties was that all the stocks of grain were in the hands of Muhamedan dealers, who could have caused a famine had they opposed him. That country does not grow sufficient rice to support its population, and the people only bought enough to last them for a few weeks' consumption.

These "Moors," as the Portuguese called them, were keen traders, and, though ready to convert inquirers to their own faith, they never, in spite of the assertions of the Portuguese to the contrary, attempted to acquire political independence save where such independence was essential to the conservation of their own community. On the Indian Coast they found a settled polity and they accepted it. We must come down late in Indian history to find a state founded by non-Europeans from over the sea, and then only by Abyssinian corsairs. The great Muhamedan states of India have been founded from the inside by armies marching over the land, not by armies carried by the sea.

[1] This is the more remarkable as there is little wood on their coasts suited for shipbuilding. Indian-built ships, manned by Arabs, appear to have been in use when the Portuguese reached India.

But while this was the history of the "Moors" in India, their history in Africa and the further East is different. On the African Coast they had to deal with savages with no fixed form of government, and here, like the Phenicians, they formed independent self-governing colonies, sometimes almost republican in their institutions; where possible, on an island, and always in an easily defensible position. Even with all their precautions an invading horde of negroes would at times sweep away their settlement. Thus, in 1598, Kilwa was destroyed when a Muhamedan treacherously showed the negro leaders a ford. [1] In the further East, where they came in contact with the semi-civilized Malays, their conduct somewhat approximated to that in India, save that their proselytizing zeal was greater. In India, where they met a religion far older than their own, their converts were mainly from the outcaste population, men to whom the change from Muhamedanism meant a complete elevation of their social status. A Poler who could not approach within a 100 yards [2] of a Nambutri Brahmin, who had to howl like a wild beast as he walked, to warn all others of his polluted vicinity, had everything to gain by adopting a faith which admitted him at once to a social equality with the best in the land. [3] On the Indian Coast, therefore, there were few converts among those of the higher castes; among the Malays, on the other hand, a very large number of the ruling families, who drew after them the people they governed, adopted the Muhamedan religion.

Malacca, the great emporium of the further East, had been a dependency of Siam, but late in the 15th century

[1] Couto, XI. Ch. 10 and 1

[2] Ninety-six steps is the exact distance.—Asiatic Researches, V. p. 5.

[3] Later, when the Malabar pirates infested the coast and paid tribute to the Samuri, the latter (though a Hindu) ordered that a certain number of the Makkuwar caste should be brought up as Muhamedans, to supply sailors to the piratical craft.—Pyrard de Laval, Vol. I., p. 389.

it declared its independence. Its air was unwholesome, and it could not even supply food for its resident population. The original trading centre was in Singapur, but early in the 15th century the defeated party in a civil war in Java fled to the Muar river, and a few years later these emigrants settled on the spot, a few miles distant, where Malacca now stands. For the navigators of that period the prevailing winds made the voyages from the East and from the West more expeditious to Malacca than to Singapur. Aided by this and by the conversion of the colonists to Muhamedanism, the new settlement grew rapidly at the expense of the old. Malacca was not a trading city in the modern sense of the word; it was during the season the site of a vast fair where the products of China and the extreme East were bartered for those of the West. There were some coins of small value current to pay wages and to buy daily necessaries, but with that exception money was not used; gold and silver were articles of trade, but the public convenience was not consulted by impressing on fixed quantities any public stamp. At the height of the season the population is said to have reached a million. This was perhaps an exaggeration, and certainly such a number were only gathered for a very short time. The arrangements for this multitude were good: each nationality had its own leader, and free use of the differing religions and customs was allowed to all.[1] The administration must have been efficient even if the standard were low, or such a fair could not have been held year after year in the territory of a petty prince.

Malacca commanded the narrows between Sumatra and the Malay Peninsula, in which all the traffic of India and China was concentrated. Ormuz similarly commanded the

[1] Dobbo in the Aru islands must be the nearest modern approach to Malacca, though falling far short of it in volume of trade. See Wallace's "Malay Archipelago," Ch. 32.

narrows through which the trade of the East with Persia, and through Persia with Europe, had to pass. Ormuz, including both the island and some territory on the mainland, was ruled by a Muhamedan dynasty tributary to Persia. The city was formerly on the mainland, and Marco Polo saw it there, but at the end of the 13th century it was, apparently to avoid the attacks of predatory tribes, moved to the island Jerun. This island had no fresh water nor any green thing; but its immunity from raids, and its harbour which allowed ships to lie close to the town, combined to bring to Ormuz all the sea-borne traffic from India and the caravan-borne traffic from Aleppo, to break bulk in its bazaars. The imaginary delights of its arid and sunburnt shores have inspired the rhapsodies of poets. From Ormuz Indian wares found their way, in smaller boats more suited to the navigation, to Basra, where the trade routes divided, —some caravans started for Trebizond and others for Aleppo and Damascus. On the shores of the Mediterranean the goods were purchased by Venetians and Genoese for distribution over Europe.

Jedda was to the traffic of the East that went through the Red Sea, what Ormuz was to the Persian Gulf branch. North of Jedda the navigation of the Red Sea is hampered by reefs and shoals, and at Jedda the sea-going vessels stopped, and goods were transferred to smaller boats that went to Suez. From Suez the merchandize crossed the desert to Cairo on camels, and thence went down the Nile to Alexandria, where it was purchased for European consumption chiefly by Venetians. When the operations of the Portuguese in the Indian Ocean interfered with free navigation, Aden at the mouth of the Red Sea grew at the expense of Jedda. It was more easy to ship through from India to Aden and back than to undertake the longer voyage.

On the Indian Coast, trade was more scattered, and there was no great emporium. Partly owing to the configuration of the coast line, and partly to the prevailing winds, most of the lines of traffic ran to points on the west coast. Chittagong was one of the chief ports in the Bay of Bengal, but on the west coast there were several trading centres more important than it. At Calicut, through, however, no favour of Nature, all the Red Sea merchants had their factors; the town is situated on an unbroken coast line open to the full force of the south-western monsoon, and it stands near no navigable river that could bring the produce from the interior. The ruler of Calicut, the Samuri, had become the chief of the numerous Nair principalities of Malabar, and the countenance which he consistently showed to the Muhamedan traders brought them to make Calicut their headquarters, and in turn they helped him, by the wealth they poured into the country, to retain his supremacy.

The profits on wares sent from the East to Europe were enormous to bear the cost of passage through so many jurisdictions and the expense of so many transhipments. There has come down to us a detailed statement of the payments made by merchants trading from India to Alexandria, which is full of interest; it refers to a time when an independent Sultan ruled in Cairo, but under the Ottoman Turks the payments would certainly not have been smaller. The Red Sea merchants lived in Jedda and had their factors in Calicut. The regulations of the Sultan of Cairo required that one-third of the imports should be pepper, and this amount must be sold to him in Jedda at Calicut prices. Say a merchant brought goods from Calicut to the value there of £300, and among them no pepper. He would have to buy in Jedda, at Jedda prices, pepper worth in Calicut £100, and resell it to the Sultan at the Calicut price. On the balance of the goods he would pay 10 per cent. ad valorem, and again on the balance after deducting this ten per cent., four per cent. more. Instead, however, of getting the Calicut price of the pepper in money, he was compelled to take copper in Jedda from the Sultan at Calicut prices,—that is, copper in Jedda was worth 7 cruzados the quintal, but this he was compelled to buy at 12 cruzados, the Calicut price. Practically, therefore, the Sultan of Cairo was, at no expense to himself, a partner to the extent of one-third in every voyage. In spite of these exactions the profits on the double journey would be very large indeed.

To continue, however, with the goods to Europe. Brought to Suez in smaller boats from Jedda, the importer had to pay 5 per cent. ad valorem in ready money; and to supply this money there were banks at Suez prepared to cash drafts. The journey to Cairo took three days; and a camel to carry about 450 lbs. cost about *37s 6d.* A mile out of Cairo the goods were registered. The value of pepper in the Cairo market was about 20*d* the pound, and a merchant buying pepper had to buy an amount equal to one-third of his purchases in the open market, from the Sultan at 25 per cent. over the market value, and, in addition, pay 5 per cent. as customs on all his purchases. From Cairo the goods were taken down the Nile in boats, and were carried from the river to Alexandria on camels. At Alexandria they were registered again, and buyer and seller had each to pay 5 per cent. ad valorem. The shipper had also to pay 5 per cent. to frank him across the sea. [1]

On the African Coast the natives were mere savages, with Arab settlements dotted at intervals. Abyssinia did not

[1] See Castanheda, II. 75. Barros, I. 8. 1.

touch the sea coast, but though the government of Massowah was in the hands of Muhamedans the King of Abyssinia had, when powerful, some influence over it. In Egypt there reigned, at the end of the 15th century, the last of the independent Mamluk Sultans, El Ashraf Kansuh el Ghori, whose sway extended over part of Syria to the north, and to the Euphrates on the east. On the west coast of the Red Sea he held Suakin, and as much to the south as his arms commanded. On the east of that sea, and indeed over the whole of Arabia there were several semi-independent chieftains whose relations to their suzerain the Sultan of Egypt and to each other were continually varying. Of these the more important were the Sharif Barakat of Mecca and Amir ibn Abdu-l-wahab, who ruled over Yemen.

Speaking generally, the Sultan of Egypt was the overlord of the western shores of the Persian Gulf, and the Shah of Persia of the eastern. Between Jask and the Indus stretched a coast that was a no-man's land, where from early times pirates made their home. In India, Guzerat was the first maritime state of any importance; it had one port, Diu, of very considerable trade and many others of less importance. Guzerat had separated from Delhi in 1408; from 1459 to 1511 the reigning prince was Sultan Mahmud Bigarha, the

> Prince of Cambay whose daily food
> Is asp, basilisk and toad

of our poet Butler. Between Guzerat and the Hindu state of Vijayanagara, that began just south of Goa, lay the states, that had sprung up about 1480 on the dissolution of the kingdom founded by Alau-d-din Bahmani at Kulbarga. They were (1) the Imad Khani of Berar: (2) The Barid Shahi of Bidar: (3) The Nizam Shahi of Ahmadnagar: (4) The Adil Shahi of Bijapur. The Portuguese were chiefly brought into contact with the two last as they alone held, the coast line. South of these Muhamedan states lay the great Hindu kingdom of Vijayanagara, whose capital was at Vijayanagara on the Tungabudra river. On the western side the Raja's coast line only extended from a point a little south of Goa to another just north of Cananor, but on the east nearly the whole littoral from just north of Cape Comorin to the Kistna river was either directly his or held by his tributaries.

South of Vijayanagara on the west coast were the numerous Malabar states. The Samuri who ruled in Calicut was the chief. Over Cananor and the states to the north his suzerainty was little more than nominal, but over Cochin and the southern states, where pepper was produced and through which it passed, it was very real. The cardinal fact of Malabar politics, and one of which the Portuguese cleverly availed themselves, was the rivalry between the Samuri of Calicut and the Raja of Cochin. In the 9th century the Perumal who ruled in Cranganor over the whole of Malabar, became a Muhamedan, went to Arabia and died there. He had, before he left, divided up his country among the several chiefs, and of these the Raja of Cochin was, at the end of the 15th century, his direct representative, and in his capital, Cochin, there was preserved the sacred stone at which certain ceremonies had to be performed before sovereign rights could be claimed over the southern principalities. The position, however, of the Raja of Cochin had become quite subordinate; he was periodically displaced and re-invested by the Samuri, and he could neither coin money nor even roof his house with tiles. [1] Both the states of Calicut and Cochin retained at that time customs which pointed back to a very great antiquity. In the reigning

[1] Duarte Barbosa, p. 156.

families of both the head was a priest in a temple, and the next in succession was the ruling chief. In Calicut also there was held that festival, every 12 years, at which if any one member of certain families could kill the reigning Samuri he became chief in his place.[1] Quilon (Koulam), south of Cochin, was a dependency of Travancore and both were included in Malabar. Of all the ports on the Malabar coast Cochin was by far the best, though it was comparatively modern, as the island of Vaipeen had been thrown up after a great land flood in 1341 A.D. Owing to shoal water for some distance from the shores, it is unsuited to modern ocean-going steamers, but for the vessels of those days the depth was sufficient. Once over the bar, a series of magnificent salt-water lagoons and creeks connected Cochin with all the pepper-producing districts.

The structure of society in Malabar was highly artificial. The ruling and military race was the Nair caste, who, like all the inhabitants of Malabar except the Brahmins, ranked socially as Sudras, the lowest of the four great divisions, because they were converts and not Hindus born. The priests were Brahmins, the descendants of the missionaries who had carried Hinduism to the south. The Nairs subsisted on the industry of those still lower in the scale. A Nair might approach, but not touch a Brahmin; but the lower castes could only come within shouting distance of his sacred presence. The Nairs practised polyandry, and consequently the sons of sisters, as their relationship was certain on one side at least, inherited.[2] The great feature of the Nair character was fidelity to an employer, and

[1] For the explanation of this custom see Frazer's "Golden Bough", Vol. I. p. 225. A similar custom obtained in Sumatra and Bengal, though in these places it was not so formal; the chief might be killed at any time, though only by men of certain families.

[2] In Europe as late as the early Middle Ages the relation of a man to his sister's son was looked on as a specially sacred tie.

advantage was taken of this to employ them as Jangadas,[1] both as guides on a journey and to guard property. The Portuguese had, for instance, a jangada for each of their forts in Malabar. It was the duty of the jangada to defend anything entrusted to him with his life, and it was a serious matter to kill him, as it involved a blood feud with all his relatives. Instances are very frequent of the great trouble that resulted when owing to any cause the Nairs shaved their heads and devoted themselves to death.[2]

When the Portuguese first went to India any general combination against them was impossible; Hindus and Muhamedans were engaged in a death-struggle over the great kingdom of Vijayanagara, and both looked on the intruding Portuguese as unclean corsairs who were unworthy of serious attention. When later the Portuguese had acquired a footing in the country, and the battle of Talikot in 1565 had extinguished the last important Hindu state outside Malabar, the Muhamedans in 1570—78 made a combined attack on the Portuguese. That failed, and soon after the increasing pressure of the English and Dutch from the sea, and of the Emperors of Delhi from the north, left no leisure for further combination.

The Portuguese were never opposed to any of the races who now furnish the recruits for the Indian fighting army, nor did their rule ever extend a day's march from their ships. Their power therefore was essentially dependent upon their predominance at sea; they were never in a position to assume the offensive on shore, and they were strictly limited to defending their factories and forts, when menaced. Owing to certain moral defects of which more will be said hereafter, the race had no power of combined action, and

[1] In Malayalam, Channadam. See Yule Glossary *s.v.*

[2] The Nairs are now one of the most progressive races in India.

consequently no administrative faculty. The history of its connection with India is thus a series of episodes, interesting as revelations of character and social life, but showing few possibilities of organic growth. There is no machinery of government to be explained, for it is of little use to investigate orders that were only obeyed as far as it was convenient, and which were disregarded when they became irksome.

At the outset there were some grounds for hope that the bold attempt of the Portuguese to found an empire at a distance of more than half a year's voyage from their homes, might be successful. Albuquerque, great as a soldier, for he could repair defeat as well as organize victory, also showed high qualities as a governor. Afonso Mexia, 10 years later, and Simâo Botelho, 20 years after him, are examples of that official class which is the backbone of efficient civil administration; and had they been samples of a body of government servants rather than isolated individuals, they would have done much to render the Portuguese power permanent. Unfortunately for Portugal, she fell under the grip of religious superstition at the very time when her vital energies, sapped by the disappearance of a vigorous body of aristocratic leaders, required renewal and not repression. It was the final blow when she passed under the dominion of Spain. The actual tragedy of the story, when the gallant little country of Portugal, her life-blood drained by her efforts in the East and the West, fell an easy victim first to the reaction of Southern Europe against the religious movements of the North, and then to the temporal despotism of her powerful neighbour Spain, falls outside the limits of this volume; but it is necessary to make some reference to this important political catastrophe in order to group and explain the events which will form the subject of my narrative.

CHAPTER II

The Portuguese—Malabar

The Portuguese.—The Portuguese nation was moulded in a hard school. Until the end of the 11th century its history was that of the rest of the Spanish Peninsula. Peopled originally by Celts, it had been thoroughly incorporated with the Roman Empire, but its subsequent history so far differed from that of Spain that the wave of invading Visigoths had spent some of its force before the Western Ocean was reached, and its nobility rarely claim Gothic descent. With the rest of the Peninsula it was subdued by the Moors in the 8th century. Its existence as a separate entity began in 1095 A.D., when Count Henry of Burgundy was given the County of Portugal as the dowry of his wife Theresa. The limits of the new county comprised, however, only the districts of Coimbra and Oporto, which within the preceding 100 years had been won back from the Moors by dint of hard fighting. This contest had not been carried on by the original inhabitants, the Celts, but by armies recruited from the north, and the first Count of the new county was himself a French Knight.

In the struggle with the Moors that occupied the next two and a half centuries, the leaders, in the absence of a native nobility, were the flower of northern chivalry. The armies, too, were at first recruited by northern crusading soldiers, and it was not until some years had elapsed that the native inhabitants of either the cities or the country were swept into the general movement. By the middle of the 13th century, however, when the Muhamedan Wars on Portuguese soil ceased, the effects of the long struggle had penetrated to all classes, the towns emerged with municipal institutions, and the people had, through the Cortes, some voice in the government of the country. Still a large share of the soil was owned by the great military orders of foreign knights, the price that had to be paid for their assistance. Early in the 14th century the connection of the knights with foreign orders was severed, and they themselves remained to form the nucleus of an aristocracy, northern in blood, but Portuguese by residence. In the civil troubles at the end of that century, which shook the foundations of the monarchy, the aristocracy and the people were found united, and in 1385 they fought side by side at the Battle of Aljubarotta.

For the next 100 years the history of Portugal is the history of the strenuous effort to discover the sea-route to the East, and the leading figure is Prince Henry of Portugal, named the Navigator, son of King John I of Portugal, and great-grandson of King Edward III of England. Early in the 15th century he settled at Sagres, and from that date till his death in 1460 he sent out annual expeditions that explored painfully the African coast. He found nothing ready to his hand. His vessels were half-decked boats, his men long-shore sailors who would not or could not navigate out of sight of land. The assistance of mathematicians and astronomers, often Jews, was called in and a school of navigators formed. Cape Boyador, on the African coast, 1,000 miles from Portugal, was not passed until 1434, for years before expedition after expedition had been turned back by the terrors of a shoal that stretched out to sea, over which the water foamed and boiled.[1] Into the history

[1] For the terrors of Cape Boyador see Barros, I. 1. 2.

of this century, during which, from such commencements. were moulded the explorers who discovered half the world, it is not necessary to enter.[1]

By the rounding of the Cape of Good Hope in 1487, by Bartholomew Dias, that route to the East for which the King of Portugal and Prince Henry had been so long seeking, was at length opened. In these explorations the leaders of the Portuguese nation were following a truly national policy; their aims were chiefly commercial. The Italian republics had for many generations been enriched by the trade with the East, and beyond the Italian merchants lay the Muhamedan merchants. The discovery of a sea-route to India promised to transfer the profits of both to the Portuguese,—that, in so doing, the hated Muhamedan would suffer, was an added incentive. They hoped also to discover an ally in a Christian prince whose territory they located vaguely in Africa,—a powerful and mysterious potentate known as Prester John. The first object was therefore commercial—the injury to their hereditary foe, the Muhamedan, supplied an undercurrent of crusading interest. An age, however, in which the spiritual head of the Christian Church, the Pope himself, was in treaty with the Sultan of Turkey as to the terms on which he (the Pope) should murder the latter's brother,[2] could not have been one in which religious aims took a very prominent position. The genius of Albuquerque brought to the front the question of empire, but in his mind empire and commerce went hand in hand; he supplied no new aim, he merely pointed out a new method of attaining an old object.

King John II (1481—95) during his short but illustrious

1 The last word for the present has been said in Major's "Prince Henry the Navigator."

2 Charles VIII of France captured the correspondence on this subject between Pope Alexander VI and Sultan Bayazid II.

reign, had been, to use the simile of Barros, roaring round Africa like a famished lion seeking an entrance to a guarded enclosure. He continued the sea exploration begun by his uncle, and he also sent out land expeditions, one of which penetrated to Timbuctoo, while another explored overland the Indian Ocean and its trade routes. At home he broke the power of the feudal aristocracy, with the result that the crown in Portugal became despotic, and there was set free a reserve of energy that would have otherwise been spent in domestic intrigue and violence. The power thus released supplied the leaders that, within 50 years of his death, carried the Portuguese to the remotest corners of the earth and brought that nation to the summit of its glory. This aristocracy, as has been already said, was foreign in its origin, and there is nothing to show that the waste of such a body in an adventurous career could be made good from a lower stratum of the people.

Prince Henry encouraged his Captains to bring home specimens of the natives of the countries they discovered, partly as valuable merchandize, and partly to open communication with new tribes by learning the different dialects. It became a settled policy to promote marriages between these captives and the people of Portugal, this was the first step in a path that has led to very important results, and it is hard to overestimate the importance to the nation of this development. The Portuguese have shown an alacrity not found in other European nations, to mix their race with others differing entirely in status from themselves.

Emmanuel,[1] who succeeded John II, was well surnamed the Fortunate. He succeeded to the results of the efforts

[1] Usually called Manoel.

of his predecessors, and he found ready to his hands the instruments they had formed; even the preparations for the expedition of Vasco da Gama were well advanced. As one of his first acts showed, Emmanuel had no personal qualifications that fitted him for the great part he was called on to play. The Portuguese Jews were among the most renowned in Europe; the whole machinery of the commerce of the country was in their hands, and they were foremost in intelligence and commercial probity. In order to gain the hand of the Infanta of Spain, Emmanuel, at the bidding of Ferdinand and Isabella, decreed their expulsion. Emmanuel married the Infanta in 1497, but he never won the prize that allured him, for he never sat on the throne of Spain. Some Jews, to escape the edict, became Christians, but they had little reason to rejoice at their apostacy when a few years later they were harried by the bigotry of the Roman Catholic Church. One result of the expatriation of the Jews was immediate, for when, by the newly discovered route, the riches of the East poured into the capital of Portugal, there was no machinery to distribute them over Europe; foreign merchants had to come to Lisbon to make their purchases. When, owing to the Spanish war at the end of the 16th century, the English and Dutch, debarred access to this market, went to the East to buy spices for themselves, the course of trade was the more easily diverted as there was no skeleton of custom formed out of existing trade routes to retard the decay of Portugal.

In his treatment of his great subordinate, Albuquerque, Emmanuel showed how unfit he was to be the ruler of men: we have not the King's orders, but seen in the reflection of Albuquerque's replies they were filled with a petty carping criticism—a constant demand for money, that goaded the recipient almost to madness. Conscious of his own entire devotion to the interests of his King and his splendid services to his country, it irritated Albuquerque beyond endurance to have to reply to every tale-bearer who, whether from resentment or malice, sent a letter of malevolent gossip to the King.[1] "But there are men here, Portuguese "whom your Highness credits... If I were a trusted Cap-"tain I would build their heads into Calicut fort, but I "have no such credit with your Highness, and they are "believed." Albuquerque's reward was to die of a broken heart. Whatever may have been the defects of the Portuguese in India, their prestige there must have been ended by the defects of their governors in Europe. Suspicion from beginning to end was the groundwork of their conduct. "The Portuguese prefer that their own deeds should be "forgotten rather than those of their neighbours praised," is the comment of their best-known historian.[2] Albuquerque says much the same.[3] "Were our emulation to "lead us to try and serve you, the one as well as the "other, such emulation would be virtue, but that which now "obtains here is to try and get a footing with your Royal "Highness through the defects of others; we rejoice at the "mistakes of others and at their disasters, and even we "strive to make others commit errors to give ground for "accusation against them." Every home-going ship was laden with slanderous letters until in the din it was impossible to say who was right and who was wrong. Even the most flagrant derelictions of duty remained unnoticed;

[1] Cartas, p. 137; see also pp. 156 to 177. On p. 304 he says, under date October 25th, 1514, that he had not received one word of acknowledgment for the capture of Malacca three years before.

[2] Barros, II. 5. 11.

[3] Cartas, p. 32. The story of the stone on which Albuquerque inscribed the names of those who distinguished themselves at the capture of Malacca, which caused such heartburning that he turned it face inwards and carved on the new surface "The stone which the builders rejected," is another illustration.—Commentaries, III. 137.

no fidalgo could be punished in India; in Portugal it was as easy to show that the charge was trumped up through enmity as it was to take away the character of an opponent by a libel behind his back. Not only did the Portuguese lose all dread of punishment for any misdeed, but the natives of India lost all belief they might ever have had in Portuguese justice.

Whatever the Portuguese were in Europe, once in the East there was nothing to improve their character or soften their defects. There may have been some exceptions, but the only women with whom they could associate were either those of that low stamp who would willingly, or those of higher standing who, degraded by force, were compelled to associate with the new comers from Europe. In the last half of the 16th century it became the custom to send out annually poor, well-born orphans, dowered by the King of Portugal, but it was many years before a respectable Portuguese woman was found who had penetrated beyond the Western Islands. Life on board ship was impossible to any woman with self-respect, and as late as his third voyage to India, in 1524, Da Gama whipped publicly in Goa three Portuguese women who, contrary to his orders, had come out in the ships. It was noted as without precedent that Jorge Cabral, the governor in 1549—1550, had his wife, a Portuguese lady, with him.

The early voyages swept away nearly all supernatural terrors, and when there remained only the material danger of shipwreck and the material discomforts of the squalor and filth of board-ship life to put against the possibility of wealth, the voyage to the East ceased to have any bracing effect on the mind. The same may be said of the enemies they had to meet on land. Duarte Pacheco and Albuquerque showed how vastly superior the European arms and organization were to those of the East, and after that demonstration fighting involved a certain physical fatigue, but, when properly conducted, little danger.

The religion which recognised Alexander Borgia as its head differed in all respects from that which bears the same name at the present day. A papal bull divided three-fourths of the globe between the half-savage Spaniards and the half-savage Portuguese; the interpretation of this bull, as accepted by the Portuguese, is to be found in the pages of the official historian, Barros.[1] According to him the Pope is empowered to distribute to the faithful all lands in the possession of the followers of alien laws. "It is true," he says, "that there does exist a common right to all to "navigate the seas, and in Europe we acknowledge the rights "which others hold against us, but this right does not extend "beyond Europe,[2] and therefore the Portuguese as lords of "the sea by the strength of their fleets are justified in com-"pelling all Moors and Gentiles to take out safe-conducts "under pain of confiscation and death. The Moors and "Gentiles are outside the law of Jesus Christ, which is the "true law that everyone has to keep under pain of damna-"tion to eternal fire. If then the soul be so condemned, "what right has the body to the privileges of our laws? "It is true," he adds, with a charitable candour, "they are "reasoning beings, and might if they lived be converted to "the true faith, but inasmuch as they have not shown any "desire as yet to accept this, we Christians have no duties "towards them."

Had these been merely the opinions of a studious pedant they would have deserved no attention, but if they were not actually put forward by the head of the Christian

[1] Barros, I. 6. I.

[2] The modern version runs, "And there's never a law of God or man runs north of 53."

Church, they afford an interpretation of its orders that was never repudiated and which indeed logically follows from its words. These doctrines which have destroyed whole tribes and nations and have affected the lives and happiness of millions, have been used to justify the most insatiable cupidity and the most atrocious barbarities. A few instances may explain the effect on the Portuguese mind of these theories.

In 1524 it was a surprise to them that Muhamedans should take revenge by killing off their outlying parties, for "up to now the Portuguese have considered that the "Moors should abide by a peace, and that they need not."[1] Cruelties were not confined to the baser sort, but were deliberately adopted as a line of terrorizing policy by Vasco da Gama, Almeida and Albuquerque, to take no mean examples. Da Gama tortured helpless fishermen: Almeida tore out the eyes of a Nair who had come in with a promise of his life, because he suspected a design on his own life:[2] Albuquerque cut off the noses of the women and the hands of the men who fell into his power on the Arabian coast. To follow the example of Almeida and sail into an Indian harbour with the corpses of unfortunates, often not fighting men, dangling from the yards, was to proclaim yourself a determined fellow. So deeply had the degraded teaching sunk into the minds of the Portuguese that there is every reason to believe that horrible as the cruelties were which Vasco da Gama committed on his second visit to Calicut in 1502, Correa, the historian, deliberately exaggerated them, not to excite pity, but to invest his hero with fresh glories.

This same spirit roused the fierce denunciations of the letters of St. Francis Xavier. In a private letter of March

[1] Castanheda, VI. 48.
[2] Ibid., II. 28.

24th, 1544, he wrote—"They" (the Portuguese) "seem to "think it an insult and an injury to them if any one dares "to open his mouth while they are trampling on rights of "all kinds... There would be more to excuse the aggression "if they denied us justice; but what plausible excuse can "we plead now when they undertake to do justice with "the utmost faithfulness, observe exactly all the conditions "of the alliance, and when they keep the peace and deal "with all the equity we could desire in their intercourse "with us."[1] And again, writing to a brother Jesuit in Europe, on Jan. 22nd, 1545,—"Do not allow any of your "friends to be sent to India with the charge of looking "after the finances and affairs of the King. To such persons "we may most truly apply which is written—'Let them be "blotted out of the book of the living, and let their name "be not written among the just.' However great may be "your confidence in one you know and love, trust my "experience and oppose him on this point, and fight to "the last to prevent him from being exposed to the greatest "of dangers.... There is here a power which I may call "irresistible, to thrust men headlong into the abyss, where "besides the seductions of gain, and the easy opportunities "of plunder, their appetites for greed will be sharpened by "having tasted it, and there will be a whole torrent of low "examples and evil customs to overwhelm them and sweep "them away. Robbery is so public and common that it "hurts no-one's character and is hardly counted a fault: "people scarcely hesitate to think that what is done with "impunity, it cannot be bad to do. Everywhere and at "all times, it is rapine, hoarding and robbery. No one "thinks of making restitution of what he has once taken. "The devices by which men steal, the various pretexts

[1] Life, Vol. I. page 193.

"under which it is done, who can count? I never cease "wondering at the number of new inflections, which, in "addition to all the usual forms, have been added in this "new lingo of avarice to the conjugation of that ill-omened "verb 'to rob'." [1]

With the end of the 15th century the complete break-up of the mediæval social system had advanced far. The authority which for some centuries had governed politics, and that which for even a longer time had governed religion had alike lost their influence. In Portugal the renaissance came late and left early, and the geographical discoveries that nation made, synchronized with the brief period of liberty she had enjoyed when relieved from mediæval sterility she had not fallen under the numbing influence of the Jesuits and the Inquisition. Cut off from the rest of Europe by Spain, she had no contact with the more bracing civilizations of the North, nor even with that of Italy. Her one outlet was the sea. For a century, speaking roughly, from 1450 to 1550, she ruled the seas of more than half the then known world. Then for another half-century her sovereignty continued in name, but the influence that guided her actions and galvanized her declining strength was not that of the Portuguese people, dwindling in number and mixed in blood, nor of its leaders who had degenerated till they could no longer lead, but that of ecclesiastics who wielded an open and often insolent control to attain the selfish aims of their own Church. At the first challenge her dominion fell without a struggle.

The causes of this fall are partly physical and partly moral, and the two are so intermixed that they can only with difficulty be separated. The most obvious of the physical causes was the small size of Portugal, which was

[1] Life, Vol. I. p. 227. Couto, V. 8. 5, traces the deterioration of his time to the canonical lawyers.

unable to supply sufficient population to stand the drain of both Brazil and the East. The drain in the East was increased by the ignorance of the elementary laws of health and the consequent excessive mortality. Among the causes partly moral, was the deterioration in the Portuguese race caused by intermarriage with native races. From this intermarriage two results stand out prominent,—a loss of vigour and a loss of prestige. Among the moral causes, one of the most potent was the adoption of Oriental methods of diplomacy which placed Eastern and Western on the same plane, and in an intrigue the Eastern won; while another was that ingrained suspicion and distrust of each other already referred to.

Malabar.—Civilization, in that part of the western coast of India first touched at by the Portuguese, had reached a high level. It was not a very progressive civilization, but it ensured personal security, it admitted the toleration of hostile creeds and it allowed great freedom in mercantile transactions. The evidence of the author of the Taháfatu-l-Mujáhidín, himself a Muhamedan, writing in the latter half of the 16th century, is valuable. He says, of course, that the prosperity of the towns was much increased by the activity of the Muhamedans, but he goes on to point out that the Hindu rulers abstained from all oppression and, although they and their armies were pagans, paid every consideration to the prejudices and customs of the Muhamedans, and that, although the latter did not number one-tenth of the population. In deference to them Friday was respected throughout Malabar, a death-sentence on a follower of their religion was never carried out without their consent, and converts to their faith were not molested.[1] In the conveniences

[1] Taháfatu-l-Mujáhidín, p. 71. The whole passage is valuable, but too long to quote.

of life the Indians were certainly behind the Europeans. To this day the words in common use in the bazaars of Agra and Delhi, to which their political influence never extended, show how many articles of this class the Portuguese introduced.

In 1442, 56 years before Da Gama reached it, Abdu-r-razák visited Calicut. As a Persian and a Muhamedan he hated the place, and he appears too to have been treated with scant ceremony by the Samuri. His description, in spite of all, is pleasant reading, and a good corrective to the continued abuse of the Portuguese. "The town is inhabited by infidels and "situated on a hostile shore. It contains a number of Mu-"hamedans who are constant residents, who have built two "mosques and meet every Friday to offer up prayer . . . "Security and justice are so firmly established in this city "that the most wealthy merchants bring thither from maritime "countries considerable cargoes, which they unload, and un-"hesitatingly send to the markets and the bazaars, without "thinking in the meantime of any necessity of checking the "accounts or keeping watch over the goods. The officers "of the custom-house take upon themselves the charge of "looking after the merchandize, over which they keep watch "night and day. When a sale is effected they make on "them a charge of one-fortieth part; if they are not sold they "make no charge on them whatsoever . . . But in Calicut, "every ship, whatever place it may come from or whereso-"ever it may be bound, when it puts into this port is treated "like other vessels, and has no trouble of any kind to put "up with." [1]

Varthema, the Italian who visited Calicut in 1505, has much the same to say. [2] He especially praises the admini-

[1] India in the 15th Century, p. 13.
[2] Varthema, p. 168.

stration of justice and the probity of the merchants,—this, too, in spite of traces in his book that he wrote with an eye to pleasing his Portuguese patrons. Pyrard de Laval, was there in 1607; he was much struck by the universal hatred with which the Portuguese were regarded and the high grade of civilization to which Calicut had attained in spite of a century of desolating war. "There is no place "in all India where contentment is more universal than at "Calicut, both on account of the fertility and beauty of "the country and of the intercourse with the men of all "religions who live there in free exercise of their own "religion."[1] "It is the busiest and the most full of all "traffic and commerce in the whole of India; it has mer-"chants from all parts of the world, and of all nations and "religions, by reason of the liberty and security accorded to "them there; for the king permits the exercise of every "kind of religion, and yet it is strictly forbidden to talk, "dispute, or quarrel on that subject."[2] "As for justice it "proceeds from the King alone, and throughout all his "kingdom there is no other judge but he. For all that, "justice is well administered, and awarded to all gratu-"itously."[3] Pyrard de Laval may be considered a prejudiced witness, as he was kidnapped from Calicut by a half-caste Portuguese and thrown into a filthy dungeon in Cochin, from which he barely escaped with his life. Still, the combined testimony of a Persian, an Italian and a Frenchman is irresistible. The Indians of that day were more civilized than the Portuguese.[4]

In nothing was their relative civilization more shown

[1] Pyrard de Laval, Vol. I. p. 366.
[2] Ibid. p. 404.
[3] Ibid. p. 407.
[4] Several traditional instances of the Samuri's honesty will be found in Logan, Vol. I. p. 278.

than in their treatment of prisoners of war. The Portuguese killed with the most horrible tortures or enslaved all prisoners whom they could not hold to ransom. They even flung the dead bodies of their captives on the shore and watched them to extort a ransom from any one who showed any interest in the corpse. [1] On the other hand, the Portuguese who were captured were in the early days treated with the greatest humanity. Malik Aiyaz, one of their bitterest opponents, wrote to Almeida that while the fight was in progress it was the duty of either side to do all they could to conquer the enemy, but once the enemy was conquered he must be treated as a brother; and, what is more, he practised as he wrote, for he treated his Portuguese captives with the greatest kindness, and after the defeat of D. Lourenço at Chaul he sought for his adversary's body to give it decent burial. [2] Things changed somewhat in later days when the natives of India had been educated by their Christian adversaries, still as late as 1559, when St. Thomé was held to ransom for the intolerant acts of some Jesuits and Franciscans, the Raja of Vijayanagara kept such faith with the Portuguese that, as one of them says, such humanity and justice are not to be found among Christians. [3]

There are traces that the better side of the Indian nature struck the more savage Portuguese with astonishment. Two pictures may be given from one voyage of Martim Correa up the coast in 1521, of which it was said, as it was of many others, that it was an unnecessary expedition, as the people they robbed were but poor people who neither followed the sea nor did evil to any one. [4] Landing at one place, Correa marched up country with 25 men till he came

[1] Correa, III. 835.

[2] Barros, II. 2. 9.

[3] Couto, VII. 7. 1.

[4] Correa, II. p. 681. The anecdotes are from Castanheda, VI. Ch. 2 & 3.

to a large country-house with courtyards and gardens, and many poor, both men and women, sitting round. Seeing the Portuguese, a man accosted them courteously, who was the almoner of a wealthy Muhamedan gentleman who lived there retired from the world and who spent his money in almsgiving. Presently the owner himself came out and treated them with hospitality. When a friendly understanding had been arrived at, Correa had the curiosity and the naivety to ask him why he gave alms and what satisfaction he could get from it. A little later, among the captives Correa took, was an old man past work, who offered £3 for his liberty, and asked that as he had no friend he might be allowed to fetch the money himself. Correa, more in jest than earnest, gave him his liberty and made him swear on his sacred cord, for he was a Brahmin, to bring the money back. A few days later, to the amazement of the Portuguese, the old Brahmin returned with half the money and eight fowls in lieu of the rest—all that he had been able to scrape together. To the credit of the Portuguese they refused to take anything from him.[1]

It is undoubted that in many cases the Portuguese were murdered on shore, but these murders were the outcome of a sudden riot, and in no case do we hear of any torture. The Portuguese were intruders who, in order to establish their own trade, had to break down the Muhamedan monopoly; and before the conditions of the country were properly understood, they were content to leave factors unprotected, trusting to the power of the native government. They were, however, completely ignorant of the religious and social systems with which they were brought in contact, and they made no attempt to understand them.

In 1498 Vasco da Gama and his men landed with the

[1] They gave him a certificate—the chit of the modern Anglo-Indian.

idea that all Indians save the Muhamedans were Christians, and they actually in this belief worshipped in a Hindu pagoda near Calicut; [1] and so little did he and his party learn of the facts, that the sailing orders of Pedro Alvarez Cabral were drawn up, after Da Gama's return, in the same belief, though it was recognised that these Christians wanted "teaching." [2] Pedro Alvarez Cabral brought back the fishermen whom Da Gama had kidnapped transformed into Christians, and sent them as envoys to the Samuri; he was ignorant that so polluted were they by their birth that the King could not even look on them. This same commander considered it a personal insult that the Samuri should have asked that the Nair hostages should be allowed on shore from the ships to eat, else they would be starved. [3] In 1504 Duarte Pacheco, who had been some time in the country, almost quarrelled with his faithful ally the Raja of Cochin when he said he was unable to make some low caste men Nairs. Andrade, in his life of D. Joâo de Castro, written after the Portuguese had been settled many years in India, speaks of D. Joâo as having sprinkled the Muhamedan mosques with cows' blood,—an animal they worship with abominable rites as the depositary of their souls! Couto's sixth decade, written after the Portuguese had been a 100 years in the country, by a man who was exceptionally well informed and who had lived many years in Goa, states that one of the assaults on Diu was led by a banner on which was painted a likeness of Muhamad horrible to see. [4] It is a well-known fact that the Muhamedan religion

[1] This fact is well attested. The author of the Roteiro thought the frescoes of the saints rather unusual. For many years Brahmins occasionally worshipped the images in Christian churches.—Castanheda, III. 130.

[2] An. Mar. e Col., series 5, p. 208.

[3] Castanheda, I. 35. The Samuri was of course referring to a strict caste rule.

[4] Couto, VI. 2. 5.

does not allow any representation of the human face to be made.

These examples of blunders are given to show how impossible it was for the Portuguese with their ignorance of the language—an ignorance which continued until a late period—and their habits which offended every prejudice, to avoid unintentionally alienating those with whom they came in contact in the new country. The Hindus were ignorant of the real power that lay behind the few vessels they could see; the Muhamedans had been with them for generations, or rather centuries, and their natural sympathies would lie with these and not with the unknown and unclean strangers. When therefore the Muhamedans determined on an active policy their decision met with no opposition from the Hindus.

Vasco da Gama was baffled in his endeavour to open trade with Calicut, but he met with no greater difficulties than were usually experienced at the first visit of ships to unknown ports. In some respects he received extraordinary civility; the Samuri transported his goods free of expense from the ships to Calicut; the personal indignities which he met with at the hands of subordinates have been grossly exaggerated, and it is clear from his conduct at the time, that Da Gama did not regard them in the serious light in which later writers have tried to place them. The line of conduct adopted on the west coast of Africa was not well chosen for the old-established civilizations of India, and Da Gama's own haughty and overbearing temper quite unfitted him to be a diplomat. The mingled sluggishness and ineptitude of Pedro Alvarez Cabral resulted in the murder of Aires Correa and his followers, and the breach with the Samuri became almost irreparable. There can be no question but that the Muhamedans took to the full advantage of the openings the ignorance and incapacity of the Portuguese gave them; more than this can hardly be said. The murder of Aires Correa in 1500 was preceded by acts of very gross provocation on the part of the Portuguese, and the subsequent discovery of Cochin with its harbour and its rivalry with Calicut, took away from the new comers all desire of a reconciliation with the Samuri.

CHAPTER III

ARMS AND METHODS OF WARFARE—VOYAGES—PIRACY LAND JOURNEYS

Arms and Method of Warfare.—In arms and methods of warfare the Hindu of the extreme south where the Muhamedans had not yet penetrated, was far behind his contemporary in Europe. "Hindus in India fight more with their tongues than their hands" is the contemptuous remark of a contemporary writer who had himself trailed a pike.[1] Chiefly, perhaps, because they had then met no serious enemy and had only fought their own caste fellows and coreligionists, war had become with them a game governed by a series of elaborate rules, and to break one of these rules involved dishonour, which was worse than death.[2] Their arms were lances, swords and shields, and much taste was displayed in lacquering and polishing, till neither sun nor rain affected them and they glittered "like a looking-"glass." The swords were of iron, not steel, some curved, some short and round, the point was never used; from the handle about one-third of the length was strengthened by an extra backing of iron; there were no hand-guards, only a small piece of elaborately moulded iron that hardly covered the fingers; this iron work carried numerous little

[1] Couto, X. 10. 4.

[2] See Correa, I. 354; ibid. III. 317 and 765; Varthema, p. 150. See also Jordanus, p. 20.

brass rings that rattled in sword play. For armour they wore coats wadded with cotton, that came to the elbow and mid-thigh; on the sword arm there was a gauntlet of a similar material. On their heads they wore caps also wadded with cotton, with flaps that covered nearly the whole face and neck.

There was neither night fighting nor ambuscades. All fighting was in the daytime when the sun had well risen; the opposing camps were pitched near each other and both sides slept securely. At sunrise the soldiers of both armies mingled at the tank, put on their armour, ate their rice and chewed their betel, gossipped and chatted together. At beat of drum either side drew apart and formed their ranks. It was creditable to be the first to beat the drum, but no attack was allowed until the other side had beaten theirs. The armies were formed in close columns. In the front were the swordsmen, who, with their shields touching each other and the ground, advanced, stooping low, at a very slow pace. Behind the swordsmen were archers, who fired along the ground to hit the enemy in the feet; with these archers were others who threw, also along the ground, either clubs of heavy black wood, or circles of iron with sharp edges like quoits; where these weapons touched a bone they broke it, or at least knocked a man over and made a gap in the ranks; in the rear of all were the lancemen with lances and javelins.

The fighting was always in the open plain and the advance —all stooping—very slow, now gaining ground, now losing, so that sometimes a whole day was spent in advances and retreats. When the drum beat both sides rose to their feet and fought no more that day. The drum could only be beaten when both sides were halted, and it was a point of honour not to beat it unless some advantage could be claimed. All the strategy was directed to capturing and defending the camp, and scribes were in attendance to write down the different turns of the battle. At times when the ranks on one side broke, the slaughter was very great, but after the drum sounded the two sides mingled together and there was no bad blood even when a man killed his own brother. In certain cases where a relative died or a vassal rebelled, the leader of the side that desired a suspension of hostilities, after the ranks were formed, advanced, stuck his javelin in the ground, leant his sword and shield against it, and stood apart; the leader on the other side imitated him, and a truce ensued. This artificial system broke down very quickly under the stress of fighting against the Portuguese. Thus it had always been the custom for the Samuri to sound a trumpet that it took four men to lift, to warn his enemy in the morning of an intended attack. In 1536 he nearly surprised the Portuguese by abandoning the custom suddenly.[1]

The Muhamedans of India were in a different class as fighting men, better armed and more ready to take advantage of every chance of the field either by day or night. In the gallant fight at Pandarani Kollam in 1504, where the Portuguese attacked a much larger force in position, many of their adversaries wore coats of mail, and as these were heavy, the owners, when they jumped overboard in a fright, were drowned.[2] Still as fighting men even they were far inferior to the troops that came in the Egyptian fleet from Suez. It was a maxim among the Portuguese that foot-men did not count; their only defensive weapon was a shield, and the bowmen had not even that.[3] None of the battles, however, described by the Portuguese histo-

[1] Castanheda, VIII. 144.
[2] Ibid., I. 97.
[3] Ibid., II. 16.

rians—and they are numerous and told in great detail—sound much more than magnified street brawls.

The interest of this description of the methods of fighting in Southern India, transmitted to us by the Portuguese writers, is enhanced by the evidence it affords that those methods were introduced from Northern India by the Brahmins, to mitigate the ferocity of the races whom they converted to the Hindu religion. The earliest form in which they are found is in the six rules agreed to by both sides in the great war of Bharata, celebrated in the Mahabharat, which embody some of the most artificial of the customs. It may be, as some have said,[1] that these six rules were introduced into that poem by Brahminical writers at a later date, to give them an historical sanction in the eyes of subsequent generations; but the same could hardly be said of their inclusion in the laws of Manu where they are also found. But whether this view be correct, that is, whether they actually governed the fight on the plain of Kurukhshetra or not is of little importance; the great fact is the proof that these passages in the Portuguese writers give, that the Brahmin carried with him in his civilizing advance over India such influence that he could impose his humanizing rules on the savage races over which he established his yoke,—rules, too, which, although they have left their trace to the present day in the chivalrous tone of some Hindu races, notably the Rajputs, laid those adopting them open to the attacks of outsiders who could reap every advantage from the artificial system that bound their adversaries.

In the middle of the 14th century gunpowder had been introduced into Europe, and by the end of the 15th a considerable advance had been made in the manufacture of gun-carriages, which had become lighter and had been

[1] Talboys Wheeler. "History of India," Vol I. p. 283.

placed on wheels; iron projectiles also supplanted stone. The English yeomen of the guard are said to have had some sort of hand-gun worked by two men as early as 1485. Vasco da Gama's ships had cannon of a kind but such weapons were quite unknown on the African Coast, while on the Malabar Coast, though not unknown, they were not in use. As late as 1506, when D. Lourenço d'Almeida visited Ceylon, the Singhalese were ignorant of gunpowder, and the noise of the cannon sufficed to drive away all thought of resistance from their minds. When Da Gama visited Calicut a second time, in 1502, and bombarded it, the Samuri had, as an eye-witness states, [1] only two inferior pieces in position; those who worked them had no idea of aiming and they took long to load. In the following year when the Samuri attacked Duarte Pacheco with all his force, he could only bring some iron guns that shot stones as hard as a man could throw them. [2] Early in 1503 two Milanese, Joâo Maria and Piero Antonio, who understood gun-founding, deserted the Portuguese for the Samuri's service. They founded a good deal of artillery and trained many artificers before they were killed in a riot a few years later, on the suspicion that they were going to desert again. [3] In 1505 four Venetians had reached Malabar in the Red Sea ships in order to cast artillery, [4] and from this time the knowledge of the art remained in India.

Albuquerque found some kind of large hand-gun in use in Malacca, which he conquered in 1511, but matchlocks were not introduced into Portuguese India until 1512, when some of German manufacture were imported, and there

[1] Thomé Lopes.

[2] Castanheda, I. 68.

[3] Varthema knew these men in Calicut, p. 274.

[4] Castanheda, II. 12.

were "found men who ventured to fire them."[1] Goa workmen were capable of making them and improving on the models. As early as 1510 Albuquerque began to enlist trained bands and give them some tincture of discipline; the officers for whom he wrote to teach them drill[2] came in the fleet with the matchlocks; they had themselves been taught in Italy. Albuquerque started a corps of 300 pikemen, 50 cross-bowmen and 50 matchlock men.[3] As they were viewed with considerable jealousy, and the innovation of drill bitterly resented, his successor reversed this, as he did many other of Albuquerque's reforms. Albuquerque devoted to his indents for arms the minute care he carried into all he undertook. "White body-armour is difficult to keep clean "in the Indian climate, leather cuirasses need no harness-"scourers' frames; pikes and lances should be sent to draw "blood; there is only one upstart barber in India, and the "fleet cannot be kept waiting his pleasure. Men must be "encouraged," he continues, with excellent sense, "to take a "pride in their arms; it is public opinion that makes men "do great deeds."[4]

Early matchlocks were not an unmixed advantage. The powder used in them and in big guns was different, and in the first siege of Diu several of the latter were burst because the two got mixed. The matchlockman had to stand up to his enemy while he reloaded,—a long operation during which an active opponent would pour in a stream of arrows;[5] in 1519 Christovâo de Sousa was beaten out

[1] Correa, II. 302. According to note to Varthema, p. 65, matchlocks were unknown in Arabia until 1515.

[2] Cartas, p. 19.

[3] Ibid., p. 83; see also p. 385. The Portuguese word used for drill is Soiça, which shows whence they learnt it.

[4] Ibid., p. 296.

[5] Barros, III. 3. 8. It is not always remembered that bows and arrows have been used in European warfare during this century. Marbot says the Cossacks at Leipzic were so armed.

of Dabul by Muhamedan bowmen in this way. As late as 1526 the Portuguese were ordered to throw down discharged matchlocks and fall on with other arms;[1] the Portuguese in consequence took their slaves into action to carry a reserve of weapons. Still their possession did confer superiority; between 1530 and 1538 the chief of Zeila nearly conquered Abyssinia because his army had matchlocks,—new weapons in that country, and it was only the landing of a Portuguese force that freed Abyssinian soil.[2] In 1536 rapidity of fire was increased by the introduction of cartridges containing the correct measure of powder and the ball.[3]

Indian guns were generally of iron and the Portuguese destroyed them as useless, but in 1634 copper ones were so frequently stolen that the Portuguese government ordered that only iron ones should be cast in future. Bombards were loaded at the breach; loaded chambers were kept in readiness, and it was the accidental explosion of some of these that stopped an attack by Pedro Alvarez Cabral on some boats at Kapukad in 1500. Cannon were dangerous to friends as well as foes; bombardments in the early voyages had frequently to be stopped, as more injury was being done to the ships from recoil than to the enemy from bullets. Aim was very erratic; thus a shot fired point-blank by the Portuguese at the hull of an Egyptian ship in D. Lourenço's fight at Chaul, in 1508, cleared the fighting-top of its defenders.[4] When Lopo Soares was at Jedda in 1517, the Turks had a "basilisk" that was said to throw a shot of three-quarters of a cwt.; it was fired

[1] Correa, II. 947.
[2] Castro Roteiro of 1541, p. 67.
[3] Correa, III. 69.
[4] Castanheda, II. 78.

from a galley at a Portuguese ship close by, and the recoil was so great that the former showed her keel and the shot flew wide. Direction and elevation could only be changed with difficulty, and on many occasions the Portuguese passed at low water heavily armed works because the guns had been trained for vessels coming at the top of the tide. As early as 1536 guns appear to have been mounted on camels and elephants, and sometimes also on bullock carts; in the last case they were fired from the back of the cart.

In the Turkish and Egyptian fleets the Portuguese had to meet guns of good quality and trained gunners, whose skill at Diu in 1546 excited the unstinted admiration of their opponents: they are described as being able to put 20 shots running into an egg, and send a 3lb. shot through a hogshead of earth. The gunners in the Portuguese service were frequently Flemings and Germans; those that came with the Turkish fleet were usually renegades from Southern Europe. The large guns were individualized and had their pet names,—thus at the siege of Chaul, in 1571, the Muhamedans had one big gun which the Portuguese called the "butcher",[1] served by a Brahmin named Rama. After the siege had been in progress some months a duel in regular form began between the "butcher" and a Portuguese "lion". Ruy Gonçalves, the Portuguese gunner, appeared in his gala costume astride of his piece, grimacing and threatening, and his opponent Rama appeared on his. The duel lasted three days and ended in the defeat of the "lion."[2]

[1] The Portuguese word is Caçapo, a form of Kasáb.

[2] See Fryer, Letter 4, Ch. 5, where another instance of the individualizing of guns is given. It was a slow business raising a mantlet and firing a gun, and a watch was always kept to warn all under cover when the enemy's mantlet was raised.

When the Egyptians came the first time, in 1508, the Portuguese found themselves at a disadvantage, as they had neither boarding-nets nor powder-pots, but they soon adopted them, and the latter especially became a very favourite weapon: they were a kind of hand-grenade, and at a pinch, could be improvized from two tiles placed with their concave sides inwards; a man carried his supply in a leathern bucket. In the early days powder was used rather for incendiary purposes than as an explosive in mines.[1] Mines were often as destructive to their constructors as to anyone else, but the one exploded at the siege of Diu on August 10th, 1546, under the bastion of St. John, when D. Fernandes de Castro and between 40 and 50 Portuguese were killed, was an exception.

In defensive armour the Portuguese were better protected than their opponents, and the mail-clad Portuguese, though he might be suffocated in his armour, could hardly be killed by any offensive weapon of his opponents; this accounts for the battles which ended in the slaughter of so many of the enemy with no loss to the Portuguese. When the Marshal was killed at Calicut armour had been thrown aside. Still, however highly we rate the superiority of the Portuguese in arms, their success does not rest on that alone—they had a vast moral superiority. Trained by their long apprenticeship in the wars of Europe, and hardened by facing the dangers of unknown seas, the early adventurers were able to meet with a gay heart uncounted odds, under circumstances which made defeat and annihilation synonymous. That, studying the facts four centuries later, we can understand the weakness of their opponents, in no way detracts from the renown of those who led the way in this conflict.

[1] It was so used in the defence of Ormuz in 1521.—Castanheda, V. 86. Bassein fort was after capture blown up with it in 1533.—Correa, III. 474.

Voyages.—It is difficult to put oneself in a position quite to understand the condition under which the early navigators made their voyages. Now that the phenomena of nature, however terrible, are known to follow some defined law, the sea presents a different aspect from the decks of a modern ocean-going steamer to what it did from the small vessels in which the earlier voyages were made. In modern tonnage Da Gama's vessels varied from 60 to 150 tons; when ships grew larger their seaworthiness did not increase in proportion, nor were the voyages shortened, in fact the percentage of losses increased very considerably. Falcâo, in his statistics, divided the ships sent to India into two periods,[1] the one from Da Gama's voyage to the accession of Philip II in 1579, the other from 1580 to 1612. They work out as follows:

PERIOD	Ships that left Portugal	Ships that stayed in India	Balance to be accounted for	Returned safely.
1497 to 1579	620	256	364	325
1580 to 1612	186	29	157	100

That is, whereas in the first period 90 p.c. of the ships, in the second only 63 p.c. returned safely to Portugal; these figures show a remarkable falling off in seamanship.

Couto perhaps gives one of the reasons when, speaking of another subject, he says incidentally:[2] "Because we are "Portuguese who do not get to the bottom of things, not "even at what is at our doors, as in Surat river and other "places which we have frequented for over 160 years. Both "the Dutch and the English know more of it than we do, "who, the very first time they went there, found anchorages "between shoals and banks where they stay as securely as "if they were at home from our fleet which cannot injure

[1] Falcâo, p. 194.
[2] Couto, IX. 24. 25.

"them. Our fleets who go in and out every day know of "them (the shoals) what the English have taught us." Again, the Italian, Della Valle, who some 20 years later travelled in an English ship from Ormuz to Surat, was struck by the instruction given to all ranks: 20 or 30 persons took the altitude daily,—the more experienced teaching the ignorant. On the Portuguese ships, on the other hand, he found the pilot took the observation alone, worked out the reckoning in secret, and quarrelled with any one who desired to take an altitude; many ships were lost in consequence. He even accuses the pilots of wrecking ships to get the insurance money, which has a modern ring about it. It was the custom too for one ship to carry the light at night, no other lights being allowed except one in the binnacle and one in the captain's cabin.[1] There are several cases on record where, through careless navigation, the light ship was lost and the others of the fleet followed her. These reasons are general and apply to both periods equally, but any dangerous practice tended to become more dangerous with increasing demoralization.

In the earlier voyages the ships were built both for fighting and for trade; with Vasco da Gama's fleet of 1502 there first went out ships destined to remain in India—that is fighting and not cargo ships. Almeida and Albuquerque both showed great interest in the dockyards of Cochin, and at the time of the latter's death he had a large ship nearly ready for launching. It was found, however, with a little experience, that large ships were unsuited to Indian warfare, in which organized fleets had very rarely to be encountered, but in which the enemy had to be followed into creeks and rivers. Vasco da Gama, in his third term in 1524, took out a

1 See Lopo Soares' sailing orders in An. Mar. e Col., 3rd series, p. 355; also Castanheda, I. 90.

Genoese ship-builder who promised to build boats "to catch a mosquito." These boats could either sail or row; they carried 30 fighting-men, and the oarsmen had arms under the thwarts and were available in a melee.

The pay of crews varied too much for any examination of their salaries to be profitable, but at first all classes received a share in the cargo. The method of reckoning the shares presents features of interest: the unit was the sailor—two "grummets"[1] equalled one sailor, and three pages equalled one "grummet". The caulker, carpenter, rope-maker, steward, barber-bleeder, and priest each equalled two sailors, and the boatswain and quartermaster one sailor and a half. Ships of private adventurers first went out with Joâo da Nova's fleet in 1501, the adventurers were often Florentines; they provided the ship complete with crew (who must be Portuguese) and rigging; government supplied arms, munitions and victuals. The amount of pepper to be brought back was settled before the ship started, the rest of the space was at the disposal of the adventurers and the crew. At the end of the voyage 22 p.c. of the profits on the King's cargo was paid to the adventurers as freight.[2]

The conditions of sea travelling seem very unfamiliar to us. Every ship met was an enemy until proved to be a friend, and for a stranger, even a countryman, to come down with the wind, was enough to justify a broadside.[3] Not only was every vessel a possible enemy, but the assistance even of a friend at a pinch could not be relied on. When four of Cabral's ships were overturned in a squall, the rest

[1] "Grummet" survives in south-east England as an "awkward boy": In the Cinque Ports navy "gromet" was a "cabin boy."—Parish Dictionary of the Sussex Dialect.

[2] Correâ, I. 234.

[3] See Mocquet's Voyages, p. 56, for an amusing account of a meeting of this kind.

of the fleet sailed on, leaving their comrades clinging to the keels; instances of this kind were to some extent due to ignorance of navigation, for ignorance breeds panic. The conduct of the great Magalhaens stands out conspicuous on the other side; he risked his life to save some sailors abandoned by their commander on the Sumatra coast; and a few months later, when the ship in which he was going to Portugal was wrecked on the Padua shoals, he refused to accompany the other officers in their flight, and set a noble example by throwing in his lot with the men.[1] Fernando de Castro, a Franciscan, set another, when in 1559 the ship of D. Luiz Fernandes de Vasconcellos began to founder and all the officers left in the ship's boat. The Franciscan alone refused to go. "The souls of these 200 men are of more value than my poor life," he said, and all were drowned together.[2]

With the instruments then in use, navigation was rather a haphazard affair. At the end of the 15th century it was necessary to land to take an observation with any approximation to accuracy. Vasco da Gama landed at intervals on his first voyage to correct his reckoning.[3] Later, navigators were more careless and often went wrong, thus in 1531 Manuel de Botelho, coming from Portugal to Cochin, rounded Ceylon without knowing it, and found himself at the Nicobars; he was apparently a careless navigator, for trying to return he was wrecked on an island near Calicare. He was given another ship and sailed for Europe in company with his brother, also a Captain, but the two vessels were never seen again, it was considered that possibly they had been

[1] Castanheda, III. 5. The story is well authenticated.

[2] See Couto, VI. 8. 3, for the previous history of this man; this story is in ibid. VII. 8. 1. For another instance of humanity, see Correa, IV. 413.

[3] Barros, I. 4. 2, has much of interest on this subject.

wrecked, but that probably they had fought out an old quarrel at sea and sunk each other.

One of the most unfortunate voyages on record was that of the homeward-bound governor, Francisco Barreto, who took 2½ years to get to Europe. He started early in 1559, all March was spent in trying to round the Cape. The ship was old and rotten, and leaked terribly; the pepper of the cargo got into the pumps and choked them.[1] Failing to pass the Cape, they returned to Mozambique and waited there for seven months for the next season, to start again; and Barreto had to spend £4,000 or £5,000 in feeding the crew and repairing the crazy ship. On November 7th he started in company with another vessel, but his ship began to leak again, and his companion actually foundered. With 1,137 souls crowded into his ship, and her sails split in a storm, there was nothing for Barreto to do but to put back again; he reached Mozambique on December 17th. In March 1560 he returned to India for a fresh ship, and left again on December 20th, reaching Lisbon finally on June 13th, 1561.

The life on shipboard itself was under conditions most unfamiliar to us. Linschoten's voyage was in 1583 and Mocquet's in 1608, and the accounts of both are very similar.[2] On the outward voyage the passengers were dieted, but on the return they had to provide for themselves; in both voyages men obtained their own fuel and did their own cooking. The ships were terribly overcrowded; and Mocquet's account of the squalor, filth and disease is quite untranslatable. Sleep was hardly possible lest the scanty dole of water should be stolen. The mortality was frightful; men crept away to die in corners and were sometimes not

[1] In describing a similar voyage, Albuquerque says, "the men always had the pumps in their hands and the Virgin Mary in their mouths."

[2] Linschoten, I. 10. Mocquet's fourth voyage is that in which he went to India.

found for days. On the average not 60 per cent. of the men who left Portugal reached India.[1] The heaviest death-roll that has come down to us is that of the ship in which the Viceroy Lourenço Pires de Tavora travelled in 1576. The Viceroy himself died and 900 of the 1,100 on board.

Piracy.—In addition to the licenses for the longer voyages granted by the crown, the Captains of fortresses were, under the Portuguese system, allowed to give licenses and safe-conducts for shorter voyages; these were often mere excuses for open piracy. The line between what was legitimate privateering and what was open piracy was so finely drawn that there was every opportunity for the enforced transfer of coveted property without any difficult enquiries into the justice of the proceeding, and, where the line was passed, a pardon was easily got. On the Indian coasts the rule of the strong had been for many generations the only law; thus on the Malabar Coast (except at Calicut) a custom was even enforced that a ship blown out of her course into a port to which she was not bound was lawful prize —she had been sent by God. The wars that followed the Portuguese intrusion fostered buccaneers. The Portuguese were too strong at sea to be opposed directly, and the creeks and rivers were well adapted to harbour light and speedy craft ready to pounce on some vessel weaker than themselves. Some of the so-called pirate leaders were, however, commanders under the Samuri, carrying on a guerilla warfare. Near Goa, in Sangameshwar, was a nest of buccaneers employed in Goa itself to prey on Goa trade, and in 1584 they defeated a regular Portuguese expedition sent against them.[2]

[1] Sassetti quoted in a note Linschoten, I. 199.

[2] See Pyrard de Laval, I. 446, for an account of the Malabar rovers of his day.

With the decay of the Portuguese nation the evil of piracy extended not only to all the Indian coasts, but also up the Persian Gulf. [1] Trade was increasing and there was no efficient police. Tavernier, in the middle of the 17th century, has many tales of the depredations of these rovers,—one of an English master mariner named Clerk, who with his crew defended the ship to the last, and left a slow match at the magazine when they took to their boats. The crew were captured, and their ransom was fixed at 4,000 crowns for themselves and 2,400 crowns at 2 crowns a piece for the 1,200 pirates they had blown up. Ovington has a story of one Edward Say, master of the "Heart's Delight" which was captured. By bribing one of the pirates, he concealed part of his money in a gun, but unluckily for Say this gun was fired to celebrate the return home of the successful craft, and the master's last penny went overboard. There were still some remnants of these pirates early in this century. Ras el Khema, one of their strongholds, was captured in November 1809. [2]

A few instances will bring the conditions here described more vividly home. In 1523, while D. Duarte de Menezes was governor, licenses to privateers were given freely. Francisco Pereira Pestana, Captain of Goa, among others issued one to Antonio Faleiro who was at one time a merchant and at another a soldier, to make prizes off Cape Guardafui. The Captain was to supply the necessary ordnance from the arsenal and receive a share of the proceeds of the cruise. [3] Faleiro was a man of some ability who knew more than one language, and he collected some

[1] Fryer gives a characteristic account in his voyage from Swallyhole to Persia.

[2] Asiatic Journal, II. p. 341.

[3] The story of Faleiro will be found in Castanheda, VI. 35 to 39; Correa, II. 760. Correa and Couto record his connection with the first siege of Diu in 1538.

20 Portuguese, some outlaws and others, promising that their beards should become gold, and manned two boats. They started in company with two trading vessels, an Ormuz *terrada* and a Cananor hooker (*huquer*). At an island beyond Diu they fell in with a vessel running from Diu to Persia, and though it was provided with a Portuguese pass, they robbed it of goods worth £ 15,000 and enslaved the crew. The hooker got lost on the Arabian coast, near Dofar, and only nine men escaped, who, when they were attacked by the country people, defended themselves until they reached Dofar, where the Shaikh helped them. Faleiro meanwhile had gone to Kalhat and there sold the goods he had robbed, and although the Shaikh there was very friendly, Faleiro, on the pretext of a debt, bombarded his house till he sent him a present of £ 200.

From there Faleiro went on to Dofar, and on the road overhauled a Red Sea ship. The crew, thinking they could ransom themselves in Dofar, would neither fight nor run. In Dofar Faleiro ordered the Shaikh to ransom this ship and to buy off the other vessels in the harbour, or he would burn them all; the nine men whom the Shaikh had helped requited his kindness badly enough, for they egged on Faleiro to rob the town. The Shaikh, however, utilized the delay of the messages to fortify himself, and when it came to an open rupture Faleiro could do nothing. The pirates left the town, and Faleiro sent off the Red Sea ship up the coast, to dispose of her lading, under the command of Afonso de Soure, and gave him six Portuguese and some Kanara men to work her. They started with little water, but the pilot knew of some place near the shore where it could be got. The mountains along the Arabian shore are high, the sea is sheltered from the wind, and the ship made so little way that the water began to give out. The crew were put on an allowance, and as the heat was very great many of the Muhamedans died of thirst. When they were opposite the watering-place the ship was 15 miles off the land, the air was calm and they could bring her no nearer in; so the Portuguese drew lots as to who should undertake the dangerous duty of landing from a boat on a hostile shore. The lot fell on Afonso da Veiga, Joâo Sirgueiro and another; they were given some cloth to quiet the country people if necessary, and started in the ship's boat with their matchlocks and some slaves to row.

They left at eight in the morning, but the currents carried them a long way down the coast, which they only reached at two hours before sunset. They sent on shore to search for water, but the men fell into an ambush of Arabs who had watched them from the hills; some were wounded, but all escaped back to the boat. Lower down the coast they found no resistance, and got water from some brackish springs under some palms near the shore. It was after sunset when, wearied with their labours in the great heat, and having had little to eat all day, they turned to row back to the ship. The Portuguese thrashed the oarsmen, but neither blows nor threats of death could get more work out of them. The Portuguese themselves rowed, but they did not find the ship, and as in the morning even the land was nearly out of sight, they returned, as their only chance, to try and get their bearings from the high land. It was near sunset when they got back to the shore, and cast their grapnel some way out lest the boat should fall into an ambush. Afonso da Veiga swam on shore with his lance held before him, and finding no one, climbed the hill and looked this way and that, but could not see the ship; De Soure had in fact waited a short time and then, concluding the boat was captured, gone on his way; and shortly after his ship was taken by the Muhamedans and all the Portuguese in her killed. To return to Da Veiga and his com panions—when the slaves heard the state of affairs they abandoned the boats and fled up country. Left to themselves, the Portuguese caught some fish, which they ate, and agreed to wait till the next day to see if anything turned up. Failing that, their only chance was to go up the coast to Muscat; their spirits were cheered by finding 8 gallons of wheat in a bag accidentally thrown in with the ballast.

That same evening a young Arab of about 18, wearing only a cap and a waistcloth, and carrying a dart, came suddenly round a rock; thinking it an ambush, Da Veiga fired his matchlock at him, and if the Arab had not ducked the ball would have killed him. When the ball had passed he ran into the sea and swam out, and after collecting the wits the hum of the ball had scattered, he told them, partly by words and partly by signs, that he had watched them while he was grazing his flocks in the hills and had seen their ship sail away,—that now they had better come to his village of Mete where the Shaikh was friendly to their nation. The Portuguese promised to pay him well if he brought them food, and the young man went off and returned the next day at the same time, with a bundle of balls of wheat flour such as the Arabs eat,[1] a gourd of white honey, five fowls and a friendly message from the Shaikh; and that night, two or three hours before dawn, they heard the song of the four African slaves whom he had sent to bring them to his village. They reached Mete during the morning, but Joâo Sirgueiro refused to land as he feared treason, until the Shaikh, who was a good fellow, heard of the difficulty, came, and telling his beads as he went, spoke to them in Portuguese and welcomed them. Two of the three eventually reached India, but the third, Joâo Sirgueiro, was drowned in the wreck of a vessel in

[1] *Apas* they are called by the Portuguese.

which he hoped to have made a speedier passage. Antonio Faleiro continued his piratical career for some time and then returned to India, where he spent the monsoon months near Chaul, and got a pardon from the Governor. Of his subsequent history we only know that he was employed in the Gogala outwork at the first siege of Diu in 1538, and was captured with the rest of the garrison; but he escaped the fate of the others, who became galley slaves, by turning Muhamedan and trying to seduce the Diu garrison from its allegiance.

Faleiro had turned pirate on the Arabian coast; Damiâo Bernaldes did the same in the Bay of Bengal.[1] When Nuno da Cunha returned from his first unsuccessful expedition to Diu in 1531, he gave a merchant, Damiâo Bernaldes, who had accompanied him to Diu, a license for a voyage to Bengal; but after rounding Cape Comorin, Bernaldes began to rob friend and foe alike. At the Nicobars he robbed a Muhamedan ship, retained the money—£9,000—for himself, and kept the ship and artillery to pacify the Governor. Before he reached Chittagong, however, letters from the Governor, who had heard of his doings, had reached there, addressed to the Wazir and to Khwaja Shahábu-d-din, a local merchant friendly to the Portuguese, asking them to arrest Bernaldes if they could,—if not to kill him and his crew at sight. There were then 17 Portuguese vessels in the harbour, and Shahábu-d-din and the masters consulted, and knowing that probably Bernaldes would work out his pardon, they decided to do nothing. All went well with Bernaldes till one day he captured and held to ransom a leading Muhamedan. When this got known in the town the Wazir seized as many Portuguese as he could before they escaped to their ships. Bernaldes refused to take in exchange

[1] This story of Bernaldes will be found in Castanheda, VIII. 46, and Correa, III. 446.

these Portuguese for the Muhamedan, and even when they were brought to the shore, stripped naked and whipped, he said they might hang them if they pleased, but for his "Moor" he must have £2,000. The Nicobar ship lay close to Bernaldes, and some men who had permission to live in her, seeing the game was up, determined to gain some credit with the Governor and take him the ship themselves. Soon after midnight, when the tide began to fall they cut the upstream cable and hauled on the downstream; they satisfied the sleepy watch on Bernaldes's ship by saying it was only the anchors dragging. In the morning, as she was out of sight, Bernaldes had to exchange his "Moor" for the Portuguese and go in pursuit; but he bumped his rudder out on the Chittagong bar and never overhauled the runaway. Bernaldes landed at Negapatam to go on to Vijayanagara and await his pardon, but the Portuguese settlement was on the alert and he was captured, thrown into irons and sent to the Governor. He was sentenced to banishment for ten years, but died in prison, not without suspicion of poison, after the Governor had got out of him all the money he had left.

Land Journeys.—During the 15th and 16th centuries the Jews were the great land travellers—the references to them are continual. To quote some instances: in 1512 three Jews came to Albuquerque with news of the Muhamedan world from Cairo; in 1543 two were sent overland from India to Portugal to spy out the doings of the Turks and report them to the King; and in 1581, after the accession of Philip II of Spain to the Portuguese throne was acknowledged in India, a Jew accompanied the envoy with the news across Persia. [1] Tenreiro, who himself travelled through Central and Western Asia about 1528, notices the extra-

[1] Cartas, p. 95. Correa, IV. 268. Couto, X. 1. 13.

ordinary ease with which Jews could pass anywhere; but Jedda from its proximity to Mecca was rather an exception, for Jews travelling up the Red Sea avoided that town and went by Kosseir. The early Portuguese passed as Muhamedans both in dress and in customs.[1]

Jews were employed by King John II in the land explorations with which he supplemented the scanty knowledge that he had of India, and prepared the way for the immediate utilization of the Cape route when it was discovered. His first expedition, headed by Antonio de Lisboa, had to return as none of the party knew Arabic. The second was better selected; it consisted of Afonso de Payva and Pero de Covilham, who started on May 7th, 1487, with £170 in their pockets. Their route lay through Barcelona and Naples to Rhodes and Alexandria. From this point they passed as Muhamedans, and travelled through Tor at the mouth of the Gulf of Suez, Suakin and Aden. Thence Afonso started to discover the country of the Prester John, and Covilham to discover India; their meeting-place was to be Cairo. Covilham visited Cananor, Calicut and Sofala, and returned by Ormuz to Cairo, where he heard of the murder of Afonso, and met two Portuguese Jews sent in search of him, Rabbi Abraham and Joseph—a shoemaker. The latter had already travelled through Mesopotamia, and he took back Covilham's account of his travels to Portugal, while Covilham and Abraham started for Ormuz; thence Covilham despatched Abraham to Portugal with a duplicate account of his travels, and started himself for Abyssinia, where he remained till his death in honourable captivity. Roderigo de Lima found him there in 1520.

The first overland journey to Portugal was in 1513, when Albuquerque sent from the Red Sea, Fernâo Dias, a Muha-

[1] One went so far as to be circumcised in Malindi.—Cartas, p. 316.

medan who had deserted to the Portuguese during the African wars. He was disguised as an escaped slave,[1] reached Portugal and returned to India in safety. The most important of the early land journeys after Covilham's is, however, that of Antonio Tenreiro, who took a new route. He had a dispute with a man in India too wealthy for him to withstand, and for this reason attached himself to an embassy sent in 1524 by D. Duarte de Menezes, the governor, to Shah Ismail of Persia. On this occasion he left the mission and wandered off to Cairo, apparently disguised as a Muhamedan. He returned in safety to Ormuz, and when, in 1528, some news of the Turks had to be sent in haste to Portugal, Tenreiro was naturally selected for the journey. He left at the end of September, and at Basra found that he had missed the Aleppo caravan. With the help of the local Shaikh he got an Arab and two riding camels, and started on his adventurous journey. They travelled across the desert in 22 days, including a halt of eight days to allow Tenreiro's camel that had staked itself in a senseless panic, to recover from the wound. The Aleppo caravan was overtaken 8 days out of that town, and the Arab and the camels were sent back. At Aleppo Tenreiro stayed in the house of one Andre, a Venetian friend of his former journey, but matters were not comfortable; Andre was wealthy and had been summoned to Constantinople to answer frivolous charges, Tenreiro therefore destroyed some compromising correspondence and hurried on to Portugal. His actual travelling time was 3 months.[2] In 1565 another traveller Mestre Afonso, the chief physician of D. Francisco Coutinho, travelled overland; he has left a very minute diary of his travels.[3]

1 Albuquerque Cartas, p. 230. Correa, II. 348.
2 Tenreiro's narrative, published some years later, is interesting.
3 Commenced in An. Mar. e Col. Series, p. 214, it runs through many numbers.

These were the more or less official travellers, but we get glimpses of a great number of Europeans in the East. To take only those who have left no written record behind them, many of them renegades and slaves: Malik Aiyaz, the first governor of Diu with whom the Portuguese came in contact, was a Russian who had been enslaved in his childhood. Sifr Agha, the second, was an Italian renegade. There were also Italian merchants who visited the East, such as the Venetian Bonadjuto de Albâo [1] who tried to warn Aires Correa of the emeute in 1500, whom Albuquerque took back to Portugal after his visit of 1503, and who returned as an interpreter in Almeida's fleet. He had gone to India about 1480 with Francisco Marcillo, a Venetian consul in Alexandria who had been sent as envoy to India. There were the two Jews whom Albuquerque captured in a Red Sea ship in 1510; one of whom turned Christian, married and settled in Goa; the other, an excellent linguist, became Albuquerque's most confidential adviser, [2] and was, in 1515, converted to Christianity with the name Alexander d'Ataide. After his master's death he went to Portugal and gave the King much information as to Albuquerque's plans; but in Lisbon a most impudent attempt was made to blackmail him, [3] and disgusted with Christianity he returned in a Venetian vessel to Cairo, where Tenreiro met him and found his account in holding his tongue as to the other's temporary profession of Christianity.

Of Gabriel, the Pole, we only get a glimpse. Couto's account of him is that "he travelled through Muscovy to

[1] This is the Portuguese form of the name.

[2] Gaspar Pereira and Antonio Real drew up certain articles against Albuquerque in 1512; one of the items was that he allowed these two men to govern India.—Castanheda, III. 123.

[3] Correa, II. 134.

"the country of the Usbegs, and was some years in the "Court of Abdulla Khan of Samarkand; thence passed to "the Mogul's, in whose house and service he stayed 15 years, "and then came to this city of Goa where we knew him; "and he told us much of those parts, which he remembered "well, for he was a clever man and of a nimble wit; and by "what he told us he had seen as much or more than Marco "Polo, the Venetian, for he travelled through Muscovy, Us-"begia, Persia, Tartary, and arrived at Cambalec, at the "Court of the great Khan, and was in part of China, and "returned to Hindustan and traversed all the country of the "Moguls and all Cambay and Scinde, and after being some "years in Goa went to Cambay, where he died."[1]

It is a noteworthy instance of the effect of religious bigotry, that the race whom the statesmen of the end of the 15th century and beginning of the 16th used with such valuable results, were proscribed by those of the middle of the 16th. By orders, dated March 15th and 20th, 1568, no Jew was allowed to go by sea to India, and captains were made responsible for ejecting them from their ships.[2]

[1] Couto, V. 8. 11.
[2] Livros dos Monçôes, Vol. II. p. 216.

CHAPTER IV[1]

RELIGION—COINAGE—REMUNERATION OF OFFICERS BANISHED MEN

Religion.—It was natural that the relations of the earlier Portuguese commanders to the few ecclesiastics then in India differed greatly from those of their successors to the priests and monks who, commencing from about 1540, bore such a large proportion to the total population.[2] Albuquerque was the master of the clergy as of all else that approached him, even when they opposed him in his marriage policy. He allowed his sailors to select wives from among the wives and daughters of the hostages he carried off at the time the Adil Shah reconquered Goa; his chaplain, however, objected that they were not married by the rites of the Church. "No, but they are by those of Afonso d'Albuquerque," was the reply,[3] and as such they continued to be known.

Albuquerque tells the story of a Dominican, in his letters, who, under threat of excommunication, had exacted £1 from every married man.[4] The story was this: the Governor had a body surgeon, one Mestre Afonso, who had kept, without his master's permission, one of the Goa women as

[1] In this chapter there have been brought together some unconnected subjects that require a separate notice.

[2] The story of Almeida told in Correa, I. 624, is probably amusing gossip embroidered on some slight foundation.

[3] Correa, II. 115.

[4] Cartas, p. 30.

a slave. Consequently, when another man wanted to marry her she was taken from Mestre Afonso, made a Christian (their methods were summary) and married. But Mestre Afonso was not to be beaten in that way. "He had such a way with him," as Albuquerque puts it, [1] that he won over the woman and induced the Dominican to call her up when Goa was collected for the Mass, and question her at the altar as to her marriage. She replied that she was married without her consent. The indignant husband carried off his wife and complained to Albuquerque. Mestre Afonso only got out of the scrape by marrying a wife of the Governor's choice, "a woman much too good for him."

His scorn of those who submitted to ecclesiastical interference was unbounded. When the Raja of Cananore was annoyed with the rough manners of Manuel da Cunha, Albuquerque selected to succeed him Diogo Correa, "a polite man." [2] Before Albuquerque sailed for Malacca there was a street fight in Cananor in which a Christian native killed a Hindu and then took sanctuary in a church. On complaint from the Raja, the Christian was taken from the church and his hand struck off. No sooner had Albuquerque sailed than the local priest interfered, fined the Captain £20 for obeying the Governor, and placed Cananor under an interdict. Albuquerque's comment to the King was—"If "Diogo Correa were as old as I am he would have laid them "all by the heels, he is a lax man and fit for little. He had "better return to Portugal while he is alive." And go he had to.

The Franciscans came out in 1517, with permission from the King to build a monastery; [3] they were given the house of Joâo Machado, the banished man who had been killed a few months before. The great revival began, however,

1 "Teve tal maneira este Mestre Afonso."—Cartas, p. 31.

2 Cartas, p. 175.

3 Correa, II. 537.

much later, and of it Miguel Vaz and his friend Diogo de Borba were the leaders. They obtained pecuniary assistance from Nuno da Cunha to start the confraternity of the Holy Faith, which was to be devoted to the conversion of the native races. The building was actually begun on November 10th, 1541, and opened on January 25th, 1543, the day of the conversion of St. Paul to whom it was dedicated.[1] After the death of the founders it was taken over by the Jesuits, and from it was derived the name by which that order was generally known in India.

In 1540 all the Hindu temples in the Island of Goa were destroyed,[2] an act of intolerant bigotry due to the direct orders of the King of Portugal. In the Goa villages, as is generally customary in India to this day, there were set aside either little rent-free plots, or else certain sums from the common fund, for the expenses of the local temple and for the payment of the blacksmith, the carpenter and the other servants required for daily life. When the temples had been destroyed the ecclesiastics determined to appropriate these grants, whether made to the temple or to the village workmen. The order[3] for this spoliation exists and is a curious and repulsive mixture of unctuousness and rapacity, for its authors take on themselves to answer for God, that in consequence of the villagers consenting to give up this income the increase in the productive power of their villages shall repay a hundredfold the surrendered money. The sum gained by this was at first only £250 a year, of which £100 went to the confraternity and £150 to local hermitages, which latter may have been intended to break the loss of the destroyed temples; any way, the grant of £150 was only temporary, and the whole income

[1] For a very interesting account see Correa, IV. 290.
[2] Ar. Port. Or., Fasc. 5, page 171, *note*.
[3] Ar. Port. Or., Fasc. 5, No. 75 of June 30th, 1541.

was soon absorbed by the central establishment. This was only the thin end of the wedge. The orders of June 1541, unjust as they were, at least professed to proceed with the consent of the villagers and recognized that where the grant was of land that land belonged to the village; but the ecclesiastical appetite had been whetted. Nine years later the confraternity, which was by this time in Jesuit hands, got not only a grant of all such land for themselves, but also the power to enquire what land that had been the subject of such a grant at any time had been concealed. [1] This power was worked so efficiently in the interest of the Church that the revenue from this source was quintupled. [2]

In 1543 one Jeronimo Dias, a bachelor of medicine, was found guilty of heresy by an ecclesiastical court, sentenced to be burned, and then handed over to the civil power, who carried out the sentence. [3] This was the commencement of the persecution; but the Inquisition was not established in Goa for many years, though the Sunday after this sentence the papal bull authorizing it was read in the Church. Dias, having confessed, was strangled before he was burned.

Miguel Vaz, the leading spirit of the revival, who went to Portugal in 1545, was there invested with very considerable powers as Vicar-General, and brought back with him a letter of the King, dated March 1546, to D. Joâo de Castro. What purports to be this letter was published in Andrade's "Life" of that governor, [4] but its terms are so intolerant that the ecclesiastical editor of the most complete edition of that work is inclined to consider it not genuine.

[1] Ar. Port. Or., Fasc. 5, No. 115 of July 8th, 1550. Nuno da Cunha wisely had forbidden any enquiry into concealed lands. Ibid. No. 73 of October 15th, 1534. More on the same subject will be found in the same Fasciculus in Nos. 129, 131 to 134, 159, 204, and 217.

[2] Correa, IV. 290.

[3] Ibid., IV. 292.

[4] Vida, p. 51.

It would have been a grateful task to have agreed in this view, but there is extant a letter of the Bishop of Goa, dated March 29th, 1550, which quotes the text of this letter of the King to D. Joâo.[1] It varies in the wording from that given by Andrade, but breathes exactly the same intolerant sentiment and bears the same meaning.[2] There can be no doubt then but that Vaz brought back with him a letter authorizing the most violent measures of persecution, including the search of private houses in Goa for idols. He also brought powers to turn all non-Christians out of their offices.[3] Vaz appears to have proceeded in a very high-handed way, and the new departure was so unpalatable that he was poisoned soon after his return.[4] The circumstances surrounding his death were shrouded in mystery, and no enquiry seems to have been made. The Bishop of Goa and the clergy were on notoriously bad terms with the religious orders, and scandal in this case accused the Bishop of complicity in the crime. Xavier was in the Moluccas when it occurred, and on his arrival in Cochin, a year later, he considered the scandal so serious that, before he even went to Goa, he wrote to the King on behalf of the Bishop.[5] Some interesting letters are printed in Francisco de S. Luiz' edition of Andrade's Vida de D. Joâo de Castro,[6] which throw a side light on the matter, but unfortunately these letters are not all printed in extenso. On December 15th, 1546, Ruy Gonçalves de Caminha, the

[1] Ar. Port. Or., Fasc. 5, No. 111. This evidence was not available when the doubt referred to in the text was expressed. See also Ibid. Fasc. 1, No. 14, § 4.

[2] Andrade undoubtedly treated documents with scant reverence. See Note to Vida, p. 387.

[3] Ar. Port. Or., Fasc. 1, No. 14, March 14th, 1549.

[4] Couto, VI. 7. 5. Faria y Sousa, II. 2. 6. The latter accuses "Portugueses poderosos en Goa."

[5] Life, Vol. II. p. 14.

[6] Page 454.

Comptroller of revenue, wrote to D. Joâo de Castro, then apparently in Chaul, warning him that Miguel Vaz was going to see him. The next letter is one from the Bishop to the same, dated February 1st, 1547, from which it would seem that Vaz had died on the previous January 11th, and his friend Borba, of grief, on January 26th. The most remarkable letter, however, is the one from Pero Fernandes, the chief magistrate, to the Governor, of February 14th, which certainly expresses no detestation of the crime and does not seem to consider that the recipient of his letter would feel any. It is light-hearted enough; Diogo de Borba was a bad Christian to die of grief and not to accept the decrees of Providence in a proper spirit. The remark that he was "credulous and believed things with neither head nor feet," and also the reference to an application, made by two priests to the Captain, regarding Miguel's death, "which the "Governor will see when he comes, and which will show how "impossible it is to live with some priests," both point to the charge of poisoning. The letter ends with a reference to another of the "gang" (quadrilha), the "Bacharel" who had gone to bed and received extreme unction merely to keep up the excitement, for, as the Magistrate told the Bishop, the Pope could cure the "Bacharel" at once by making him a bishop. These facts are detailed with some minuteness, not because they lead to any definite conclusion as to who actually committed the crime, but as showing that persons powerfully placed were certainly not out of sympathy with the result. Miguel Vaz was a mere vulgar persecutor, but at the time of his death Francis Xavier had been already at work for some years in India.

There came out in the ships of 1548 some monks of the Dominican order, with great powers from the King to acquire land in Goa for a monastery. The acquisition of this land involved them in difficulties, and four years later the dispute was still in progress.[1] The Dominicans, with a worthy zeal, took up the cause of the most miserable class in Goa, the slaves, whose lot it is impossible to describe.[2] The intention was good, but it is very doubtful if they did not injure those they attempted to assist.

Botelho, one of the few honest and clear-headed men then in India, saw the danger into which the country was drifting, and in 1552 wrote to the King in terms that leave nothing to be desired for directness.[3] "The religious "in this country desire to spend so freely and give so "many alms at the expense of your revenue that a large "part of it goes in this. There are already so many who "desire to favour Christianity that a great part of the "revenue is alienated, and the country round Bassein is "depopulated. I believe they act from the best motives, "and that our Lord and your Highness are well served; but "there seems to be a mean which might be the best "course, as there are some who want to force people to be "Christians and who worry the Hindus so that, as I say, "people fly from the land. Let your Highness do what "is right."

1 According to Correa the Dominicans brought out a skull of one of the 11,000 virgins. It came well attested, for it miraculously stopped a leak in the ship on the way out. At Goa it was received with a procession and taken to a monastery. The Bishop and clergy would not take part in the reception, through jealousy; this caused scandal, as the people favoured the monks at the expense of the clergy, whose lives were evil. Correa, in the same passage, reviews the ecclesiastical buildings then in Goa. The Dominicans were to get £ 20,000 to build the monastery, besides the value of the houses occupied. The Franciscan Monastery had cost £ 20,000, and there were forty monks. The cathedral cost £ 6,000, with more than 30 canons and priests, and there were also in the city 14 churches and hermitages with over 100 clergy "besides vagabonds." There was also the College of St. Paul with an income of £ 1,800 a year. The vagabonds are also mentioned in Ar. Port. Or., Fasc. 4, page 39. Decreto 11.

2 Mocquet relates some horrors, page 259.

3 Botelho's Letters, p. 35.

Botelho, had, when he wrote this, just completed his return of the income and expenditure of Portuguese India. Excluding the cost of hospitals which, though managed by the clergy, represented rather our poorhouses and hospitals combined than anything else purely religious, the annual expenditure in ecclesiastical establishments by the state was £6,944—say £7,000, which Botelho considered excessive, having regard to the size of Portuguese India. When Falcâo prepared his return in 1612, the area had certainly not increased, but the total cost of the same establishments paid by the State had risen to £25,978, say £26,000. The cost of hospitals in the same period rose from £4,445 to £6,376.

The letters of Xavier to the King more than anything else produced this change.[1] This is not the place to enter into any examination of the missionary labours of this remarkable man,[2] which lie entirely outside the limits of this work. It is sufficient for note to be taken of the important share he bore in the ecclesiastical revival.

The records of the first provincial Council of Goa, held in 1567, on which was founded the law passed on December 4th, 1567, embodying the recommendations of the ecclesiastics that composed it, may be mentioned, as they show the drastic methods adopted by the state at the command of the Roman Catholic Church, for the conversion of Muhamedans and Hindus.[3] No Christian could have infidel servants in his house, be cured by an infidel doctor or be shaved by an infidel barber. Neither Hindus nor Muhamedans could

1 See especially Life, Vol. II. p. 6—letter of January 20th, 1548.

2 An appreciative account of Xavier will be found in Stephen's Essays in Ecclesiastical Biography, pp. 120 to 158.

3 See the first 75 pages of Fasc. 4, of Ar. Port. Or. Some of the Decretos of the Council, notably those on pages 55—60 dealing with the relation of Captains of fortresses with those trading in their ports, appear to our ideas to deal with subjects strangely outside ecclesiastical jurisdiction.

5

have any public worship, purchase anything appertaining to their religion—whether books or other articles—and all their priests were banished, even a twice-born Hindu required by his caste custom to wear the sacred cord (janeo) was forbidden to do so. Nominal rolls of all Hindus were to be made, 100 in each roll, and fifty from each batch were to attend alternate Sundays to hear sermons of one hour in length on the benefits of the Christian religion.[1] No compulsion was to be used to convert anyone to Christianity, but if anyone complained that a person had been forced into conversion, the Roman Catholic prelate and not the civil power was to judge the complaint. If either husband or wife was converted (no one could marry more than one wife), the unconverted wife or husband was to be kept in the house of some virtuous person as long as was considered necessary in order to discover his or her real intentions. When any infidel father died, leaving minor children, they were to be taken over by the State to be made Christians.[2]

One of the points most strongly impressed on Viceroys leaving Portugal for the East was that the spread of the Christian religion was to be encouraged, not only by missionary efforts properly so called, but also by affording new converts all temporal aid and advancement.[3] Judging from the miscellaneous instructions issued, this order was faithfully obeyed, as a selection from some—all before 1575—will show.[4] When a man died without sons his nearest Christian

[1] Even in Rome the Jews had only to attend one sermon a year, according to Browning's "Holy Cross Day." It must be remembered that at this time there were few if any mosques or temples left in Portuguese territory.

[2] Mothers killed their children rather than subject them to this cruel law. See p. 92 of Ar. Port. Or., Fasc. 4.

[3] See, for instance, the orders of the King to D. Luis d'Ataide, of February 27th, 1568. Ar. Port. Or., Fasc. 3, p. 3.

[4] The numbers given in brackets in the text refer to the number of the document quoted—all from Ar. Port. Or., Fasc. 5.

relative could claim his property (285), and if he had no Christian relative, it went to the Cathedral (435). On becoming a Christian a native of India could at once claim all the privileges of a born Portuguese (288), while on becoming a Jew or a Muhamedan he was sent to the galleys for life (524). Children or other heirs who became converts could claim partition of any property in which they had a heritable right (292), and, similarly, wives could, under such circumstances, claim all their ornaments and half their husband's property (427). Female converts could claim inheritance as if they had been males, to the exclusion of other heirs (304). Hindus could not enter the village assembly for the management of village business, and were compelled to sell any petty village office they held (575). The archbishop could turn any non-Christian he pleased out of Goa (575). To discourage litigation a native of India could only compel enquiry into charges of (1) Murder, (2) Grievous hurt, (3) Perjury, (4) Forgery (95 § 6), but a non-Christian could only prefer a complaint of even one of these crimes before one official in all Portuguese India, and then he had to deposit £50 (767), this was practically denying justice at all to non-Christians. Finally, those who were not Christians must wear a distinctive dress, and must not ride on a horse or in a palanquin or carry an umbrella in Goa or its suburbs (781.) Under these circumstances it is not surprising to learn that as early as 1561, Goa and the surrounding islands were depopulated, and that before the end of the century even the fertile Salsette was a desert. (391 and Note.)

Coinage.—Indo-Portuguese coinage offers some difficulties of its own.[1] There were three classes in circulation: (1) Good—

[1] Carmo Nazareth gives on his p. 7 the names of 74 coins current at different times in Goa, and in the catalogue of his own cabinet he describes

which was current at its face value; (2) Poor—current at the rate of the good metal the coin contained; (3) Bad—which was not current at all. No prudent person received money until it had been tested by a shroff or money-changer. Every petty governor all over India coined at least his own copper, and travellers found that small change received in the morning was useless at the evening's halt. It will be convenient to take the *Real*, which is the Portuguese money of account, as the standard, but this money of account has been progressively declining in value. For clearness of conception it is convenient to take the fractional value of a penny worked out by Yule in his Glossary;[1] at the same time it will be understood from the history of the Goa coinage to be given, that the fluctuations in the value of the *real* have been much more violent than these figures would lead us to suppose.

	Decimal of one penny.
Value of a real at beginning of 16th century .	.268
Value of a real at beginning of 17th century .	.16
Value of a real at beginning of 18th century .	.06

The value of a real now is about .035 of a penny. The early copper coins of Goa were called *Leals;* 4 leals were worth 5 reals. There was also a local copper coinage called *bazarucos* by the Portuguese (corrupted to *budgrook* by the English), and 5 of these were equal to 6 reals. In time the bazaruco supplanted the leal. It was many years before the Portuguese authorities started either a gold or silver coinage of their own, and the people of Goa regarded all their attempts with a noisy suspicion that was undoubtedly abundantly justified.

294 varieties. There was a standing order that all items of accounts must show the coinage in which payment was made.—Ar. Port. Or., Fasc. 5; No. 10, March 23, 1519.

[1] Underheading Pardâo, p. 837.

The current value of the different coins stated in terms of the real were:

	Reals.
Muzafarshahi new of $23^1/_2$ tangas (gold) . . .	1,410
Muzafarshahi old of 21 tangas (gold)	1,260
San Thomé Portuguese gold coin of 1549 . .	1,000
Venezeano, Sultani, Ibrahimi	420
Cruzado	400
Pardâo	360
Ashrafi of Aden and Maldives	360
Ashrafi of Ormuz, Cochin and Ceylon . . .	300
Tanga	60
Fanam	40
Vintem	20

The history of the copper coinage is a good introduction to the shorter one of the gold and silver currency. When Albuquerque took Goa (1510) copper was valued at 13 pardâos the quintal—128 lbs.—and he coined that weight of copper into 3,736 leals, which represented the true value.[1] Alcaçova, the short-lived Comptroller of Revenue in 1517, calculated that 3,744 leals should be made from a quintal of copper at a cost of 1,042 reals; the lynx-eyed Afonso Mexia could not, however, let this pass, and he ordered that whatever the number of leals struck, the cost of coining a quintal of copper must never exceed 450 reals.[2] In the time of Nuno da Cunha (1529—38) copper had risen to 16 pardâos the quintal, and the number of leals coined was increased accordingly. Under his successor, D. Garcia de Noronha (1538—40), copper rose to 18 pardâos—and owing to the fall in the value of money he raised subsistence allowance (mantimento) from 4 to 6 tangas

[1] 13 pardâos at 360 reals each=4,680 reals, which at 4 leals=5 reals is 3,744 leals.

[2] Ar. Port. Or., Fasc. 5, No. 5.

(5*s* 4*d* to 8*s*). Martim Afonso de Sousa (1542—45) was the first who tampered with the coinage. Copper was worth from 18 to 20 pardâos the quintal, but he coined that weight into bazarucos nominally worth 36 pardâos. As the Portuguese lived in settlements scattered along the coast, they were dependent upon their neighbours for the necessaries of life, and naturally those not living in the settlements refused to take these coins at more than their value as metal. Workmen declined to work and merchants to bring goods for sale. D. Joâo de Castro (1545—48) remedied the abuse and reduced the number to 25 pardâos' worth. His successors gradually lessened the size of the coin until, in the time of D. Constantine de Bragança (1558—61), it had risen to 42 pardâos' worth. As the old evils reproduced themselves D. Francisco Coutinho (1561—64) reduced the number to 35. Matters remained fairly quiescent until the second term of D. Luis d'Ataide (1578—81), when he, "against all justice human and divine," tampered with the coinage all round, and coined 56 pardâos' worth of bazarucos from copper barely worth 25. The next change was back to 42. Taking 25 pardâos the quintal as the standard when the real was worth .268 of a penny, it was worth .16 when the same amount of copper was coined into 42 pardâos' worth, and .06 when it was coined into 56 pardâos' worth. The value of the real was subject, therefore, to far more violent fluctuations than Yule's account shows, but the figures that he gives may be taken as an approximation to the truth for the sake of clearness. [1]

Albuquerque is said to have struck some silver coins; their names never appear in mercantile transactions, and they would seem rather to have been medals than coins. [2] Garcia de Sa's new coin, the San Thomé, worth about

[1] The facts stated above were not efore Yule when he made his calculations.

[2] The words of Nunes, p. 31, imply that there was no special coinage for

£ 1, met with considerable opposition when first struck in 1549, but it was worth its face value and held its own. D. Afonso de Noronha (1550—54) began experiments in silver coinage soon after 1550, when he issued "Patecoons" on the pattern of pieces of 8. Their exact value is not recorded, but was some fraction of 2,400 reals, that is of 8 Cochin ashrafis. Their originator kept them at full value, but his successors, D. Pedro Mascarenhas (1554—55) and Francisco Barreto (1555—58) could not let the coin rest. They kept the weight and fineness the same, but raised the nominal value of the unit from 2,400 reals to 3,540 reals (3,300 for the silver and 240 for the coinage). There was thus on the silver alone a profit of $37^1/_2$ p.c. on the coining, and genuine coins struck in the country round poured into the Portuguese settlements. In 1566 D. Antâo de Noronha tried to stop this flood of foreign money by stopping the coining of Patecoons in Portuguese territory, but naturally those made outside continued to pour in until D. Luis d'Ataide in his first term rendered them uncurrent, much to the relief of the people of Goa, who called them the "devil's scourge." On his second return to India (1578—81) he lost, however, all the good name he had acquired, by striking ashrafis of which five-sevenths of the weight was silver and two-sevenths copper. This raised the exchange 50 p.c. against Portuguese India. His successor, Fernâo Telles (1581), remedied this abuse.

Nothing has been said of the decrease in the purchasing power of money. Yule is undoubtedly correct in saying

Goa except copper when he wrote (1554). See also Ar. Port. Or., Fasc. 2, p. 174, where it is clearly said that Albuquerque only coined copper as there was plenty of gold and silver coin. See also Ar. Port. Or., Fasc. 5, p. 326, *note*, which shows that by a refinement of cupidity the debased coinage was only received in payment of Government dues at its current and not at its face value. Correa's account of Albuquerque's coining must refer to medals.

that up to about 1860 the purchasing power of money in India had remained almost unaltered within historical times. The rise there has been has taken place since that time.[1]

Remuneration of Officers.—The social system of the Portuguese recognised roughly two classes,[2] (1) Fidalgoes, (2) Soldiers; there was in India a cross division into married and single. The higher classes were possessed of privileges, but the lowest, that is the bachelor soldier, had none; he was the mere sweepings of Portugal. Pay on the Indian establishment was calculated on a rather elaborate plan, there was (1st) *Soldo,* or pay of a man's rank—this depended on classification founded chiefly on birth; (2nd) *Mantimento,* or subsistence allowance, which to some extent depended on place of service;[3] (3rd) *Ordenado* or pay of an appointment. A man who received ordenado got neither soldo nor mantimento, though a person who received soldo generally got mantimento. In time another element grew up which overrode all the others, and this was *percalços* or profits. A man willingly gave up everything else to keep the profits of an appointment. As soldo could only be drawn on a special order of the Governor and after an audit by the central pay-office, first at Cochin and afterwards at Goa, it was often in arrear. Mantimento could be drawn anywhere.[4]

In that extraordinary monument of industry, the accounts which Luiz de Figueiredo Falcâo prepared for his master in 1612, the pay and profits of every office in India are

[1] See Ar. Port. Or., Fasc. 2, Nos. 54, 61—both very important papers, and A. Nunes Livro dos pesos e medidas e moedas. Many of the facts have been extracted from statements scattered up and down the historians, and complete references would be lengthy and at the same time unsatisfactory.

[2] For a more minute division see Linschoten, Vol. I. p. 187.

[3] Yule Glossary *s. v.* Batta suggests that it and Mantimento corresponded.

[4] Ar. Port. Or., Fasc. 5, Nos. 10, 11.

scheduled. Take Sofala; the pay of the post of Captain in three years was £850 and the profits £57,000. As the pay of an office was a matter of indifference it remained unchanged, or even decreased, in spite of the depreciation of money. Thus in 1550 the Captain of Ormuz received £600 a year and £216 as the salary of his guard, which represented the £450 a year and the share of the cargo fixed by Albuquerque. By 1612 there was a considerable change. Owing to the fall in the value of money the Captain's pay had sunk to £400 a year, but the pay of his guard had risen to £540, and he was also allowed £860 as the pay of 40 hangers-on supported out of public funds.

In the earlier voyages a man received pay from the day of embarcation, but, commencing from about 1540, men at arms were sent out with no pay (Soldo); with some it was to commence on arrival, with some six months later, and with some one year later. It grew to be the custom for soldiers to receive no pay for months after they came out, and from this a vast amount of misery resulted. The newly arrived Portuguese ("Reynols" as they were called) were the sport of the older inhabitants, and they had no chance of earning an honest living; they starved in the streets, begged from wealthier men, hired themselves out as cut-throats or bullies, or turned robber on their own account; some deserted to native states and changed their religion. Certain of the leading men kept a table open to their immediate dependants who were bound to follow their patrons in all their enterprises. When an opportunity occurred for service the soldier fought under his patron's banner and was paid by the King. On return from the service he produced at the registry office (Matricola) a certificate of his Captain, which entitled him to one from the office, and when a man obtained enough certificates from the Matricola he returned to Portugal to claim some reward for his services. The usual form this took was the reversion of an office, but these grants were given so lavishly that Couto tells us he met a man of 40 who had got one of which he could not avail himself until 30 grantees who preceded him had enjoyed and vacated the office, When it was pointed out to him that there was no chance of entering on the office for nearly one hundred years he replied that at all events he could make a good marriage and dower his son well. [1] It resulted that no troublesome questions of fitness interfered to delay an appointment, and when a man or his heir after long waiting did obtain the post, he made the most of his three years' term to enrich himself.

Another method of rewarding service was by the grant of a voyage. The licenses to make trading voyages were valuable assets and as such they were the subject of sale, sometimes therefore one was given to a religious or charitable institution. There is a case recorded at the end of the 16th century where a man purchased three of these voyages to Japan,—one from the heirs of his own father, one from the Church of St. John in Goa, and one from the Goa hospital which required rebuilding, and he took all three at once. Falcâo has transmitted to us their estimated value. In 1612, voyages to Pegu, Tenasserim, Banda, Sunda and Bengal were extinct. The China and Japan voyage was worth £25,000; St. Thomas by Malacca, £5,600; Goa by Mozambique, £6,000; Moluccas, £7,000; and Ceylon, £500.

On May 2nd, 1614, soon after Falcâo's report had shown the large profits individuals could make in India, the King of Portugal suspended all royal grants and ordered the Viceroy to put up for sale by public auction all commands

[1] Couto, XII. I. 10. Offices were even given to the man (unknown) whom such and such a woman may be pleased to marry. In one such instance after marriage, the man and his wife each sold the reversion to a different person. See Ar. Port. Or., Fasc. 5, Nos. 339 and 375.

of fortresses, all other offices and all voyages, and give them—on a vacancy occurring—to the highest bidder. The document, which is quoted with textual incorrectness in Bocarro. Decada 13, p. 367, will be found in full, stripped of Bocarro's softening additions, in Fasciculo 6 of the Archivo Portuguez Oriental, No. 353, p. 1059. It stands as one of the most remarkable state confessions of utter demoralization on record.

Banished Men.—It was the custom to take out banished men to be sent on any desperate service. Some of these were criminals of a bad type, who wandered off, besmirched the Portuguese name, and sometimes even caused the Portuguese considerable direct trouble. Thus, Antonio Fernandes, a ship's carpenter, sent out with Pedro Alvarez Cabral, turned Muhamedan, and, as Abdulla, led the attack on Anjadiva in 1505.[1] Joâo Machado, on the other hand, did his countrymen good service. He was a man of good family in Braga, who, disgraced in a love affair, was banished in Pedro Alvarez Cabral's fleet for a technical offence. He was left on the East African coast in 1500, but wandered to India, and in 1510, when Albuquerque took Goa, was in the service of the Adil Shah. At the darkest time of the defence of Goa in 1511, he restored confidence to the Portuguese by deserting to them. He was a man of education, was made thanadar of the city in 1513[2] and was killed in a senseless expedition organized by the Captain of Goa in 1517.[3]

1 Barros, I. 10. 4. Correa, I. 584.

2 Ar. Port. Or., Fasc. 5, No. 1.

3 History repeats itself. In a recent war with Morocco it was stated that a regiment of criminals had been enlisted by Spain for desperate service. Banished men were sent out in some of the earliest English voyages to the East.

APPENDIX

The Portuguese historians seem to show that scant justice has been done to Alvaro d'Ataide, Xavier's antagonist at Malacca, by ecclesiastical writers. It is very doubtful if he was doing more than insisting on his just rights in claiming to appoint the commander of the ship for the China voyage, while in requiring the command for *protégé* a Xavier was overstepping the boundary of his province. Alvaro d'Ataide was a son of Vasco da Gama; there are black sheep in every family and he may have been one, but his brothers, Estavâo da Gama, Christovâo da Gama and Paulo da Gama, were all men of exceptionally high standard. There had, too, been ill blood between the Captain and the ecclesiastic before. Xavier was closely allied to that Governor, Martim Afonso de Sousa, who had worked Alvaro d'Ataide a cruel wrong. All three had come out in the same fleet, and while waiting for a wind at Mozambique, De Sousa had suspected that d'Ataide intended sending ahead a message to warn his brother, Estavâo da Gama, then Governor, that a successor was on his way to oust him, as was indeed natural. On this suspicion De Sousa deprived d'Ataide of his ship, and kept him in close confinement for several months after the fleet had reached India. He could not certainly have borne good will either to De Sousa or to those whom he could only look on as De Sousa's allies, and any intercourse between d'Ataide and Xavier must have been interrupted by asperities. I have not seen this noted by any writer on Xavier's history. The facts fall within the period of Couto's sixth decade, there is, therefore, no trustworthy secular historian of them.

CHAPTER V

1497—1501

By the end of the fifteenth century, the Portuguese had, by a series of expeditions extending over nearly a century, explored the African coast down its whole Western face and up some leagues of its Eastern, beyond the Cape of Good Hope. From the notes of the overland traveller, Covilham, they had also gained some knowledge of the trade routes and trade centres of the Indian Ocean. In the last decade of that century, then, the Portuguese were in a position to join their land and sea explorations and make the final effort to discover the sea route to India.

The command of the expedition organized to outflank the Muhamedan trade monopoly by opening out the passage by the Cape of Good Hope, was entrusted to Vasco da Gama, a man of 37 years of age, of whose previous history we are ignorant. His personality had more influence on the early connection of the Portuguese with India than the mere events of his first voyage. He is described as a man of medium height, stout build and florid complexion, harsh in manner, bold in attack, much to be feared in his anger, and with no feeling of mercy to temper his justice. His physical powers of endurance, and his energy were exceptional, and his firmness indomitable. Combined with his inflexibility his temper was cruel, violent and passionate, —he could wait for years for his revenge, and then take one at which the world still shudders. He was accompanied by his elder brother, Paulo da Gama, a man whose sweetness of character was curiously reproduced in more than one of Vasco da Gama's sons, more especially in that noble Christovão da Gama, who led the expedition into Abyssinia in 1541. The two brothers were inseparable, and it is to Paulo and his influence over the crews that the success of the voyage was to a great extent due. His kindness and helpfulness to those sick of that dreadful disease—scurvy—which raged on the ships, was ever after held in affectionate remembrance. Paulo died at Terceira on the homeward voyage, broken down by the hardships he had undergone. Vasco da Gama appears never to have recovered from the blow, for the more repellant features of his character became from this time accentuated.

The three vessels which formed Vasco da Gama's command varied from 60 to 150 tons burden,[1] they left Portugal on July 8th, 1497, and anchored off Kappat, a small village 8 miles north of Calicut, on May 17th, 1498. The Portuguese had treated the Arab colonists with whom they came in contact on the east coast of Africa with the same high-handed disregard of all rights which they had always shown in their dealings with the negroes of the west coast, and there can be no doubt but that news of this had preceded Da Gama to India and predisposed against him that powerful body of Muhamedan traders which formed such an important element in the society of the Malabar Coast. This predisposition, however, merely anticipated the inevitable. The Portuguese came to the East with the determination to wrest from the Muhamedans their commercial advantages, and whether the latter learned this earlier or later mattered certainly but little in the eventual history. At the same time the fact of this speedy communication

[1] I have added 1/5th to the nominal tonnage to reduce it to the denomination of the present day.

between the two distant countries is not only interesting in itself, but it also explains some of the difficulties which Da Gama encountered.

The first act of the Samuri, the Hindu ruler of Calicut, was, however, friendly. The south-west monsoon was blowing in its first strength, and on that exposed coast there were few harbours safe from its fury. At Pandarani Kollam, a few miles north of Kappát, however, lay then and lies still one of those remarkable mud banks which form one of the natural features of this coast.[1] Although in very heavy weather the sea sometimes makes a breach, still, partly from the shelter of the bank and partly from the effects of the oil discharged through the mud by natural vents, there is between the bank and the shore a stretch of smooth sea where in ordinary years vessels may lie in safety. The Samuri's pilot conducted the ships to this anchorage, and the first dispute with their new acquaintances occurred over the berthing of the vessels. The pilot considered that the only safe holding was close in shore; Da Gama, fearing too close proximity to an unknown people adhered to his own view, and the ships lay some distance out. The long row from the shore to the ships on one occasion when, one squally evening, the shore boatmen refused to take him off to his vessels, led to the so-called "imprisonment" of Da Gama.

On the invitation of the Samuri, Da Gama with thirteen companions landed to travel overland to Calicut, a distance of twelve miles, to visit him.[2] Misled by the idea that all natives of India (excluding of course Muhamedan settlers)

[1] For more about these mud banks see Logan, "Malabar", Vol. I. p. 36. The H.E.I.C. ship, "Morning Star", took refuge in the monsoon of 1793 behind this very bank—the storms were unusually violent, the sea breached the bank and the ship was wrecked.

[2] Da Gama's ships never visited Calicut.

were Christians, the little party worshipped in a Hindu temple, though they certainly marvelled at the frescoes of the saints whose teeth projected a thumb's length from their mouths, and who had four or five arms apiece. They mistook the *janeo*, or sacred cord of the Hindus, for a stole. This visit had not a successful termination—Da Gama had no present to offer the Samuri. "Did you come to discover stones or men? If men, and your king is so great—why did he not send a present?" asked the angry ruler. The permission to trade which Da Gama requested was only granted in a very indeterminate form. That the Muhamedan traders seized the opportunity given them by the irritation of the Samuri to inform him of the proceedings of Da Gama on the African Coast, is certain, they could hardly under the circumstances be blamed for so doing. In spite of this his conduct to the Portuguese continued to be marked by considerable courtesy. Da Gama's wares do not appear to have been well selected for the Calicut market, and this under the circumstances is not surprising. When five days after his return to his ships Da Gama complained to the Samuri that the Muhamedans would not buy his goods at his own price, the Samuri first sent a broker to help, and this failing, he, towards the end of June, conveyed them at his own cost to Calicut.

The relations of the Portuguese with the people of the country continued very friendly, the shore-going parties met with a most hospitable reception, and the ships were encumbered with the numbers that came off.[1] It is interesting to learn that even then the population pressed so closely on the means of subsistence, that none of the sailors could appear with a piece of biscuit in his hand that it was not begged from him by children or even grown up people.

[1] "Que nos aborreciam", says the Roteiro.

By the middle of August, when the strength of the south-west monsoon had begun to decline, Da Gama prepared for his return to Europe. He had disposed of but few of his goods, but he had secured specimens of the articles obtainable in the Calicut market, and had gathered a good deal of information as to what was most in demand there. He appears to have been assisted to some extent by an Italian who had then lived on the Malabar Coast for nearly twenty years, but chiefly by a Tunis Muhamedan, who could speak Spanish, whom the Portuguese called Monçaide. Monçaide so openly took their side that he found it convenient to leave for Europe in Da Gama's ships. The expedition did not, however, sail without a further misunderstanding with the Samuri. Da Gama, seeing the country people friendly, asked permission to leave a factor and his merchandise in Calicut. This request was met by a demand for customs' dues, and, failing immediate payment, both Da Gama's messenger and all the goods on shore were seized. Da Gama in reprisal captured a dozen natives of the country, who ventured on board his ships, and although after a few days the Portuguese and the goods were returned, Da Gama eventually left the Coast with five of his captives still prisoners on his ships. Having done so much to render the position of his successor difficult, he finally sailed on August 29th, 1498.

He spent some days of September refitting at the Anjadiva Islands off the Indian coast,[1] and while there captured a Grenadine Jew, who, enslaved in his youth and made a Muhamedan, had drifted to India and was then employed as

[1] Anjadiva Islands have their place in English history. When, in 1661, an English force was sent to take possession of Bombay under the then recent treaty, the local authorities refused to acknowledge the orders from Portugal. Pending diplomatic negotiations Lord Marlborough landed the troops on Anjadiva. Sir Abraham Shipman, the General, and 300 of the 500 troops died there in a few months.

a spy on Da Gama. As Gaspar da India or Gaspar d'Almeida he played a distinct, though subordinate part, in the events of the next eleven years.

Two of Da Gama's original ships reached Portugal after an absence of two years, with 55 survivors of the 170 who had started on the expedition.

Poets and even historians have surrounded the comparatively simple facts of this voyage with fictions, but stripped of its romance, the story does not suffer in interest. It stands out as one of the epoch-making landmarks in the world's history. Apart from its effect on the course of events, the first meeting since the days of Alexander, 1,800 years before, of the civilizations of the East and West must always retain its interest. That the Samuri failed to grasp the significance of the arrival of three weather-beaten ships on his coast is true, but many generations elapsed before Indian rulers of far greater political sagacity than he, understood fully what the advent of strangers from over the sea did mean. Throughout the whole stay of the Portuguese the Samuri showed no signs of treachery, he was an Oriental ruler bound by custom, and when those customs were violated by navigators coming to his harbours, he enforced them with the means at his disposal. On the other hand, Da Gama's conduct in carrying off the 5 men he had entrapped on board his ships is indefensible.

Vasco da Gama returned to Europe with ideas strangely incorrect as to the India he had visited, for to him all the East that was not Muhamedan continued to be Christian. Hindus, Buddhists, Syrian Christians and pagans were alike confounded.[1] Considering the scanty intercourse that he and the chief men of his fleet had with the shore, this is not surprising.

[1] See list of the Indian countries at the end of the Roteiro.

No time was lost after the return of Vasco da Gama in utilizing his discoveries. The new fleet of which Pedro Alvarez Cabral was the commander, consisted of thirteen vessels, carried 1,200 men and started on March 9th, 1500. Among the captains were Bartholomew Dias, who first rounded the Cape, and Nicholas Coelho, the companion of Da Gama. Even at this early date rumours of the gold mines of Southern Central Africa had reached Europe, and one of the objects of the expedition was to explore them. The sailing orders were very voluminous [1] and assumed that the Samuri and all the inhabitants of India, save the Muhamedans, were Christians, but Christians who required teaching. Cabral was to land Baltazar and the other Malabaris whom Da Gama had brought home, who had been instructed in the Christianity of the West. [2] Cabral was not to land without hostages, and he was to endeavour to awaken the Samuri to his duty as a Christian prince, to turn all the Muhamedans out of the country. Failing a satisfactory settlement with the Samuri, he was to leave Calicut and go on to "Callimur," by which Cananor is apparently meant. After all the minute instructions, he was given a discretion to use a free hand if he found anything contrary to the custom of the country in them. Unfortunately for Cabral, he obeyed his orders to the letter and neglected the saving clause.

The misfortunes of the unlucky expedition began early; one ship parted company off Cape Verde, the remainder stretched across the Atlantic to take advantage of the winds, and discovered Brazil. Another ship had to be sent home

[1] It is interesting to compare the reality in An. Mar. e Col., 5th series, p. 208, and 3rd series, p. 351, with Barros, I. 5. 1, who has tinted them as he considers they should have been.

[2] It is certainly remarkable that in the process of instructing the Indians it had not been discovered that they were not Christians, but the fact remains.

with the news of this discovery. The remaining eleven left the American coast for the Cape on May 3rd; on the 23rd the ships handed their sails for a north-easter, the next day was a dead calm and they hoisted them again; a threatening cloud came up unnoticed, and the sails were left flapping against the masts. Four vessels, including that of Bartholomew Dias, were overturned in the squall and all on board perished. Seven ships then rounded the Cape—one ran up the coast of Madagascar, which island it discovered, and reached Berbera, with many of the crew sick. As the Arabs seemed friendly, fifty of the sick and ten sound men were put on shore, leaving twenty too ill to move and about the same number of able-bodied men on board. The Arabs, seeing their chance, killed those on shore. Fortunately for themselves, those on board, warned by the tumult, were able to cut their cable, hoist some sail, and get an offing. When at length she reached Europe, only six of her original crew were alive.

On August 7th Pedro Alvarez Cabral, with his six vessels, started for India from the African Coast, and reached Calicut on September 13th. Acting on his instructions, he sent on shore the five returning Indians, all low caste men, dressed as Europeans; he did not know that the Samuri could not even look on such polluted wretches. On September 18th Cabral and the Samuri met at a house near the shore. The latter had yielded the—to him—unusual demand for hostages, and two Nairs remained on board while Cabral was on shore. A request by the Samuri at the end of the interview, that the commander should return to his ships to release the hostages to allow them to eat, made Cabral, who thought he was being flouted, lose his temper; he did not, of course, know the strict caste rule. As he was leaving the Samuri in a rage, he was told that in consequence of an oral message the hostages had tried to escape from the ship, but had failed. Leaving the Portuguese and his goods on shore to their fate, he hurried back.

The following day the Malabaris put off with the abandoned Portuguese, and those in the ships started to meet them with the hostages. The two sets of boats remained facing each other all day, neither side trusting the other; the silence was only broken by the dismal wails of the captive Portuguese to their friends to save them. The next day the Samuri shewed his manliness by returning the Portuguese and the goods in an unarmed boat. No further intercourse followed for some days, and then a factor, Aires Correa, was sent to arrange a peace; the negotiations were long, and it was not until two and a half months had elapsed since their first coming that peace was concluded; the terms, which are not known, were engraved on plates of metal. The position of the Portuguese at this time was very favourable, they had a factory and leave to fly their own flag.[1]

Cabral was suffering from intermittent fever, and the worries incidental to his position overwhelmed him; every quintal of pepper cost him a quartan fit, as one writer puts it. The Portuguese were ignorant of the ways of the country, and the interests of the larger portion of the Muhamedan traders were opposed to theirs. It is no matter of surprise therefore that, at the end of three months from the date of their arrival, only two ships were loaded. The Portuguese arrogated the sole right to buy pepper, and finding the supply came in but slowly, they complained to the Samuri that the Muhamedan traders were secretly loading their vessels with what should have come to them. It is not

[1] The Samuri also got them to bring to a ship laden with elephants, when he wanted to buy one. A great deal has been made out of what was apparently a simple incident.

quite certain exactly what reply they got, apparently it was to the effect that the Portuguese might take any pepper they found, provided they paid cost price for it. Whatever it was, no attempt was made to allow its tenor to be generally known, but the Portuguese at once proceeded to act on their interpretation of it.

On the morning of December 16th they seized a ship belonging to the Arabs that was at anchor in the harbour. The news of the outrage spread quickly through the city, and the riot that ensued swelled so quickly that the Italian, Bonadjuto de Albâo, [1] though he ran to warn the factory, only reached there just ahead of the mob. The people had hitherto been so friendly that the seventy or eighty Portuguese on shore had only seven or eight cross-bows and their swords: among them were Father Henry, afterwards Bishop of Ceita, two other priests, and the anonymous pilot who wrote the account in Ramusio. With their scanty weapons the Portuguese made a desperate defence, but the Malabaris had lost all fear of death, and literally pulled the factory to pieces. Aires Correa and some thirty or forty Portuguese were killed—some thirty, including those above named, escaped to the ships, mostly wounded. Some of the wounded were sheltered by the townspeople, and were alive years afterwards. The two children of Aires Correa, who were playing in a harem with the children of a friendly Muhamedan, were saved; one of them lived to make himself a reputation as a soldier. At the commencement of the riot, Correa had signalled to Cabral; the latter was in a fever fit, and thinking it merely a factory brawl did nothing. The boats were sent off in time to pick up

[1] This is the Portuguese form of the name. He was a Venetian who had lived twenty-two years in India, having originally gone there with Francisco Marcillo, a Venetian consul in Alexandria, who was on a mission. He went to Europe with Albuquerque in 1503 nad returned with Almeida.

a few stragglers, with energy more might have been saved.[1]

Cabral was now in a most difficult position, he even waited twenty-four hours in case peace might still be possible; but when all hope of this had gone he showed his energy by seizing 600 boatmen, sailors belonging to ships from other parts, who had nothing to do with the quarrel, and slaughtering them; many were roasted alive in their own boats.[2] Calicut was bombarded for two days, the destruction of the flimsy houses was not much loss, but it was said that many people were killed. As the recoil from the firing did more damage to the ships than the bullets did to the town, the bombardment was stopped.

The Portuguese position was now very serious, the season had nearly passed, only two of the ships had any cargo at all, and they knew of no port on the Indian coast where they could safely pass the monsoon. In one of the councils, Gaspar da India suggested Cochin as a place where they might possibly get cargo. They were off that port on December 24th, a message elicited a promise of help; prices were arranged without any formal treaty or meeting with the Raja,—and in less than a fortnight the ships were laden.[3]

On January 9th, 1501, came the news that a Calicut fleet of 80 or 85 ships was sailing down the coast to attack Cabral. Cabral refused all offers of help from Cochin, and that night, extinguishing all his lights, stole away. He left so hurriedly that he took with him some Nair hostages—

[1] Albuquerque lays the blame for this catastrophe on the Portuguese. —Cartas, p. 130.

[2] Three elephants were killed in one of the boats and the flesh salted for the crews.

[3] While here, there came to the ships from Cranganor two Christians, Mathias who died soon after, and Joseph who visited Europe. See Grynaeus, "Novis orbis regio", under head of Josephus Indus, for his account.

men changed every day during the lading—and left behind Gonçalo Gil Barbosa of Santarem, the factor, and some thirty Portuguese in the factory. Among those thus abandoned was Duarte Barbosa, whose work on the African and Malabar Coasts has been translated into English.[1] He was brother-in-law of Magalhaens and accompanied that great man on his voyage round the world, and was killed with him.

The following day Cabral and the Samuri's fleet lay becalmed in sight of each other, but when the slant of wind came the prudent Cabral sailed away. Passing Cananor, the Raja there offered to supply any deficiencies in the cargo; the offer was accepted, and this was the beginning of the long connection of the Portuguese with that place. The troubles of Pedro Alvarez Cabral did not end when he left the Indian coast. On the night of February 12th—13th, the ship commanded by Sancho de Toar was wrecked, but the crew was saved. Five laden vessels reached Portugal in safety, and the cargo was so rich that it more than repaid the cost of the whole fleet.

The voyage of Pedro Alvarez Cabral is very important because, through the incapacity and ineptitude of its commander, the breach with the Samuri became irreparable, and because the discovery of Cochin entirely altered the policy of the Portuguese. Cochin harbour was far superior to the open roadstead of Calicut, and the magnificent inland communications it had with the pepper country were unlike anything obtaining at its rival. Calicut owed its importance partly to the ability of its rulers, but mainly to the assistance they received from the Muhamedan traders that frequented it. By adopting Cochin, therefore, the Portuguese

[1] Published by the Hakluyt Society. Gaspar Correa has a great deal in praise of his linguistic accomplishments.

were certain of having the chief on their side, as he could look to them only to support his position.

The fleet of 1501 under Joâo da Nova was a trading fleet of 4 vessels, which went and returned in safety. Da Nova heard at Mozambique of the events of Cabral's stay, and avoided Calicut, though he had a brush with the Samuri's flotilla. St. Helena was discovered on the return voyage.

CHAPTER VI

1502—1504

THE information brought by Pedro Alvarez Cabral changed the whole policy of the Portuguese towards India. It was recognized that the Indians were not Christians, and that Cochin was the natural rival of Calicut. Some idea, too, of the natives and traders of Southern India as a fighting force had been gained. With the consent of the Pope, the King of Portugal assumed at this time the high-sounding titles of Lord of the Navigation, Conquest and Commerce of Ethiopia, Arabia, Persia and India, and to enforce the claims these titles carried with them, Cabral was first appointed to the command of the largest fleet hitherto sent, but the feeling of his inefficiency grew so strong that he was put on one side in favour of Da Gama. The fleet that was to command the sea, and divert all the trade of the East with Europe to Portugal, consisted of twenty ships. Fifteen started on February 10th, under Da Gama, and five of these, under Vincent Sodre, his relative, were to remain permanently in the Indian Seas; five other vessels, under Estavâo da Gama, another relative, left on April 1st.

After reaching the Indian coast where Anjadiva was the rendezvous, [1] the ships spread out to intercept a rich ves-

[1] Thomé Lopes, who has left such a valuable record of this voyage, was in the Ruy Mendes de Brito, Captain João de Buona Gracia. This ship was one of the last to join at Anjadiva, when she caused considerable excitement. Da Gama, thinking she was a Red Sea ship, hurriedly left Mass to attack

sel known to be on its way from the Red Sea. She was met with on Sept. 29th, and found to carry 240 men besides many women and children.[1] She made no defence, possibly on account of the women and children, possibly because the 10 or 12 wealthy Calicut merchants on board, whose leader was called according to the Portuguese, *Joar Afanqui*,[2] expected to ransom her. None of Joar's offers, however, were accepted; all the men were disarmed and everyone was told to give up what property he pleased. The boats of the fleet were next ordered to dismantle the Muhamedan ship; her sails, rigging and rudder were removed and she was set on fire, but the Muhamedans extinguished the conflagration, collected the very few arms that were left, prepared to sell their lives dearly, and beat off the boats sent to rekindle the flames. Vasco da Gama, says Lopes, looked on through his port-hole and saw the women bringing up their gold and their jewels and holding up their babies to beg for mercy, but there was no mercy.

João de Buona Gracia was ordered on October 3rd to capture the Muhamedan vessel by boarding. "It was a day I shall remember all my life," says Lopes.[3] Though they grappled, they could not board, the sides were high, and as they disdained to wear armour to fight unarmed men they were beaten below by showers of stones, and only now and again could they shoot one of their opponents with a cross-bow bolt. The Muhamedans cared neither for death nor wounds; they plucked out the arrows, even

her. Lopes was told that on the way across Da Gama had gone far north towards the house of "Mecca", and entered a river where was a town called Calimal, where the people were friendly. The author of Calcoen calls it Combaen on the Colar River. It is not clear what place is meant.

[1] The author of Calcoen says 380 men and many women and children; Lopes has been followed—the number would only approximately be known.

[2] Jauhar Effendi?

[3] See the account in Thomé Lopes, beginning at page 179.

from their own bodies, to throw back. By evening the Portuguese captain was badly wounded and his battered helmet torn from his head, the forecastle was entered and captured, the sailors began to fling themselves into the sea, and the few defenders of the ship would have been overwhelmed had not another ship—the "Joia"—drawn off the attention of the Muhamedans by a feint of boarding, and given the "Ruy Mendes de Brito" breathing time to escape. For four more days and four more nights the Portuguese followed the doomed ship, firing into her with their bombards. As they were on the point of giving up the attack in despair, a traitor swam off and offered to fire her if they would spare his life, his offer was accepted and he became a slave; the ship was burned with all in her, save a few children.[1] It is difficult to exaggerate the horror of that death-agony, prolonged for eight days.

Calicut was reached on October 29th: Da Gama refused to listen to any suggestions of peace until the Muhamedans were turned out of the country, and naturally these terms were not accepted. Calicut, said the Samuri, had always been a free port, and should remain so; if they wished for trade, on the security of his word, they could have it; if not, they must go. Meanwhile the fishermen, thinking there was peace for them at least, had gone out to fish, but Da Gama captured them and also the coast sailors from the rice vessels to the number of 800 men. On November 1st the Portuguese bombarded the town at their pleasure, till near nightfall. The Malabaris had two inferior guns mounted with which to reply, but they could fire them but seldom, and they could not aim. If Da Gama's name had not

[1] Correa says 20 children were saved, and a hunch-backed pilot to tell the Samuri. Lopes agrees that some children were saved. Perhaps the hunchback was the traitor. Calcoen says nothing of any survivors.

been marked by his conduct to the pilgrim ship, his treatment of his 800 prisoners would for ever have branded his reputation; he hanged them at the yard-arms, cut off their hands and heads, loaded them in a vessel and allowed it to drift ashore.[1] All that night the shore was thronged with the crowds searching for the remains of their murdered friends. The bombardment was continued on November 2nd, over 400 shot being thrown into the town; on the third Da Gama left for Cochin.

Vincent Sodre, while left behind in command of six vessels and a caravel, patrolling the coast, did an act whose consequences involved his nation a few years later in some trouble. The Raja of Cananor had a dispute with a Muhamedan merchant, "Mayimama Marakkar", and on the complaint of the Raja, Sodre grossly outraged him. The merchant from that moment plotted his revenge, and he got it. He was in the Egyptian fleet that attacked D. Lourenço in Chaul in 1508, and though he lost his own life in the encounter, the Portuguese flag-ship was destroyed and its commander killed.

At Cochin the Raja was still sulking at the kidnapping of the hostages by Cabral, but Da Gama carried matters with a high hand, beating down the rates as he had done at Cananor.[2] He organized the Cochin factory, and strengthened that at Cananor by a palisade across the neck of the promontory.[3] In this, the first voyage in which a definite claim to the dominion of the seas was put forward, and a definite war to the death with the Muhamedans was declared, Da Gama gave a term of merciless cruelty to the Portu-

[1] Correa's account is far more horrible. It is to be hoped that he exaggerated the cruelties to exalt his hero.

[2] These low rates caused much trouble. The King of Portugal could only get refuse pepper; the good went to those who paid a fair rate.

[3] Lopes says that while he was at Cochin the Raja impaled three Muhamedans who sold a cow to the Portuguese.

guese policy, exceeding even the cruelty of that age, of which he must bear the odium. The cargo ships under Da Gama reached Portugal on September 1st, 1503.

The departure of Da Gama was the signal the Samuri awaited to commence action against the Portuguese factory in Cochin. He sent several envoys to work on the Raja's caste and religious feelings to induce him to abandon the Portuguese, but in vain. Before Da Gama had left it was certain that the Samuri would revenge himself on Cochin; and the former had assured the Raja of Cochin that Sodre had been left to support him. The Portuguese both in Cananor and Cochin endeavoured to induce the latter to remain on the coast, but to all representations he turned a deaf ear. His excuse was that in the creeks, in the monsoon months, his ships could be burned; he forgot that the honour of his nation was worth many ships. When he started for his cruising ground at the mouth of the Red Sea, it is to their honour that two of his captains preferred to give up the command of their ships rather than abandon their countrymen in Cochin.

Sodre was successful in his object, and took several rich prizes. [1] On April 20th his squadron put into a bay in one of the Curia Muria islands. In May the Portuguese were warned that a gale from the North, to which the bay was exposed, would be on them soon, [2] and that their only chance of safety lay in running to the opposite side of the island. Three of the ships left while it was yet time; but Sodre with his brother, Bras Sodre, remained, for he imagined that possibly the advice was given to save merchant vessels that might be expected. When he saw the

[1] From one of them the Portuguese first learned the importance of coir for ropes.

[2] Correa says that the islanders knew by the movements of shoals of fish that the gale was coming.

islanders moving their own houses from the shore, it was too late, for the wind had fallen to a calm and a long oily sea was rolling into the bay. He did what was possible, but the wind came up from the offing, Vincent Sodre's ship was driven on shore, the masts sloped seaward, and all on board perished. Bras Sodre was more fortunate; his ship was wrecked, but the crew escaped. [1]

Affairs in Cochin went on badly. The people were opposed to their Raja's policy, but he, with rare good faith, refused to abandon the Portuguese; he refused also to allow them to retire to Cananor, or even to allow them to venture themselves in the fight. On March 31st and April 3rd the Samuri was defeated by the troops of the Raja of Cochin, but in a later battle at the Eddapalli ford the latter was defeated, and three of his nephews, including the heir apparent, Narain, were killed. Public feeling ran higher than ever against the Portuguese, but in his retreat to the Island of Vaipeen, a sanctuary the Samuri dared not violate, he took them with him. [2] The Cochin territory was overrun, and the sacred stone at which the Samuri was made the Lord of the Southern Malabar States, was removed from Cochin to Eddapalli. [3]

Only 200 of Narain's immediate following escaped from the disastrous battle in which he was killed. As they had survived their master they shaved off all their hair, even to their eyebrows, and devoted themselves to death. [4] They made their way to Calicut territory where they slaughtered all they met; twenty survived to reach the neighbourhood

[1] In some long-winded sailing orders of 1508 Vincent Sodre's fate is mentioned to point a moral.—An. Mar. e Col., 3rd series, p. 491.

[2] The two Italian gun-founders, Joâo Maria and Pero Antonio, deserted from the Portuguese at this time. Their assistance to the Samuri was invaluable.

[3] For more about this stone see page 251.

[4] Castanheda uses "Chaver", the proper word as applied to them; the usual Portuguese word is "Amoucos."

of the town, killing as the chance offered. In turn they were killed off one by one, until in five years the last was destroyed.[1] In September the reinforcements from Europe came. As Indian affairs were considered finally settled by the establishment of factories in Cochin and Cananor, no large fleet was sent in 1503. Three ships under Afonso d'Albuquerque, afterwards surnamed the Great, sailed on April 6th; three under his cousin, Francisco d'Albuquerque, on April 14th, and a third squadron under Antonio de Saldanha still later. The discovery of Saldanha Bay has kept alive Saldanha's memory which else might well be forgotten.

Francisco d'Albuquerque, with the loss of one ship, reached India before his cousin, to find the Raja of Cochin and the Portuguese still in sanctuary. He succeeded in ejecting the Samuri from the immediate outskirts of Cochin, and then, with the Raja's permission, began to build the first fortress the Portuguese had in India. On the arrival of Afonso d'Albuquerque the remainder of the Cochin territory was reduced, but the very Homeric battles of the operations are of little interest except as the occasion for Duarte Pacheco to acquaint himself with the field where he was to reap so much renown.[2] As the result of these defeats the Samuri sued for peace, which the Raja of Cochin was anxious to conclude.

The wishes of an ally who had put everything to the stake could not be ignored; the loyalty of the Raja to the Europeans was certainly extraordinary, for up to this time his only experience of Portuguese honour had been that Cabral had carried his hostages to Europe, and that Sodre, to go on a piratical cruise, had abandoned him to his fate.

[1] A similar case occurred in Cochin in Jorge Cabral's time; see p. 323.

[2] The battles resembled massacres rather than anything else: in one, for instance, eight thousand of the enemy are said to have been killed to three Portuguese.

Peace was concluded on the condition that the Samuri should pay 1,500 bahars of pepper;[1] and the heir-apparent of the Samuri came in person to Cranganor to deliver it. There was no dispute on the first consignment, but on the pretext that the second was overdue the Portuguese attacked some laden boats, and in the fight six of the Samuri's men were killed. The Portuguese, who in reality did not want peace, refused all satisfaction, and war began again. Duarte Pacheco, with ninety men and some small vessels, was left to defend Cochin, and on January 31st, 1504, the Albuquerques started. Francisco d'Albuquerque and Nicolas Coelho (the companion of Vasco da Gama) were lost; where or how was never known. The vessel of Afonso d'Albuquerque and one other reached Portugal in safety.

The defence of Cochin by Duarte Pacheco against the whole power of the Samuri is one of the most brilliant feats of arms that illustrates Portuguese history in the East. A review of his position when the homeward-bound fleet left, must have shown him that, though very difficult, it was not quite hopeless. The larger part of the native population was against him, but later experience proved, even if his earlier experience had not taught him, that on such auxiliaries no reliance could be placed. Cochin could nominally dispose of 30,000 men,—of these 8,000 only were faithful to their Raja, the remainder were actively hostile. The country round Cochin did not produce enough grain to support its population; there were patches of cultivation, but rice, the staple food of the people, had to be imported from the Coromandel Coast, and was distributed throughout the country by Muhamedan traders on whom householders depended for their daily supplies. These traders, at whose head was one Muhamad Marakkar, could therefore, if hostile, create a famine in

[1] A Cochin bahar was a little over 3 cwts.

Cochin. By a judicious mixture of threats and cajolery Pacheco got the headman's family into Vaipeen, where they were hostages, and Muhamad Marakkar himself was of the greatest help to Pacheco throughout the operations.

The Samuri was advancing at the head of 60,000 men against Pacheco's hundred; but all Eastern armies had vast numbers of foot-men, almost unarmed, among whom immense slaughter was made in every battle. It was far, indeed, from uncommon for a ruler, starting on a campaign, to burn his capital, and command all the inhabitants to follow his armies, where the women and children were at least pledges for the fidelity of their male relatives. In efficiency of arms Pacheco's advantage was almost incalculable, and he had, too, the advantage of information. The spy system, favoured by the caste organisation, was so perfect in both the camps that either side knew exactly what his opponents were doing. Thus, while Pacheco and his Portuguese could keep their own counsel, they could learn what the Samuri was planning. In Calicut, also, Pacheco had Roderigo Reynol and the Portuguese from Cabral's time, as well as friendly natives, all of whom regularly corresponded with him.

The season of the year was somewhat in his favour, the rains—when active operations would be difficult—were near, and when they were over reinforcements might be expected. As Pacheco could forecast the Samuri's movements the configuration of the country helped him, for it was a point of honour with the latter never to change the direction of his march when once that had been definitely fixed.[1] The Cochin frontier was defended, and the territory to some extent intersected, by salt-water creeks and channels, which were fordable at a few places at low water; at others, on

[1] Porque avia por injuria deixar de ir por aquelle passo por amor de Duarte Pacheco que lho defendia.—Castanheda, I. 70.

the other hand, there were ferries practicable for a certain time at high tide; in these channels the tide ran strongly. It may have been for this reason, combined with the little skill of the boatmen, or more probably from the Nair custom of fighting in close serried ranks, that no very serious attempt was made to cross the stream in boats. The Samuri's object was to capture the fort just erected by the Portuguese, and to use it against them to prevent their again landing in Cochin, and it was practically certain that his advance would be over the Eddapalli ford.[1] This ford was knee-deep at low water, except then impassable. a crossbow-shot long, with deep water at either end.

The preparations for the defence were kept secret until the Samuri was definitely committed to attacking it. On various pretexts posts 12 feet long, sharpened at one end, and fitted with cross pieces, were got ready; so that when the time came a stockade was quickly erected in mid-channel, running the whole length of the ford. At low tide the posts showed five feet above the water, and room was left between them for lance-thrusts, and even for the use of a small field-piece. At either end of the ford there was a caravel and some attendant boats, all with artillery, and strengthened with coils of rope and mantlets to fend off arrows. The approach to the ford was so narrow that the assailants could make no use of their preponderating strength, but crowded together, offered a fair mark to the Portuguese artillery.

The first attempt to cross was made on Palm Sunday, March 31st. The position was impregnable to a front attack with the arms the Samuri's men possessed; apart from that, their strategy was good. An advance was made on either flank by 20 boats, to draw off the artillery fire of the

[1] Repelim of the Portuguese.

caravels and the boats, while a storming party of 200 men with hatchets and mallets to demolish the stockade, supported by a column of 11,000 Nairs made the direct attack. The Samuri's artillery could only project stones as hard as a man could throw them, and the Portuguese guns decided the day's contest. Of the boats 21 were destroyed and three captured. The small body of defenders suffered little inconvenience except from the crowding of their antagonists. There were further attacks on Good Friday (April 5th) and on the following Wednesday, which were repulsed with even greater ease.

Of the many attacks of the next 3½ months, the most serious were, first, that in which the Samuri attempted to cross contemporaneously both the Eddapalli and the Vallanjaka ford (a little used one to which a road had to be cut), that compelled Pacheco to divide his small force; and secondly, an attack in the end of June at which certain lofty castles, each on two boats, the invention of one Khwaja Ali to command the caravels and the stockade, were used. To meet this last attack Pacheco prepared booms; some of the castles could not be steered, and these were caught on the booms and burned, while the rest were knocked into matchwood by the guns. A night attack was planned on the advice of the Italians, but it was contrary to the genius of the Nairs, and of the Samuri's force one-half furiously attacked the other half in the darkness, and many were killed before the mistake was discovered. To crown all the other disasters, a terrible outbreak of cholera swept through the Samuri's camp, kept too long in one place, and carried off 13,000 men.

Pacheco's gallant defence inspired even the low caste men to fight for their homes. A body of some 2,000 Nairs crossed by a seldom used and unguarded ford, to find themselves in an extensive rice swamp at the side of a creek, through which they had to get to take Pacheco in the rear. This rice swamp was divided up into fields by narrow earthen banks that were the only available paths. The fields were irrigated by opening small sluices in these banks. At the time the Nairs began to cross, some polers, the lowest of all the castes, were working in the fields, and when the former were well entangled in the swamp they were attacked by the latter with the tools of their husbandry. That a poler should dare even to come into the presence of a Nair was almost incredible, and so amazed were the latter, and so afraid of ceremonial defilement that all discipline and martial ardour were lost, and they were killed to a man. Pacheco was annoyed that the Raja could not make Nairs out of these polers—he had not mastered the mystery of the caste system; they had, however, substantial rewards, including the right to meet a Nair on the high road.

Pacheco, who was a born leader of men, received no reward or advancement for his gallant defence;[1] he, however, obtained a curious document from the Raja of Cochin—a grant of the Portuguese title of Dom, and of certain arms, set out with all the jargon of mediæval heraldry "on a scarlet field, to signify the amount of blood he had shed.[2]

Lopo Soares commanded the fleet of the year,[3] which consisted of 14 ships. His orders were to prevent any ships leaving Cochin except those of the Portuguese, and if the Raja objected he was to be told that this was for his benefit. Lopo Soares visited Calicut at the request of the Samuri to arrange a peace, but the Italians were an insurmountable obstacle; the Samuri would not deliver up men whom he considered his guests, and his unlucky capital

[1] See Camoens, "Os Lusiadas", canto X. 15 to 25.
[2] For this extraordinary document see Castanheda, I. 88.
[3] See An. Mar e Col., series 3, p. 355, for his sailing orders.

had to stand another two days' bombardment. The King of Portugal had, in consequence of the steadfastness of the Raja of Cochin to his allies during the early part of 1503, —of which alone he had heard at the departure of Lopo Soares—sent him valuable presents, and, in spite of the disturbance caused by the war, the ships were not long in finding a cargo.

Cranganor lies 15 miles north of Cochin, and commands several ramifications of the inland navigation; and as the passage thence to Cochin was easy and safe at all times of the year, the Samuri was collecting there the material for an extensive campaign against Cochin directly the Portuguese left the coast, but his action was anticipated, and the destruction of the town by a force under Lopo Soares was a severe blow. A worse one was to follow. At Pandarani Kullam[1] were collected 17 vessels of large size, with their bows on shore, fastened together with chains. At the entrance there was an earthwork mounting guns, and the defending force was 4,000 strong, all fighting men from the north, who, driven from Malabar by the prolonged war, were returning to their homes. It was a bold enterprise for 360 Portuguese in 15 boats and two caravels to attack vessels so defended. The two caravels were no help, but the boats, led by Lopo Soares in person, pushed home gallantly, and after a fight that lasted from morning to mid-day of December 31st, the ships and all their cargo were burned. In this dashing exploit the Portuguese had 23 killed and 170 wounded—or more than half their force.

The parting between the Raja of Cochin and Pacheco was a sorrowful one, especially to the former, for the surly

[1] Correa puts this fight at "Trampatão, a port of Cananor." This is perhaps Vallarpattanam—Dharmapattanam is nearer his name, but far too small a place. The other authorities place the fight at Pandarani Kullam—a more likely site.

demeanour of Lopo Soares repelled any request that Pacheco might remain. The Raja, impoverished by his long continued struggle with enemies his alliance with the Portuguese had brought against him, had nothing to offer Pacheco save a little pepper for a private cargo, which the latter could not take. Manuel Telles, his successor, did everything to make his gallant predecessor regretted.

CHAPTER VII

ALMEIDA, VICEROY, 1505—1509

THE Portuguese interests in the East had already passed beyond the stage in which they could be managed by an annual fleet; while the experiment of leaving a subordinate in charge in the interval between the departure of one fleet and the arrival of another had not proved satisfactory. It was therefore decided to appoint a Viceroy for three years, and the choice fell on that uncouth seaman—rough even in a rough age—Tristâo da Cunha, whose name has survived in the islands he discovered. Before he could sail, however, he was struck with temporary blindness, and D. Francisco d'Almeida was selected in his stead. Almeida was a man 45 years of age, of noble birth, the seventh son of D. Lopo d'Alméida, first count of Abrantes. He took with him a large fleet and 1,500 men at arms, and he was accompanied by his only son, D. Lourenço, a youth of great bodily strength and great proficiency in the use of all arms. [1] Almeida's orders were to build fortresses in Kilwa, Anjadiva, Cananor and Cochin. [2] He was to take with him the Captains and the staff for the fortresses, and should any of the rulers object to a foreign power putting up fortifications within their limits, a suitable

[1] For the story of his death see Camoens Os Lusiadas, X. 29—32.

[2] Similar orders were issued to him in 1506 as regards Malacca. If the ruler objected—well, he was still to build it. See these orders in An. Mar. e Col., series 4, p. 112, dated April 6th, 1506.

base was to be selected and war made until they submitted. [1]

After building a fort at Kilwa and sacking several towns on the African coast, Anjadiva was reached in time to commence a fort there on September 14th, 1505; experience showed this fort to be useless and it was dismantled in 1507. Negotiations were also begun with the authorities on the mainland, but before any definite conclusion had been arrived at, a vessel coming from the north found herself, when she opened the south of Anjadiva, in the centre of the Portuguese fleet. She turned towards the mainland, but her pursuers followed so closely on her heels that the crew had barely time to run her ashore and escape up country, leaving in her 19 horses. Before the Portuguese, however, could remove these horses, a sudden storm arose which drove them to the shelter of Anjadiva, and in the morning the horses were gone. The governor of Honawar, under Raja Nara Sinha Rao of Vijayanagara, in whose territory this happened, denied all knowledge of the animals, but offered to pay their value. This offer was refused; but in the Honawar River lay some trading vessels, and when, after some fighting, they were burned on October 16th, the Portuguese accepted the proffered price.

After the peace had been concluded, one Timoja had no difficulty in proving to Almeida the mistake he had made in attacking his natural ally, the Hindu power. The Raja of Vijayanagara was at perpetual war with his Muhamedan neighbours, and, as no horses fitted for military purposes were bred locally, it was of great importance to either side to command the import trade from Ormuz of the horses now known as Gulf Arabs. The Raja had obtained

[1] A journal of this voyage was translated into English from the Flemish, and published in 1894 as the work of Albericus Vespuccius. It seems more than doubtful if it is by him. It adds nothing to our knowledge of the events.,

at one time a considerable supply of these through his ports, but owing to the spread of Muhamedanism among the Hindus there had grown up a body of so-called Naiteas or converts who favoured their coreligionists at the expense of the Hindus. In 1479, acting on recognized lines of policy, the Raja of Vijayanagara arranged, without warning, a simultaneous attack on the Naiteas. Many were killed and the balance were driven to Goa, which from that day grew at the expense of the Raja's ports. To secure any trade at all, Vijayanagara was compelled to keep the fleet of which this Timoja was commandant, to make perpetual war on Goa. From the date of his interview with Almeida, Timoja was closely allied with the Portuguese, and in the time of Albuquerque attained some prominence.

João Homem was a captain of one of the caravels in Almeida's fleet, he was a scatterbrained man of whom many stories were told. While dropping down the Tagus when the fleet was starting, his crew, fresh from the ploughtail, did not understand the pilot's orders to larboard and starboard [1] the helm. Homem was equal to the occasion: he hung a bundle of onions on one side of the ship and a bundle of garlic on the other—"Now," he said to the pilot, "tell them to onion their helm, or garlic their helm, they will understand that quick enough." No sooner were they over the bar than he divided up all the food among the crew, to each man his share,—for he was no purser, he said,—and told them to help themselves to the water and the wine. Naturally they were still far from India when the crew came to him, weeping, to say they had no food and only water for a day. "Oh! men of little faith," said Homem, "God will provide." The very next day they reached an island with a store of good water, and wild fowls that they split and dried in the sun.

[1] These words are of northern derivation.

When the fleet reached Anjadiva, Homem was sent down the coast with orders to the different factories. At Quilon he found some Muhamedan ships loading pepper. "What "is the good," he said, "of complaining to the chief? He and "they are black together, and to take their rudders and sails "is better than all the King's orders." He stored the rudders and sails in the factory and sailed away, leaving his countrymen defenceless. Homem, on his return voyage, captured two vessels loaded with rice. He left in them the original crews of 16 men, and put in each a prize crew of three Portuguese. The prize crews went to sleep and were overpowered and killed by the original crews, who took the vessels into Calicut. When the Viceroy reached Cochin he heard that, owing to Homem's acts at Quilon, the populace had, on his departure, risen suddenly on the factory and burned alive in it all the Portuguese. Homem, who had nearly lost his caravel for his carelessness in the matter of the rice boats, was now deprived of his command.

The Viceroy started down the coast on October 18th, 1505, and at Cananor laid the foundations of a fort of stone and lime on the end of the promontory.[1] The Muhamedan party in Cananor was both powerful and wealthy, and to retain their hold on the place a fort was necessary, but Cananor rapidly sank into a place of second-rate importance.

The chieftainship of Cochin had, at the time of Almeida's arrival there, become vacant through the operation of an old custom. The head of the Cochin line was always a priest in charge of the worship of a temple—the next in succession was the ruling chief. On the death of the head, therefore, the ruling chief—who, in this case, was Trimumpara, the early friend of the Portuguese—was promoted to the temple. The question was—who was to succeed him? The senior of the

[1] The present fort stands on the site of this old one.

sister's sons in the direct line was closely allied with the enemies of the Portuguese, and the latter arranged, though not without difficulty, to set him aside for another nephew more favourable to themselves. Trimumpara died in 1510, when the Portuguese found it convenient to abolish this custom.

Owing to the presence of the Portuguese fleets on the Malabar coasts, the Muhamedan ships, trading between the extreme East and the Red Sea, had taken a new route through the Maldives, that kept them clear of their enemies. The Viceroy despatched D. Lourenço, his son, to close this route and to explore Ceylon, but, owing to the ignorance of the pilots, he missed the Maldives, though he reached Ceylon. He did little, however, there but put up a pillar at Point de Galle, and no definite occupation of the island was made for many years.[1] On his return D. Lourenço was sent northwards to Cananor on convoy duty. One day in February 1506, as he was sitting in a room in the Cananor fort, a man, who turned out to be Varthema the Italian, came in dressed as a Muhamedan, and begged for a private audience.[2] At this audience he told D. Lourenço of the extensive preparations the Samuri was making in secret. The Samuri had been, in fact, thoroughly alarmed at the attack on the towns of the African coast, at the new fortresses, and at the news that year in year out a powerful fleet and a Viceroy would stay in India. His preparations were defensive

[1] Correa, to magnify his hero D. Lourenço, describes a monster he slew in Ceylon. Apparently it is a distorted description of a crocodile. Correa was shown the bones in Ceylon in 1538.

[2] This was the Varthema whose travels were published by the Hakluyt Society in 1863. It shows the discredit into which Portuguese writers have fallen, that the editors of this work, who have ransacked the libraries of Europe (except the Portuguese) to elucidate the history of Varthema, have missed the passages which explain the dark places of his history. He returned to Europe in the fleet of Tristão da Cunha, and it is practically certain, as Yule suggested in the bibliography to his Glossary, that he never visited the further East. For Varthema's account of his escape from Calicut see page 270 of the translation.

rather than offensive. Assisted by the Arabs and other Muhamedan traders he had armed and loaded a large convoy, and the two Italian deserters, Joâo Maria and Piero Antonio, had cast for him about 500 cannon, chiefly small pieces. Varthema, as their countryman, had been much with the Italians in Calicut, where they were virtual prisoners with no hope of ever returning to their homes; they dared not trust themselves to the Portuguese, and they were far too valuable from their special knowledge to have been allowed to pass through any other part of India,—indeed, soon after Varthema left Calicut they were killed on the suspicion that they intended to abscond.

In March 1506 this armed convoy, consisting of between 200 and 300 vessels, the greater number being merely row-boats, started from the Malabar Coast; Abdu-r-Rahman, a relative of the Captain of the Red Sea ship burned by Vasco da Gama, was in command.[1] The Portuguese fleet of 3 large vessels and a brigantine brought this force to action on March 16th. There was but little fighting properly so called, but the massacre lasted two days, no Portuguese was killed, and the number of the enemy slaughtered was from 3,500 to 4,000, the largest vessels were captured and many of the smaller ones sunk.[2]

The Portuguese were by this time beginning to settle down in Cochin, but they found, as all emigrants must find, that although in the new country some articles of food were cheap, others which were almost necessaries of life could not be obtained at all. All the wheat, for instance, that came to Cochin was grown beyond the tropics to the north, in the country of their enemies, the Muhamedans, and was seldom tasted save by those of rank sufficient to dine at the Viceroy's table—its importation at all was a

[1] Varthema, p. 274.
[2] Varthema was in this fight, p. 274.

novelty. There were some fowls and a little fish in the market, but the great majority of the Europeans only had rice from captured prizes; naturally they sickened on a diet of rice and bananas varied very occasionally by meat, and to men so weakened in health the labour of building the Cochin fort was heavy. The factor had taken advantage of the interregnum between the promotion of the old Raja and the selection of the new one, to dig the foundations of the new fortress, and Almeida, directly the cargo ships were despatched, put his whole energy into finishing it; but the work was delayed as he could not find the necessary craftsmen in Cochin.

Towards the end of the year D. Lourenço d'Almeida was in command of a strong fleet that was sent northwards to convoy the trading vessels from the ports friendly to the Portuguese past the hostile harbours. He was appealed to by the crews of some Cananor and Cochin ships in one of these, for help against a superior force of blockading Calicut vessels, but the council which D. Lourenço held decided not to fight, and the Portuguese left their allies to their fate.[1] The Captains who had signed the decision of the council were deprived of their commands by the Viceroy and sent prisoners to Portugal.

Trouble had meanwhile been rapidly brewing in another quarter. While D. Lourenço's fleet was sailing north one of his ships had lagged behind to water, and hurrying after her consorts, had sighted and brought to a vessel manned by Muhamedans, who showed a pass in the usual form, signed by Lourenço de Brito, Captain of Cananor. As the captain, Gonçalo Vaz, affected to believe that the pass was

[1] Castanheda hints that D. Lourenço was afraid. He says that at the supper the evening before the Council he was pensive and expressed his wonder whether they should all meet again. The Council would hardly have gone against the strongly expressed wish of D. Lourenço.

a forgery and the ship from Calicut, he killed the crew, sewed them up in a sail, and sent the ship and the crew to the bottom. The vessel was from Cananor, owned by "Mamale Marakkar," a well-known Cananor merchant; its cargo was valuable, and his nephew was on board. The sail split, and the bodies were washed on shore and recognized. Gonçalo Vaz was deprived of his command, but no further punishment was awarded him. The Cananor Raja with whom the Portuguese had had at first to deal was dead, and as in a disputed succession the arbitrator was a Brahmin selected by the Samuri and favourable to his interests, the new Raja's views were coloured by those of the supporters of his appointment, he was therefore ready to listen to the Muhamedans that he should league himself with the Samuri against the Portuguese. Lourenço de Brito, the Captain of Cananor, only heard of this alliance late in March, and his message reached the Viceroy on Maundy Thursday, April 1st, 1507, while a miracle play was being acted in the Cochin church. No time was lost: the Viceroy went in person from house to house to collect arms, and, to show the press, it is said that the very centurions in the miracle play had to restore their borrowed doublets and greaves. In the heavy weather of the opening monsoon D. Lourenço took the reinforcements and returned in safety.

The so-called fort of Cananor consisted of a wall, cutting across the neck of the promontory from sea to sea. The two sea faces were undefended save by the stormy ocean in the monsoon months, and by the Portuguese fleet at other times. The weakness of the position lay in its water supply; the one sweet water well was outside the wall, towards the land.[1] For the first month of the siege the Portuguese, when they wanted water, had to

[1] Logan says the Cananor fort is to this day dependent on this very well for water, p. 315.

fight their way to the well and back, and lost heavily in consequence, until one Thomas Fernandez, who, from the frequency with which his name recurs, was a skilful engineer and architect, made an underground tunnel to it and covered in the top to prevent the water being poisoned. The garrison was only about 300 strong; there was certainly a large contingent of slaves which brought the total number in the fort almost to 1,000, but they were a source of danger to the garrison; for when hard times came they deserted in numbers and carried to the besiegers the news of the fortress. Whether by the design of a slave or whether by accident, one night the inflammable materials of the huts were fired, and all the food stores of the garrison, public and private, were destroyed. When all the cats and dogs and rats in the fortress had been eaten and famine stared the Portuguese in the face, and when the moderating seas of the monsoon left two sides of the settlement defenceless, the arrival of Tristâo da Cunha with the ships of 1506 raised the siege.[1] Peace was easily concluded with Cananor, for the Viceroy felt that the war had been provoked by an outrage of the Portuguese.

It is necessary to bring forward the history of this fleet of Tristâo da Cunha that arrived so opportunely. Tristâo da Cunha, who left Portugal in April 1506, commanded ten cargo vessels, and a squadron of four vessels accompanied him, under Afonso d'Albuquerque, afterwards surnamed the Great,[2] who was to build a fortress in Socotra and then go on to Ormuz and render it tributary to Portugal, thus closing, it was hoped, the mouths both of the Red Sea and of the Persian Gulf. After the expiry of Almeida's three years as Viceroy, Albuquerque was to

[1] Varthema, p. 281, says he was in this siege which, he says, lasted from April 27th to Aug. 27th. His account is rather vague and general.

[2] Albuquerque was part owner of his ship the Cirne.

succeed him as Governor of India. As the flagship was but a poor sailer, the fleet went so far south that it discovered the Tristâo da Cunha islands, and did not reach Mozambique until December, too late to save the Indian voyage that year. Of the ships which came straggling in, there was one that had coasted the east side of Madagascar; it brought ginger, cloves and silver [1] enough to fire the imagination of Tristâo da Cunha, who was at heart an explorer and adventurer, and too glad at the chance of seeing a new country to remember Socotra, Ormuz or the Red Sea.

Brave deeds were done in Madagascar among savages armed with bones tied to sticks—negroes in appearance and Muhamedans in religion, but nothing save provisions was got. Albuquerque seeing the inutility of this excursion, got leave to return with his ships to Mozambique. [2] Tristâo da Cunha continued south, towards the Matatana river, where rumour promised him an Eldorado. One night they ran before a smart breeze along an unknown coast, and in the morning one of his ships was gone; she had torn her bottom out on a reef, and only the master, pilot, and 13 men escaped. After this Da Cunha returned to Mozambique.

Malindi was the next halt. The chieftain there had two enemies, Ozi and Barava, and when Da Cunha learnt that these places were malignant because of Malindi's friendship with Portugal, and also that they were wealthy, no rigorous proof of the origin of the quarrel was asked, but the two places were sacked. Bringing off the Barava plunder, an overladen boat with the chaplain of the flag-ship on board was overset, and the priest and most of the crew drowned. Barros piously suggests that Providence was angry with

[1] The ginger turned out to be of no commercial value, the cloves from the wreck of a ship, and the silver from bracelets come from no one knew where.

[2] Cartas, page 30.

some sailors who, to get at their bracelets more quickly, had hacked off the arms of living women; it was but a blind justice, after all, for the commander who hounded them on escaped, and it is to be hoped the chaplain was innocent. None of the Portuguese were killed by the Barava men, who fought with javelins, bows and arrows and hives of bees, but so honourable was the feat of arms that, at his special request, Albuquerque knighted his commanding officer, Tristâo da Cunha.

The next halt was at Socotra, which was reached in April 1507. Among the natives of that island there still lingered some memory of Jacobite Christianity,[1] but the memory was little more than the reverence for a symbol in the shape of a cross, and the names by which their children were distinguished. They were low in the scale of civilisation; they had no arms, offensive or defensive, except slings and some small iron swords. Their habits were pastoral and not agricultural, and they had not even the skill to catch the fish that swarmed on their shores.[2] They had, at the time of which we are writing, been for about 50 years subject to the Arabs of the opposite coast, who had a small garrison under a captain, Khwaja Ibrahim. The only attraction to the Portuguese was that it lay in the fair way of ships from the Red Sea to Southern India, and its possession would, they hoped, close the mouth of that sea to the Muhamedans. The Arab fort was captured after a sharp skirmish in which Albuquerque was severely wounded by a stone. In connection with this assault, there is a characteristic story of Tristâo da Cunha; he saw his son,

[1] So named from Jacob Baradœus, Bishop of Edessa in the 6th century, who taught that Jesus Christ had but one nature and that the Divine.

[2] For an interesting account of Socotra by an eye-witness see De Castro's Roteiro of the voyage of 1541, page 16. The men, he says, are tawny and well shaped—the women "honestly pretty."

Nuno da Cunha, afterwards (1529—1538) Governor of India, racing with Albuquerque's nephew, Afonso de Noronha, for the fort; his blood was warmed with the fight, and the old buccaneer lost enough of his Portuguese stateliness to shout to Albuquerque—"Let us blood these puppies—Hie on! Nuno, hie on!" When the fortress was built Afonso de Noronha was made Captain. Tristâo da Cunha started for India on August 10th, 1507, and Albuquerque left for Ormuz ten days later.

After Cananor had been relieved and the cargo loaded at Cochin, the Viceroy and Tristâo da Cunha started with their fleets to destroy the Samuri's ships defended by a large body of men who had thrown up stockades and batteries. The attack on November 25th ended in the complete triumph of the Portuguese,[1] and, as usual, Tristâo da Cunha gloried in the fight. There was a mosque in front, thick with Moors: "D. Lourenço," he shouted, "christen "me that youngster of mine with your sword in yonder "mosque; with you for a godfather he will gain honour."[2] All the booty was burned, and on December 10th Tristâo da Cunha sailed for Europe. On his return voyage he discovered Ascension Island.

Trouble was meanwhile brewing in the north. Kansuh el Ghori, the last independent Mameluke Sultan, was at this time reigning in Egypt. The effects of the Portuguese policy in Indian waters were quickly apparent in the

[1] This fight is interesting as an example of the difficulty of arriving at any exact idea of the semi-mythical D. Lourenço d'Almeida. In Barros he disposes of one Nair champion, whom he cleaves to the breast. In Castanheda the Nair wounds D. Lourenço, who turns sick, and his friends kill the Nair. In Correa he begins by eating marmalade and drinking water, and then starts to meet 14 Nair champions, who challenge him and who all attack at once: he disposes of them in a series of most tremendous thwacks. All agree in the story of Tristâo da Cunha.

[2] Varthema (p. 286) was in this fight and was knighted by the Viceroy, with Tristâo da Cunha, he says, for sponsor.

Egyptian custom-houses, and the deficient revenue gave a point to the complaints of the Muhamedan traders, and especially of "Maimama Marakkar" who had been so grossly outraged by Vincent Sodre. The Sultan breathed fire and fury; he would destroy the Jerusalem Temples, the relics in the Holy Land, and the Monastery of St. Catherine at Mount Sinai, and would order all Christians to leave his territory or else become Muhamedans. The head of the Monastery of St. Catherine, terrified at these menaces, undertook a mission to the Pope of Rome. He visited both Rome and Portugal, but failed to get much comfort from the interviews he had, beyond sympathetic donations for his monastery. It was clear to the Sultan that his only chance lay in an armed force, and as there was no timber fit for ship-building to be got in the Red Sea, he obtained a supply in Scanderoon, which was sent in 25 boats to Alexandria. This flotilla, however, encountered the Rhodes fleet, five were sunk and six captured; of the remainder four foundered in a storm, and only ten reached Alexandria.

The wood was taken up the Nile in boats, worked up in Cairo, and sent across to Suez to be built into twelve vessels there. Mir Hashim, a native of Asia Minor, commanded. There were 1,500 men at arms, and the crews were Levantines of all nations. Suez was left on February 15th, 1507. Diu was reached on September 20th, where some time was spent in refitting. The Governor of Diu was then Malik Aiyaz, a Russian who had been enslaved in his youth by the Turks. He was a man of very considerable ability, who held his own through many years till his death, and who foiled all the efforts of the Portuguese to establish themselves within the limits of his governorship, without ever losing any of their respect.[1]

[1] For an interesting and full account of this man from the Mirát-i-Sikandarí see Bailey's "Guzerat," pp. 233—235.

In January 1508 D. Lourenço d'Almeida started up the coast on the usual convoy duty; no reports of the arrival of the Egyptians had reached him, and he took only 8 vessels; the usual burning of ships and slaying of crews on the way did not give him much chance of gaining any information. At Chaul he heard some confused rumours, but disregarded them, thinking they were set on foot to frighten him; and when his father sent him more definite information, though with hardly credible supineness, he sent him no help, he hardly believed it. Even when the enemy's fleet was off Chaul bar they were taken for the ships of Albuquerque coming from Ormuz. "I see no crosses on "their sails," said a cautious old warrior to a group of youngsters laughing at him for buckling on his armour, and this was the first intimation they believed. It was then March 1508.

A cannonade, as the Egyptian ships sailed through the Portuguese lines, was the inconclusive result of the first day's encounter. A council that night determined to board the enemy, but the attempt in the morning failed as the Egyptian ships, though bulkier, drew less water than the deep-keeled Portuguese, and the fight became an artillery duel. Towards evening there was a shout from the enemy to welcome the arrival of Malik Aiyaz with 60 foists, and this reinforcement decided the battle. That night the Portuguese agreed to fly: all was got ready, and with the morning light and the ebbing tide they started; all escaped safely save D. Lourenço's ship, which took a wide sweep to avoid the enemy's shot. A cannon-ball entered her rice store-room at the stern, between wind and water, and it was afloat before the damage was discovered; the rice then prevented all efforts to stop the leak. The bow was in the air, when the ship running foul of some fishing stakes, was so jammed there in the race of the tide that no cutting away of stakes was of any avail, and there was no breeze to help. The enemy gathered round the doomed vessel, but four attempts to board were beaten off. D. Lourenço himself with half his leg carried away by a cannon-shot, sat on a chair by the mainmast and encouraged his men to fight on, until another shot in the chest flung him lifeless on the deck; he was carried below, and his body sank through the shattered planks and was never recovered. Another attempt to board was successful; 19 men, mostly wounded, were made prisoners, and the ship itself sank, carrying some of the Egyptians with her. The loss of the Portuguese in the fight was 140 killed and 124 wounded.[1] It is to the credit of Malik Aiyaz that the wounded prisoners were treated with very great humanity. The whole bent of the Viceroy's mind was now turned on taking vengeance for the death of his son. "He who has eaten the cockerel "must eat the cock," he said. This, his attitude, must be understood in order to get an explanation of his later actions, which are otherwise unintelligible.

Albuquerque left Socotra on August 20th, 1507, with 7 ships and 450 fighting men to attack Ormuz. Of this small force 120 men were sick, and he had no provisions on board his ships. The King of Ormuz at this time was a boy—Saifu-d-din—12 years of age, but the entire power lay in the hands of his ministers, Khwaja Atar and Rais Nuru-d-din, not merely because the King was a minor, but because these puppets only retained the title of king as long as they did not interfere with their powerful ministers; an inquisitive or obstructive monarch was at once made away with. As Albuquerque's instructions were explicit he did not consider that any pretext was required for making

[1] For the Indian accounts of this battle see Bailey's "Guzerat," p. 222. They put their own loss at 400 men and claim to have killed many "disorderly Europeans."

war on a Prince with whom neither he nor his master had had any previous communication. Each town of the Ormuz state was attacked as it was reached: Kariat, Muscat and Khurfakam were sacked and burned. The carnage was great, and the unfortunate prisoners were only released when the women had had their noses and ears cut off, and the men their noses and right hands. These actions were not committed in hot blood, for very few Portuguese were killed; they were committed in cold blood to produce an impression of fear.

In Ormuz Albuquerque had to hide the smallness of his force from the city by countermarching and manœuvring as if on the stage, for his demand was no less than that the King should become tributary to Portugal and pay for the peace which the fleet of that country imposed on those who followed the seas. The subsequent history of Ormuz is a bitter satire on the pretensions involved in this barefaced aggression: even his own captains professed to be shocked at the naked robbery, but at this distance of time it is difficult to say how far they were biassed by their previous disputes with their commander, because he never took them into his counsels. There were some 400 vessels in Ormuz harbour when the Portuguese reached it, of which 60 were ships of some size—one from Guzerat was of 800 tons with 1,000 fighting men. There were also some 30,000 men with arms of sorts in the city, of whom 4,000 were Persian archers. As the negotiations hung fire the ships were attacked and quickly destroyed by artillery; when troops landed, the King of Ormuz at once surrendered and agreed to the terms imposed—namely, £1,600 down for the expenses of the expedition, a tribute of £5,000 a year, and a site whereon a fort could be built. Over the proposal to build a fort the captains raised difficulties: their ships were not fit to remain at sea, nor had they men enough to leave a garrison of 200 in the fort, and with neither sea power nor a garrison, the fort was but a pledge in the hands of the Muhamedans. The division of the £1,600, too, raised other debates. Albuquerque considered that half should go to pay for the fortress and half be sent to India to buy pepper for the King; the captains claimed the whole for the men. In this miserable quarrel, that grew apparently out of the discontent of the captains that they could not go prize-seeking at the mouth of the Red Sea, everything was done to thwart Albuquerque.

The quarrel culminated at a council where Albuquerque, stung by some words of Joâo da Nova, drew his sword and seized him by the shoulder. Da Nova, weeping, picked up some hairs from the deck,—hairs he declared plucked from his beard,—wrapped them in his handkerchief, and swore he would have justice from the King. [1] Da Nova was for a time deprived of his ship and under arrest. Albuquerque's great qualities never shone so brightly as when at bay before an enemy who outnumbered him by 100 to 1; with his captains and crews mutinous, his ships hardly seaworthy, and any reinforcement months distant, he held his own through many weeks. [2] The foundations of the new fort were laid on October 6th, but as information of the dissensions in Albuquerque's ships had filtered through to the city, the King's ministers were waiting for some opportunity to prevent the work continuing.

The King of Ormuz employed in his negotiations an Armenian, one Khwaja Bairam, who knew Portuguese, and

[1] For Joâo da Nova's protest of September 12th, 1507, and Albuquerque's reply of October 27th—both very interesting documents—see An. Mar. e Col., series 3, page 443.

[2] In his letter of February 2nd, 1508, to the Viceroy, Albuquerque says that when news was brought to Ormuz that the Egyptian fleet was coming to attack him, he ordered another anchor down to show he had no intention of moving.

Albuquerque learned from him the news of the city.[1] He was able therefore to gauge the effect that the desertion of two Greeks, a Biscayan and a Portuguese that happened at this time, would have on his enemies. The deserters, in fact, told enough of the weakness and dissensions of the Portuguese fleet to make Khwaja Atar refuse to give up the masts and yards of the fleet Albuquerque had defeated in the harbour.[2] "If you interfere with me in any way," said Albuquerque, "I will build the walls of Muhamedans' "bones. I will nail your ears to the door and erect the "flagstaff on your skull." This menace kept Khwaja Atar quiet for a time, but the four deserters, in spite of reiterated demands, were not given up.

At length work was stopped on the fortress, the factor was recalled from the town, and, after the usual protests from the captains in a signed letter dated January 5th, 1508, Albuquerque bombarded the city till his powder ran short and the touch-holes blew out of his guns.[3] The bombardment was then turned into a blockade, and the supply of sweet water from the mainland cut off, and when the city cleared out the brackish wells of Toranbagh they were destroyed.[4] For greater security Albuquerque, besides his orders to the captains, had taken written agreements from the masters and pilots, but all was in vain; the captains traitorously opened communications with the enemy against whom their commander was acting, and three ships stole away secretly to India. Thus weakened, there was nothing for Albuquerque but to break the blockade and go to

[1] Khwaja Bairam left Ormuz with the Portuguese, and was rewarded in Portugal for his services.

[2] Cartas, page 12.

[3] Cartas, page 14.

[4] See Cartas, pages 6 to 19, where Albuquerque's case is fully stated. He hanged some of the pilots afterwards in Goa.

Socotra. On the way there João de Nova, who had been restored to his ship, took a chance that offered, and bore up for India.

The Socotra fortress was suffering from famine, and the island in insurrection: a few prizes and the arrival of two new ships from Portugal gave the needed relief. In the rains the crazy ships were patched up, and on September 13th Albuquerque was again before Ormuz, but matters had changed very considerably. Arrived on the Indian coast, the rebel captains had met the defeated fleet returning from Chaul to Cochin with the news of D. Lourenço's death. They were received by the Viceroy with no marks of displeasure, and the right of their conduct in leaving their commander in the face of the enemy did not trouble his mind, filled with only one idea; on the whole, perhaps, he inclined to think they had acted correctly, chiefly because their ships were a reinforcement to his avenging fleet, but to some extent, perhaps, because he disliked Albuquerque and his methods. Some reason of the nature of this last one is necessary to explain his conduct in writing to Ormuz to say that he was satisfied with the tribute agreed to by the King, but that Albuquerque had done many things at Ormuz for which he should chastise him when the time came. This letter certainly justified Albuquerque, after the event, in not following his captains hot foot to India, where he would have involved himself in a wrangle with the mutineers, that would have given Almeida a pretext for sending home his successor designate with heavy and aggravated charges against him.

The effect of this letter was evident enough in the conduct of the Ormuz ministers to Albuquerque on his return; still, although they refused any concession to him, he remained there six weeks in the hope of some reinforcement from Portugal; when it did not arrive he, on November

4th, perforce sailed to India.[1] Albuquerque reached Cananor on December 5th, where he found the Viceroy pushing on the loading of the home-going ships. In the fleet of 1508 the King of Portugal introduced some changes: the Viceroy was ordered—it is true—to make over charge of India to Albuquerque, but the latter was only to hold command from Guzerat to Cape Comorin. Two independent governors were appointed, Jorge d'Aguiar from the Cape of Good Hope to Guzerat, and Diogo Lopes de Sequiera from Cape Comorin eastwards.[2] The idea of this arrangement, if indeed it had any underlying idea, appears to have been that, if the mouth of the Red Sea were closed, the trade of India would of itself fall into Portuguese hands. Fortunately for the Portuguese, d'Aguiar was lost on the Tristâo da Cunha islands,[3] and his successor, Duarte de Lemos, had little authority; Sequiera failed at Malacca; and Albuquerque was on the spot to remedy the mistake of his master.

In India Albuquerque found himself in a sea of intrigue with no pilot; he evidently trusted rather to the advice and judgment of Gaspar Pereira, the Viceroy's secretary, who was out of favour with his master. There is a good deal about the man in Albuquerque's letters, written after the King of Portugal had sent him out for a second term of office under Albuquerque. Albuquerque had by then discovered his true character; but there was some reason for his at first trusting Pereira and his protestations, for the

[1] Albuquerque's ship, the Cirne, was so rotten that fish came in with the bilge water, and 80 slaves at the pumps could hardly keep her afloat.

[2] For Sequiera's sailing orders in which he is particularly told to enquire everywhere for the "Rio Gramjes", and where it falls into the sea, see. An. Mar. e Col., 3rd series, p. 379.

[3] For an account of his voyage out and all that was known of the loss of d'Aguiar see the letter of Duarte de Lemos to the King of Portugal, of Sept. 30th, 1508.—An. Mar. e Col., series 3, page 525.

man had been a chamber-lad of his uncle's, and had been taken into the royal service only after his pertinacity in soliciting for him. "He could stir up a whole army to strife "and escape himself" is Albuquerque's comment on him when he knew him better.[1] Albuquerque at once demanded some explanation of the Viceroy's conduct in receiving the mutinous captains, and the immediate relinquishment to him of the Government of India. The Viceroy promised to give him every satisfaction on his own return from Diu, and Albuquerque, recognizing that further protest was unavailing, went to Cochin.

Almeida sailed for Diu on Dec. 12th, 1508, with 18 ships and 1,200 men. Diu, which has now been a Portuguese possession for more than $3^1/_2$ centuries, and which plays a large part in Indo-Portuguese history, is an island seven miles long by two miles broad, south of Guzerat, separated from the mainland by a narrow channel that passes through a considerable swamp. To the north the channel is only navigable by small boats; but to the south, under a sandstone cliff, there is a small harbour where craft not drawing over 12 feet of water can anchor. Gogala on the main, called by the Portuguese after the events of Almeida's time, Villa dos Rumes, belongs also to that nation. To collect his force Almeida had depleted both Cochin and Cananor; all else must be sacrificed to regain the command of the sea. Coast towns were sacked, but nowhere could any refreshments be obtained; for, alarmed at the news of the Portuguese armada, the people had hastened to hide the scanty store they had saved from the locusts which had swarmed that year. Diu was reached on February 2nd, 1509. There can be no doubt but that there had been

[1] Cartas, pp. 275 and 284—291, are especially valuable, for they give Albuquerque's business habits—habits that are now, as they were then, the right ones for an administrator.

negotiations between the Viceroy and Malik Aiyaz, the Captain of Diu, and that the latter had been won over, if not to espouse the Portuguese interests, at least to agree to assist them secretly as far as he was able.

Besides the 12 Egyptian ships there were about 100 sail of other vessels, including some from Calicut, but none of much value as fighting machines except four large ones of Guzerat. Contrary to the judgment of Mir Hashim, the Muhamedan vessels awaited the expected attack at anchor. The Portuguese advanced on February 3rd, and from midday to nightfall there was a confused melee, which ended in the discomfiture of the Egyptians and their allies, with comparatively little loss to the Portuguese. The 17 surviving Portuguese prisoners were released, and the Viceroy, it is recorded, trimmed his beard for the first time since his son's death. No damage was done to Diu or to any of the Guzerat ports, but in a triumphal procession down the coast the Viceroy celebrated his victory at every halting-place where there was a Muhamedan town, by firing the limbs of his captives, who were executed in batches for that purpose, over the city. Cochin was reached on March 8th.

Returned to Cochin, the Viceroy still refused to give over charge to Albuquerque, on the ground that he had been ordered to return in a particular ship (that of d'Aguiar) which had not yet arrived,[1] and that, as the giving over charge and leaving India were to be simultaneous, Albuquerque must wait. Although, looking back some years afterwards, Albuquerque thought that he had paid too much attention to Gaspar Pereira, yet he must be pronounced to have behaved himself irreproachably under great provocation. His avowed enemies had the ear of the Viceroy, and for some months he was subjected to every petty annoyance

[1] It had been wrecked.

that malice could suggest. His private servants, even his surgeon and his personal friends, were removed from him, and he was not allowed to leave his house; some of his adherents were imprisoned and some degraded, others banished to Malacca in the fleet of Diogo Lopes de Sequiera. The Viceroy further demeaned himself by receiving a petition got up by the faction opposed to Albuquerque, and which Sequiera, who had reached Cochin on April 21st, even signed, asking that Albuquerque should not receive charge of the Government. Albuquerque haughtily refused to reply to the allegations of this petition: the King alone could be his judge, he said. Even deprived of his friends and a prisoner in his own house Albuquerque was too formidable to be left alone, and it must have been a relief to him when, in the worst of the early monsoon, he was sent up the coast in a crazy ship to Cananor. In Cananor fort he was the prisoner of the Captain; but Cananor was not Cochin, for there was neither the Viceroy nor the opposing faction, and with the sympathy of the residents he broke his arrest and lived freely, if quietly, in the settlement. Early in September a fleet of 14 ships under the Marshal of Portugal, D. Ferdinando Coutinho, a friend and relative of Albuquerque, reached Cananor. Coutinho had powers superior even to those of Almeida, which there was no resisting. Almeida left Cochin on his homeward voyage on December 1st, 1509, after giving over charge to Albuquerque. Most of the latter's enemies accompanied him, but Joâo da Nova was too ill and died soon after; it adds to our estimate of Albuquerque to learn that, forgetting his griefs against the dead, he followed his old comrade to the grave. Almeida rounded the Cape safely, but at a watering-place on the west of the Cape there were quarrels with the natives, whose conduct he thought he must chastise in person. After the cattle were rounded up at a village where the disorder had happened, the Portuguese—150 strong—(who, despising their enemies, wore no body armour) started with the herd to return; about an equal number of natives attacked them in their retreat, cut off stragglers, and used the herd of cattle accustomed to their voices as a moving fortification against their enemies. The Portuguese, who had only lances and swords, began to fall fast, and the late Viceroy, 12 leading fidalgoes and 50 other Portuguese were killed. This rout happened on March 1st, 1510.

CHAPTER VIII

ALBUQUERQUE, GOVERNOR, 1509—1515

AFONSO D'ALBUQUERQUE, who now became Governor of India, was a man of fifty-six years of age; considering, therefore, the period in which he lived, he was an old man. He had accompanied two expeditions from Portugal against the Muhamedans, in which, although he acquitted himself manfully, he was in no way particularly distinguished; in 1503 also, he had, as has been said, commanded a squadron of ships from Portugal to India. He had on this occasion done well in clearing the Cochin territory of the enemy, and to him must be given the credit also of being one of the selectors of Duarte Pacheco; but putting all together there was nothing that is known of his past career which foreshadowed the lustre that surrounds his term as governor.

Directly Almeida left Cochin, at the end of 1509, the Marshal pressed Albuquerque to assist him in carrying out the King's orders by destroying Calicut. The new Governor as well as those who knew India were opposed to any attack; there would be some immediate plunder perhaps, but the Portuguese had no intention of retaining the town, and the destruction of the houses composing it, mostly thatched huts, would not break the Samuri's power. However, as the Marshal explained at the Council, the King's orders were definite, and admitted of no discussion; the Council had only to decide on the way the attack was to be made. The Samuri happened at the moment to to be away from Calicut, but secret though the preparations for the attack were, the townspeople had ample time after the news reached them, to concert their measures of defence. The Portuguese fleet of thirty sail with 1,800 men on board arrived on January 2nd, 1510, and under his patent the Marshal at once took supreme command of the forces. Save a sea beating heavily on the coast, a few fishermen's huts on the point, and a dense forest of palms, there was little to be seen but a "Cerame", so called by the Portuguese, a room raised on posts, occasionally occupied by the Samuri.[1] According to the plan, the Marshal with 800 men was to land on the north of the Cerame, and Albuquerque with 700 on the south. Both forces were to meet at the Cerame, and then, if necessary, go to the city —but under all circumstances the Marshal was to have the honour of place.

Eager to childishness, the Portuguese buckled on their armour and sat all night in the boats, replying to the defiant shouts of their enemies; they were of course tired out when the signal was given at dawn. The Marshal, carried too far north by the current and encumbered by a field-piece, only reached the Cerame after it was in the possession of Albuquerque, who had occupied it after a sharp fight. Some of the spoil which the Marshal coveted had been carried for him to his boats,[2] but when he came up, beside himself with rage, he ordered it to be thrown overboard, and called out that he was ashamed to fight naked negroes who scuttled like goats. He gave his helmet and lance to his page, shook his cane in the air, and said he would tell the King what these travellers' tales of India were, and how he took the Samuri's palace with a cane in his hand and

[1] See Yule Glossary, *s.v.*

[2] He had promised the King to take back to him the doors of the Samuri's palace.

a skull cap on his head; Gaspar the Jew was ordered to lead the way,[1] and in spite of Albuquerque's remonstrances the Marshal started. The palace was three miles off; the road thither ran along a hollow way on whose high banks stood houses; the heat and dust were stifling. There was a continual skirmish with the enemy posted on the high banks and at every point where a cross road cut through them; but the Portuguese in the end won their way to the palace, where on higher ground they could at least get some air.[2] The party spread over the palace to loot, and arms even were thrown away to allow laden Portuguese to stagger back under the booty, these men were cut off by the enemy.

In the meantime, Albuquerque had, to create a diversion, fired the town, and following the Marshal, prevented the Nairs closing in on the party in the palace. Repeated messages were required to rouse the Marshal to a sense of his position. At length Albuquerque started to fight his way back to the beach, and the Marshal followed; the latter was stout, and the heat of midday was great; he had thrown off his armour and could with difficulty fend off the arrows with his shield. As long as the field-piece could be dragged it kept the enemy at bay; when the road was blocked with beams and stones it was abandoned, the Nairs and Muhamedans closed in, and the Marshal and his immediate following were killed.[3] Albuquerque had kept his men in hand, and fought wherever he could see an enemy, and when he heard the Marshal was in difficulties he tried to return, but the stream of fugitives bore

[1] Gaspar disappears after this day, he was probably killed in the rout.

[2] The Samuris are still crowned on the mound where this palace once stood.—Logan, Vol. I. p. 317.

[3] See Cartas, p. 79, for a curious account of this retreat—Albuquerque minimizes the difficulties the party encountered to prove his then thesis, which was that Calicut could be easily taken.

him back. An arrow through the left arm [1] and a blow on the head rendered him unfit for further effort; his standard bearer was killed by his side, and he was carried off the field on a buckler. Albuquerque had, with great foresight, left a strong guard at the boats, and with their help the wounded were embarked. In this disastrous day the Portuguese lost 300 killed, of whom 70 were fidalgoes; and 400 wounded, of whom many died or were maimed for life. The damage to the Samuri was of course great, but he retained the field of battle, the Marshal's banner, and nearly all the arms offensive as well as defensive of the Portuguese.

Albuquerque had now to restore the discipline impaired by the late Viceroy's favour to the mutinous captains, and the morale impaired by the defeat at Calicut. Fortunately, general opinion recognised that he was not to blame for the mistake of the Calicut attack. He profited, too, by the death of the Marshal in retaining his ships and troops, which else would have returned to Portugal. Albuquerque threw himself into the work of reorganisation with characteristic energy,—he formed the soldiers into trained bands and wrote to Portugal for officers to drill them, he introduced business habits into all branches of the Government, [2] he issued a number of passes to Muhamedan ships to trade in all things save spices; a greater mind had come to the control of affairs. Like all hardworking men, he neither rested himself nor gave his subordinates rest, either by night or by day, it seemed as though the check at Calicut had spurred him to extra exertion.

The two governors who had independent jurisdiction to

[1] He never had the full use of this arm again.

[2] Before he introduced them there were no registers either of orders or of property. Alhuquerque at this time suffered a great loss in the death of his nephew, D. Afonso de Noronha, wrecked on his return from Socotra.

the west and east of India were both in difficulties. Duarte de Lemos had remained within his own limits off Arabia, where there was no shelter, and nothing to do except be a pirate. He could get no help from Albuquerque by writing, and when his ships were so rotten they could hardly swim, and his crews so weak that they could hardly navigate, he passed on to India. The other governor, Diogo Lopes de Sequiera, met with actual disaster, for he was both careless and indolent. At Malacca he received repeated warnings both from the captains of Chinese junks, with whom he had made friends, and from the Malay women on shore, that an attack was intended, but he had allowed his boats to be drawn away on the pretence of cargo, and when the crews and the men in the factory were cut off from the ships they were attacked. Francisco Serrào, the friend of Magalhaens, was one of the very few on shore who got back to the ships, and he only because Magalhaens and some others went in the only boat left in the fleet to rescue him; 60 Portuguese were killed and 33, including Ruy d'Araujo, the factor, made prisoners. The Malays refused to restore the prisoners; the Portuguese Council decided that without boats they could not attack, and the fleet sailed away and left their comrades to their fate. Of his five ships only three returned to India, and his force would have been smaller but for the devotion of Magalhaens. At anchor off the Sumatra coast, a junk that had no anchors was tied to Sequiera's ship: a storm arose and Sequiera cut the rope and would have left his sailors to their fate but that Magalhaens saved them at great personal risk.[1] In January 1510, Sequiera reached the Indian coast, and hearing that Albuquerque was governor, headed

[1] Castanheda, II. 116. It was on his return to Europe after this voyage that Magalhaens was shipwrecked and stayed by the crew on the reef when all the other officers abandoned them.

his own ship straight for Portugal and sent the other two to Cochin.

By the end of January 1510 Albuquerque had collected 1,200 Portuguese and a fleet of 23 vessels; he allowed it to be believed that his objective was Ormuz and the Red Sea. It is, however, very doubtful if he entertained such an idea, for directly he took over charge he had raised the scornful laughter of Almeida's following by sending to sound the Goa bar; and as, whilst De Lemos was in the East, Ormuz and the Red Sea were within his jurisdiction, and as any failure of De Lemos would more quickly bring the reversion of his government to himself, Albuquerque was not likely to help him to success. After a meeting with Timoja, who has been already mentioned in Almeida's time, the project of attacking Goa was mooted in a meeting of the captains, and agreed to. The moment was propitious. Yusaf Adil Shah, who almost 40 years before had obtained possession of the city, was just dead, and as was customary, all the neighbouring potentates were ready to try the mettle of his successor, Ismail Adil Shah, whose hands were so full that he had little leisure to devote to Goa. The town of Goa stands on an island formed by salt-water creeks, that intersect the narrow belt of level ground which divides the Western Ghats from the sea. The soil is fertile, and the situation of the town renders it easily defensible by sea power. Standing in the centre of the west coast of India, it was, in the days of ships of light draught, a peculiarly favourable site for a colony, and for a colony Albuquerque designed it.[1]

[1] Albuquerque's designs and general policy will, not to break the narrative, be considered later. The early Portuguese writers call the ruler they found in Goa, the Sabaio, and Albuquerque himself used this word. It was apparently derived from the information of Gaspar, the Jew, who gave it as the name of his master when he was captured at Anjadiva. Yule adopted the explanation of Barros, that it was derived from the name of Yusaf Adil

The first capture of the town presented no difficulty. The fleet anchored at the bar, and Albuquerque's nephew, D. Antonio de Noronha, started with some boats to sound the channel. Rounding a point, the Portuguese came unexpectedly on a small fort, which they carried with a rush, a surprise equally to the victor and the vanquished. Although the fort was some way from the town, the effect of the capture was immediate, for Goa capitulated, and on March 1st Albuquerque made his triumphal entry. The spoil was considerable,—horses, elephants, and dock-yard stores, 16 ships complete, and 8 on the stocks. Timoja was made Thanadar of the city, an office of profit, as all crimes could be compounded for a fine, but the old buccaneer was too hard on the Muhamedans, and at their special request a coreligionist was appointed over them. [1]

Two months were busily spent in the arrangement of the new conquest, when rumours began to circulate that the troops of Ismail Adil Shah had been seen in motion near the frontier. The Portuguese, too, were grumbling at being kept away through the rains from the flesh-pots of Cochin. Albuquerque had also ordered the execution of a Muhamedan Kazi who had suffocated a Muhamedan to prevent him turning Christian. The execution was possibly justifiable, but the Muhamedan community were annoyed and sided secretly with Ismail Adil Shah. That prince had

Shah's birth-place. He has overlooked the correction of this statement by Couto (IV. 10. 4), who says that the Sabaio was a Hindu chief in Kanara, whose sons he knew personally. These sons laughed heartily when Couto read them Barros's derivation of the word Sabaio; their father, they said, was neither a Turk nor a Yusaf. The name of this petty Hindu Chief has thus got transferred in error to the Muhamedan King who held Goa.

[1] Albuquerque's verdicts on Timoja vary amusingly, as his moods: on Nov. 30th, 1513, he writes—"if any were ever condemned as a traitor and evil, then Timoja should have been." But the next day he was a "Boom homem"; see Cartas, pp. 148, 175; 179. Albuquerque never trusted him after he was driven from Goa, he suspected him of embezzlement

patched up a hasty truce with his enemies on the mainland, and early in the monsoon months put himself at the head of his troops to retake Goa. He was dominated by a desire to get rid of the Portuguese dominion, and he was willing even to give a site for a fortress to gain this end, but Albuquerque, when the offer was made, refused to entertain the idea.

Across the creek that makes Goa an island, there were certain definite crossing-places where the water was fordable; such a frontier could only be defended if the officers conducting the defence worked harmoniously, but they did not, and Albuquerque, himself new to this kind of warfare, did not utilize his forces to the best advantage. In a dark rainy night on May 16th the creek was crossed, the artillery in position to defend the fords was lost, and the whole population rose against the invaders, the very shop-keepers produced their hidden arms to attack any helpless Portuguese. By May 23rd, the town was indefensible and boats were being sunk in the fairway to cut off the retreat of the ships. Before he left the city Albuquerque, enraged at the spirit of the townspeople, killed in cold blood the chief Muhamedans as well as their wives and children, whom he had collected as his hostages. He reserved a few of the wealthiest of the Muhamedans to hold to ransom, the more beautiful of the women to marry to the Portuguese, and some of the children to turn into Christians. Albuquerque delayed the advance of his enemies through the streets by dropping valuables for them to pick up, [1] and the Portuguese, not without heavy loss, reached their ships.

Albuquerque was caught in a trap; Goa was in the enemy's hands, batteries on the shore commanded the anchorage, and the bar was impracticable in the south-

[1] At Delhi, in 1857, cases of brandy were used for a similar purpose by the mutineers.

west monsoon; the very guns mounted in the batteries were those which had been lost at the fords. The weeks that followed were a time of great trial; one of the batteries was carried by surprise, and this afforded relief, but famine stared the Portuguese in the face. Some of the Muhamedan prisoners were ransomed for food, but the crews were reduced to 4 ounces of biscuit a day. The Adil Shah had prepared a flotilla of boats to attack the ships; Albuquerque's counter stroke was completely successful, but in the flush of victory his nephew, D. Antonio de Noronha, was mortally wounded. The loss of D. Antonio de Noronha was felt throughout the fleet, for he often stood as a mediator between the Governor and the objects of his sudden passion; he was "brave, of "good counsel, and friendly to all, even those who were on the "worst terms with the Governor, were still friends with him." There occurred a difficulty immediately after, in which his advice might have been of assistance. As Albuquerque discovered that the presence on the ships of the Muhamedan women led to certain irregularities, he collected them on the flag-ship. One Ruy Dias, a man of good birth, was caught in an intrigue with one of them; he swam in the night from his own to the flag-ship. Albuquerque ordered him to be hanged, and hanged he was, but not before several of the captains had broken into open mutiny.[1] Three of the more noisy were invited on board the flag-ship to see the governor's powers: "These are my powers," he said, drawing his sword; he clapped all three into irons and gave their ships to others.[2]

[1] It is difficult to follow Camoens in his bitter attack on Albuquerque for this act.

[2] Both Castanheda and Correa have an account of a theatrical carouse of his famished crews on viands they were not allowed to touch, to deceive the Adil Shah's Ambassador who came to suggest a peace. Perhaps the Ambassador saw through the device, certainly Albuquerque knew how vital a peace was to Ismail.

He took his ships over the bar with considerable risk on August the 4th; one, the Flor de la Mar, struck and remained fast in the falling tide. Her crew were ready to abandon her, but Albuquerque, disregarding the remonstrances of those around him, went on board her, and stayed there till she floated off with the next flood.

Albuquerque had good reason to despond; his career in India so far had been marked only by failure; driven from Ormuz by the mutiny of his Captains, beaten at Calicut by the fault of another, at Goa he could impute his ill success to none but himself. Yet during the weary time of waiting at the Goa bar, he was forging the discipline with which during the few remaining years of his life he was to command success.[1]

In 1510 three fleets left Portugal for India, one under Diogo Mendes was destined for Malacca and was independent of Albuquerque; the second was composed of adventurers' cargo boats that could not assist him; the third was only intended for Madagascar; there was no help for Albuquerque. Out of these unpromising materials, however, he began to strengthen his fleet. Duarte de Lemos had not many vessels, they could hardly swim, and the commander was making difficulties by his punctilious claims; but orders came for him to return to Portugal, and Albuquerque appropriated his ships and patched them up. Some of those destined for Malacca, under Diogo Mendes, were private property, but for all that Albuquerque determined to annex them. He began by pointing out to Diogo Mendes the difficulties that Diogo Lopes had encountered, and then dangled before him the hope that if he would only help to recover Goa, he should be helped in his attack on Malacca. Diogo Mendes, whose force unassisted was too

[1] It was to his advantage that communication with Europe was so slow.

weak to deal with Malacca, agreed to assist Albuquerque, and then he, his captains and pilots had to swear not to leave India without Albuquerque's permission, and obey him in everything. Diogo Mendes when he found that he had been tricked, continued to complain pathetically, and he was allowed to put in numerous protests in writing, but he never got his fleet again. Albuquerque was now in fact, as he soon afterwards became in name, Governor of all the Portuguese East.

Albuquerque left Cananor on October 3rd, with 1,700 men[1] and 28 vessels to attack Goa. At Honawar he nearly lost his fleet, for while he and the chief officers were on shore, dining with Timoja to celebrate the latter's wedding, a storm arose which prevented their returning for three days, and even then they lost 2 boats and 30 men, including one of the Governor's secretaries. Ismail Adil Shah had left the defence of Goa to his Captain, Rasul Khan, with 8,000 men; he himself had been called off by the capture of Raichor by the Raja of Vijayanagara. The Portuguese were doubtful, fearing they could not take the town, certain they could not hold it if taken, and to satisfy them Albuquerque gave out that his only intention was to burn the shipping.

The defences of the city had been strengthened, the ships especially, which were drawn up on the beach at the dockyard, were protected by a stockade parallel to the city wall, that at either end turned in to meet it. The only communication with the city, except that at either end, from the yard thus enclosed, was through a narrow door; Albuquerque founded his plan of attack on this defect. Over night, on November 24th, the ships were sent forward to threaten the city frontage to the east of the stockade;

[1] Cartas, p. 36, gives 1,680 men of whom 380 were from merchant vessels.

they served a double purpose, they drew the enemy's forces to defend a fancied attack at this spot, and they prevented any reinforcement entering the dockyard from the eastern end. The attack was made on the stockade on the morning of November 25th, the day of St. Catherine. Albuquerque himself, with 600 men, took up a position on the hillock, where now stands the parochial church of the Rosary; his force took little part in the actual fighting, but it hung on the western flank of the stockade and closed that end to reinforcements as the fleet closed the eastern. The defenders of the stockade could, therefore, only be reinforced through the one narrow door in the wall. Including fighting slaves, the Portuguese mustered some 3,000 men, and of these 1,600 under Joâo de Lima and Manuel de Lacerda, attacked the stockade, which they rushed. The fugitives blocked the one door and the Portuguese prevented it being shut by thrusting in their pike staves, while some of them climbed the wall to the embrasures and thence drove the defenders from its back; the city was entered and after much street fighting cleared. For three days the slaughter continued; Hindus were spared, Muhamedans, men, women and children were killed, either individually or burnt in batches in their mosques; the hill men of the Ghats even turned out to attack the fugitives, and the pursuit from the Goa side was continued by native troops led by banished men, for the work had its danger and if they were killed it mattered little; the total number of slain was 6,000.[1] The Portuguese had 40 killed and 200 wounded, among the former was Jeronymo de Lima the brother of Joâo de Lima, who led the assault. Struck by an arrow in the breast he fell, his brother ran to help him: "Go your way, brother," said the dying man, "and

[1] Albuquerque in his letter of December 22nd, 1510, gives 6,oco "per comta."

I go mine;" his brother returned to the fight, and he soon after died. The plunder was not large as the place had been used only as a fortress.

Albuquerque allowed no grass to grow under his feet; within a week of the capture of the city on December 1st, the foundations of the new fortress were laid.[1] The city walls were repaired, a hospital endowed from the lands belonging to mosques was started, and a chapel to St. Catherine built. All these buildings were of mud, thatched; the chapel had only an altar and a rude painting on the wall; for fear of fire the vessels were kept in a building in the masonry part of the fort, and there mass was said. There was a general objection to the return of Timoja to his old post, he had been involved in several piracies, some on ships that held Albuquerque's own safe-conduct, and one Malhar Rao, a relative of the Raja of Honawar, was appointed, and the revenue and police farmed to him for £14,000 a year.[2] The protests of Diogo Mendes continued, and finding them fruitless, he and two of his captains determined on a secret flight. They dropped down one night silently with the tide; in the morning their absence was discovered and Albuquerque sent his galleys after them. They were overhauled, beating up against the sea breeze; fire was opened, two men were killed on Diogo Mendes' ship and the halliards of his sail shot away; the three ships then yielded and were brought back to the anchorage. Albuquerque hanged two of the pilots;[3] Diogo Mendes and the other officers were sentenced to banishment to Por-

[1] Thomas Fernandes of Cananor fame was the architect. He also built the Calicut fort, two years later.

[2] Cartas, pp. 47 and 48. Timoja was made over to the charge of Malhar Rao, accompanied him in his flight in 1511, and was poisoned.

[3] The two pilots hanged had been on board the mutinous ships at Ormuz. The King had pardoned them, but Albuquerque refused to accept their statements to that effect as they had not their pardons with them.

tugal, Albuquerque's defence of this high-handed action against a man in independent authority was absolute necessity.[1] The Portuguese in the East were too few to split up the Government, and it is noteworthy that no attempt was again made for 60 years to divide it. Having given the finishing touches to the Goa administration, Albuquerque collected his troops for an expedition against Malacca. He started on April 20th, 1511, with 18 ships and 600 men at arms besides slaves.

The town of Malacca stood on either side of a salt-water creek into which the marshes at the back of the town drained: communication between houses on either side of the creek was kept up by a bridge. The thatched and wooden houses stretched for a league along the shore, but the danger of fire was so great that merchandize was kept in underground cellars, closed at the top with clay, called godowns. The streets were wide, and the houses of the better sort were surrounded by walls that separated them from their neighbours and the streets. The marshes guarded the back of the town and rendered it secure from attack in that quarter, but the environs were infested by wild beasts, the air was pestiferous, and no supply of food was locally produced. The ruling chief was called Sultan Muhamad. The nationalities the Portuguese found in Malacca were numerous: there are especially mentioned, Persians, Guzeratis, Burmans, Malabaris, merchants from the Coromandel Coast, and what struck the Portuguese most, ships from the Lew Chew Islands with crews of people they called Gores, men of reserved speech and apt to take the law into their own hands.[2] On the way Albuquerque touched at Pedir and Pasai, in Sumatra, and on July 1st anchored

[1] See defence in Cartas, page 59, based on necessity.

[2] They may have been Japanese.

at Malacca.[1] Of the Portuguese who had been made prisoners from Diogo Lopes' squadron, 9 were found in Pedir whither they had escaped, Ruy d'Araujo and 5 others were in Malacca, the rest had died or turned Muhamedan. A demand for the release of the captives was evaded until Albuquerque burned some houses along the water's edge and some ships. The further demands of the Portuguese that they should be given permission to build a fort, compensated for the damage done to Diogo Lopes, and for the expenses of Albuquerque's fleet, were not accepted: the Chinese with whom Albuquerque had fraternized suggested reducing the city by starvation, as the sea-borne supplies on which the town depended could be easily cut off, but Albuquerque had no time for this. In all, including slaves, he could muster 1,100 soldiers, to attack a strongly fortified city defended by 50,000 men. His plan was to seize the bridge and thus cut the city into two parts.

Either end of the bridge was attacked on St. James's day, July 25th, but with its capture the success of the assailants ended, they lost 70 or 80 men wounded and many of these died. The troops, cowed by the effects of the poisoned arrows, were withdrawn the same evening. Recognizing that he was not strong enough to carry the city by assault, Albuquerque used diplomacy, and opened communication with Utimute Raja, a Javan who occupied one side of the town, and obtained his promise to remain passive. He loaded a lofty junk with materials for rapid field fortifications,—casks filled with earth to make a stockade, and field-pieces to fire between them; beams to stand in the casks, and sails to stretch from beam to beam to conceal the men behind; he also provided an awning

[1] See Cartas, p. 59, for the story of the Malay in a captured ship who fought on though covered with wounds that did not bleed. When a bracelet of bone was taken from his wrist he bled to death.

for the bridge to shelter the wounded. Tide by tide the junk was worked nearer the bridge: the full depth of the spring tides was needed to bring it close, and the second assault had to be postponed until August 8th. In its slow approach the men in the junk suffered from the enemy's fire, and part of the face of its captain, Antonio d'Abreu, was carried away by a bullet.[1] Once close up to the bridge the men from the upper works cleared it of its defenders, and one boat at either end kept all succour from approaching. With the help of the materials in the junk the Portuguese were soon fortified on the bridge, and a mosque hard by was also stormed and occupied as a subsidiary position.

There followed nine days of street fighting and nine nights of bombardment before the town was cleared;[2] after the Malays had been driven out, rough stockades were built at the outskirts. Safe-conducts were given to some Hindus, Javans and Burmans who had treated Ruy d'Araujo with kindness, and a systematic sack of the place began. The amount of plunder was enormous. Correa, in one of his rare personal references, says that he had heard Albuquerque swear that he was bringing home a million in gold for the King; the currency is not mentioned. Castanheda more soberly puts the King's share at £95,000. As almost all, including the bronze lions which Albuquerque had reserved as ornaments for his own tomb, were lost by shipwreck, the exact sum can never be ascertained. The capture of this fortified city defended by an army of 30,000 men, by 1,100 Portuguese was a most brilliant feat, but

[1] Albuquerque, hearing of the wound, annoyed d'Abreu greatly by sending a substitute. He declined to give over charge as long as he had feet to walk on and hands to fight with.

[2] The King's elephants were met in this street fighting and defeated with lances only.

characteristically Albuquerque never received even any verbal acknowledgment from his king for the service. No time was lost in building a fort with forced labour, it was completed in four months, on a site defended on one side by the creek, and on the other by the sea. Ninachetty was appointed head of the city, into which no Malay was admitted. Albuquerque next turned his attention to the Javan colony headed by Utimute Raja. This man was descended from a Hindu family settled in Java; he had become a Muhamedan, and fifty years before had migrated to Malacca, where he had amassed great wealth. Albuquerque considered him too powerful to be left behind. A friendly visit was arranged: he, his son, son-in-law and grandson came to intercede for a friend, whom they desired to see appointed Kotwal or governor of the city. At this visit they were all taken prisoners and immediately executed. This treacherous act was followed by ten days' hard fighting before Utimute Raja's following was dispersed: subdued they were not, for under another son-in-law, "Patequatir," they remained a thorn in the side of the Portuguese for many years. An expedition was sent to explore the Moluccas, and after the return of Duarte Fernandes from Siam, a more formal embassy was despatched to that State. The Captain of the fortress also had standing orders that when any ship left Malacca for a new port a Portuguese should sail in her to bring back information of the unknown countries of the further East. [1]

Albuquerque left 300 men for the garrison of the fort and 200 for the crews of the ships, and in December started on his return to India. He had three ships and a

[1] Barros, writing in 1545, has a very curious passage in II. 7. 1., in which he says he has seen letters from Albuquerque to the Royal Chronicler, Ruy de Pinha, to whom he sent valuable rings. He implies that Albuquerque had, in modern phrase, tried to influence the press.

junk, in which last were only 13 Portuguese, the rest of the crew being Malay craftsmen and their families, sent to work in Indian dockyards. The spoils of Malacca were in Albuquerque's ship and the junk;—the former was the Flor de la Mar, João da Nova's ship at Ormuz, now old and leaky, and selected as flag-ship because if the governor had not sailed in her no one else would have. The voyage was unfortunate: Albuquerque's ship struck on a shoal, broke in two, and sank just after a raft had been rigged upon which the Portuguese part of the crew was saved. All her riches sank in her, and though divers were employed nothing was ever recovered. The Malay craftsmen in the junk rose and killed the Portuguese, ran her on shore and looted her; thus of the plunder of Malacca all was lost.

Early in February 1512, Albuquerque, to the joy of almost every Portuguese in India, reached Cochin, for matters had not been going on well during his absence. Throughout his whole term he was persistently followed by a clique of enemies, the most inveterate of whom was Antonio Real.[1] Apparently, in one of his letters, the King had written recommending this man to Albuquerque's goodwill. In reply he spoke his mind: "You recommend "Antonio Real to me—considering how he has abused me, "calling me thief, Moor and coward, and the confidence you "place in him, it is I who want a letter of recommendation "to him." It is needless to rake up all the old scandals, but this clique intercepted Albuquerque's letters to the King, read them and published their contents, and it was their action that in the end ruined Albuquerque. The information they sent to Portugal while the Governor was in Malacca, induced the King to write the querulous complaints which drew the very angry series of replies that went home

[1] For the history of his son, see page 240.

at the end of 1513, replies which led the King to send out a new governor in 1515. The quarrel with Real began out of a simple incident. A larger church was needed at Cochin, and as a commencement a share of the proceeds of prizes taken at sea was devoted to a building fund. With £160 thus collected some stones and lime were purchased, and while Albuquerque was absent from Cochin, Real used the materials partly to repair the fort and partly to repair his own house. For this Albuquerque fined him heavily.

But the news from Goa was more disquieting than even the intrigues of faction. After Albuquerque's departure the forces of Ismail Adil Shah, under Fulad Khan, cleared the mainland of the Portuguese officials, crossed the fords, defeated and killed Roderigo Rabello, the Captain of Goa, and closely besieged the town.[1] To the disappointment of the invaders the townspeople, among whom no Muhamedans were left, showed no disposition to join them. Diogo Mendes was taken from the prison where he awaited his removal to Portugal, and appointed at the general desire to succeed the dead Captain; he did not show, however, much sagacity in his new post, for when Ismail Adil Shah grew suspicious of Fulad Khan and sent back Rasul Khan to supplant him, and the latter found himself too weak to take action alone, the Portuguese actually helped him to defeat and capture Fulad Khan. Naturally, Rasul Khan once in power, demanded the cession of Goa itself. The garrison were 1,100 strong, of whom only 450 were Portuguese; the supply of food was scanty, though some was obtained by natives resident in the town, who had relatives cultivating in the outskirts. By Easter, which in 1512 fell on April 11th, 60 Portuguese had deserted to the enemy, and there was even a conspiracy in the garrison itself to give up the place.

[1] By a fatal error Albuquerque's orders to fortify Benasterim, that commanded the chief ford, had been neglected.

There were about 100 Europeans in Goa married to native wives, and their acknowledged leader was the illegitimate son of a Portuguese fidalgo, one D. Fernando, whose record in Lisbon had been a bad one. Several of the native wives had been taken prisoners at the capture of Goa, and some of them had husbands, brothers and other relatives in Rasul Khan's camp: there was thus a constant communication between the two forces, and Rasul Khan had availed himself of this communication to win over about forty of the married men, including the leader, to open the gates by night to the invaders. Married men were, under Albuquerque's arrangements, exempt from night duty; but their leader, the better to carry out his designs, suggested to the Captain that at such an anxious time all must bear their share of the burden. Orders were issued accordingly; but one married man—Fernâo Braz, a barber—not in the conspiracy, and doubtful how far he could with safety leave his wife alone in his house, complained loudly and got a thrashing from D. Fernando for his pains. When Fernâo Braz, sore from his beating, returned home, his wife who knew the whole story of the conspiracy told it him, and he immediately disclosed it to the Captain.[1]

This conspiracy was of course thwarted, but it left an uncomfortable feeling of insecurity behind, from which the Portuguese were relieved by the action of Joâo Machado, the banished man then in command of some of Ismail Adil Shah's troops, for he with eight other Portuguese deserted and entered Goa. The return of a man who had been so many years among the Muhamedans and who had risen to a position of trust among them, not only effectually stopped any further desertions, but supplied the Portuguese with much information as to their enemies' forces and plans;

[1] The history of this conspiracy was concealed, as the married men were implicated, and there was no public enquiry.

but the garrison was not strong enough to undertake any operations outside the town. Albuquerque, who learned on his arrival at Cochin that Rasul Khan was strongly fortified in Benasterim, 6 miles from the walls of Goa, was not, either, in a position to go at once to its relief; men and arms were both greatly needed, and he had therefore to await the arrival of the ships of 1512.[1] In these ships came 1,800 men as reinforcements, and the first matchlocks sent from Europe.[2]

In October the relieving force left Cochin, and Goa was reached on November 8th. The operations which followed for the relief of Goa were among the most gallant of Albuquerque's exploits, and his letter to the King describing the event brings out vividly the devotion he inspired in his men.[3] Benasterim fort stood on the Goa bank of the creek that made Goa an island.[4] The fort had been strongly built under the orders of Rasul Khan, and two lines of beams at either side of the ford served to defend those crossing from the mainland and to prevent an attack on them by boats. The fort could be approached by water from either side, either by the creek passing north from old Goa, or by that coming south from the Goa river; Albuquerque selected the former route for his first advance. While the ford connecting the fort with the mainland was in the hands of the garrison, any attempt to capture the fort from the land side would have been a lengthy operation; the first thing then was to cut the line of

[1] Cartas, pages 42 and 91.

[2] Correa, the historian, came out in this fleet.

[3] Cartas, p. 101, dated Nov. 23rd, 1512. I have added anecdotes of Albuquerque's heroism from the historians. He called his sailors "my cavaliers."

[4] Benasterim is not marked on the Indian atlas, but is marked on the map to Fonseca's Goa. In the former it should stand where the road from Goa to Hurcan crosses the creek

communication, the isolated fort could after that be attacked with some hope of speedy success. The river face of the fort was defended by a numerous artillery trained along the water line, and to attack this Albuquerque specially prepared six vessels, covering them with coils of rope and with planking. In the one that was to approach nearest to the walls an inverted boat was slung over the deck to fend off missiles—raw hides were freely used as a protection from fire. The men at arms were removed from the vessels, and only sailors and gunners left; the fewer the men the less the chance of their being hit.

Albuquerque sat in the leading boat that towed these armoured vessels. Near the fort a Malabar man was shot close to him, and the garrison, seeing the blood sprinkled on Albuquerque, raised a shout that he was killed; standing up amidst the cheers of his own men he disabused them. He berthed his ships a gunshot from the walls, to let his crews lose their fear of the artillery, and though the ships were pierced through and through by the shot, but few men were killed. In return the ships did some damage to the fort, but as they could not subdue some heavy guns served by renegades, Albuquerque made a raft, mounted on it a powerful gun in charge of a master gunner and six gunners; and anchored the contrivance by night close under the walls; his orders to the gunners were to fire only at the enemy's big guns. They were successful and the renegades were killed. On one ship, the Rosario, owing to an explosion, the deck and the forecastle were blown into the air; the crew in a panic jumped into the water, and the captain only was left in the burning vessel. Albuquerque got into a skiff alone with some oarsmen and shamed the crew into returning to help their captain, the flames were extinguished and the ship was temporarily withdrawn from the line of fire. When the fire of the fort had been got under and the Portuguese crews were seasoned, Albuquerque grappled the beams that guarded the ford, pulled them out and cut the crossing. He never left the ships during the whole eight days' fighting, till he saw the San Pedro anchored in the ford with her bowsprit touching the walls of the fort. In these eight days the ships had fired 4,000 rounds from their big guns; the hulls of the vessels were riddled, and the masts, rigging and decks were studded with arrows.[1]

The land forces had meanwhile been organized. Soon after Albuquerque's return to Goa, the beacon fires and the church bells warned the citizens that Rasul Khan was advancing to deliver an attack against the town. Albuquerque was against any fighting before he was quite prepared, as he thought, and rightly as it turned out, that the Muhamedans would not await the onset; he was, however, overborne by the eagerness of his men, who got out of hand at the sight of the enemy, drove them back to the walls of their fort, which they then tried to scale without ladders, and from which they were beaten with the loss of 150 men. Albuquerque, delighted at the bravery of Pero Mascarenhas who commanded the trained bands, kissed him on the cheek and nearly caused a mutiny by the signal honour.[2] A few days' battering at a short range compelled the garrison to capitulate, and had not Albuquerque demanded the surrender of the deserters the garrison would have yielded sooner. Rasul Khan left secretly, and but for the arrangements of Albuquerque the garrison,

[1] The captains and the men were deaf for some days after. The hulls of the vessels could not sink as they had shores under them.

[2] All the historians are agreed on the incident. Castanheda adds that one fidalgo turned the general indignation into a bitter laugh by saying, "Se ho Governador por cousa tâo pouca beijava na face a Pero Mascarenhas avia dalia poucos dias de beijar a eles no traseiro por outros muyto grandes que aviâo de fazer." III. 91. Mascarenhas was, in 1526, Governor for a short time.

including many women and children, could not have escaped to the mainland. Reinforcements from the Adil Shah arrived shortly after the fort was surrendered and had to retreat.

The deserters were given up by Rasul Khan on a promise that their lives should be spared, but the promise was kept to the letter and not to the spirit. "I gave them their "lives at the request of Rasul Khan, but I ordered their "limbs to be mutilated and amputated and their ears cut "off, for a warning and in memory of the treason and evil "that they did." [1] Of the 19 surrendered, half died under the tortures, and at the end of the three days the survivors were hardly human in form. The after history of two of them is recorded. One, Pedreannes "of the hands", lived in Cochin for 20 years doing menial acts of charity; another, Fernâo Lopez, was the first colonist of St. Helena, living as a hermit and raising vegetables for passing ships. By order of the King of Portugal he was brought to Europe and received absolution from the Pope in Rome, but he returned to St. Helena and died there in 1546.

The numbers of envoys from the countries of India [2] and its neighbourhood that waited on Albuquerque's pleasure, was of itself sufficient to show the status that the conquest of Goa had given the Portuguese among Eastern powers. Ormuz, Siam, Pegu, Guzerat, and Abyssinia all appear in the goodly list. At Ormuz there had been some changes, for Albuquerque's old opponent, Khwaja Atar, was dead, and Nuru-d-din had succeeded him; the King too had accepted the "cap" from Shah Ismail of Persia and acknowledged himself to be an adherent of the Shia sect.

[1] Cartas, page 116.

[2] In 1514 the Portuguese received a rhinoceros as a present from the Sultan of Guzerat. It was then an almost unknown animal, and was sent to Portugal, and being sent on to the Pope it died just as it reached the Italian shores. It is the very animal immortalized by Dürer. Castanheda's description—III. 134—is quaint. The Portuguese used the Hindi name Genda.

There was something here to be remembered when the time of reckoning came, but in the meanwhile the embassy was complimentary, and there was the horse trade that called for immediate regulation. No horses suited for military purposes were bred in Southern India; all used there were imported from the Persian Gulf. It was a matter of life and death to the states warring in the Deccan to obtain the command of this horse supply, and Albuquerque intended to control it by his power at sea and bring all the imported horses to Goa, whereby he would gain two objects,—fill his coffers by the high import duty charged, £17 a horse, and obtain command of a lever that would give him great influence in Deccan politics. The thorny question of Persian rights over Ormuz could therefore wait; it was enough for the present to settle that horses exported from Ormuz should be consigned to Goa. In 1514 Vijayanagara offered £20,000 for the exclusive right to buy 1,000 horses, but Albuquerque rightly refused the offer on the ground that such an exclusive privilege would destroy the trade he was trying to foster; his mind, however, constantly reverted to the idea: it is better than any gold mine, he explains. [1]

The Abyssinian envoy was undoubtedly the one of all the envoys that roused the most interest in Albuquerque's mind, as his arrival was the first result of the many years of effort to reach that semi-mythical prince. Even now the message was brought by a doubtful messenger. The man was a Cairo Muhamedan, who said that he had been made a Christian, with the name Matheus—that the King of Abyssinia had sent him off at an hour's notice as his envoy to the Portuguese, and that he had been robbed both at Zeila and at Dabul. He had some letters done up in a wax cloth, and a piece of wood wrapped in a rag, which

[1] Cartas, page 343.

he said was part of the true cross. He was first heard of with his wife in Dabul, and Albuquerque got him from there by a stratagem lest the Muhamedans should intercept him. He questioned him, and found that he knew of the two men whom Albuquerque had landed some years before at Cape Guardefui, disguised as Muhamedan merchants, who had been robbed by the Portuguese; and that, on the other hand, the Abyssinian captives in India knew him. Albuquerque argued too in his favour that there could be nothing to gain by a forged embassy: the Egyptians could discover all they needed without a cumbrous scheme from which there was no escape for the envoy except to be landed on Abyssinian soil. It turned out many years later when he was taken back to Massowah, that Matheus was a genuine envoy; but the wretched man had to suffer indignities of all kinds from the faction opposed to Albuquerque, who took advantage of the Governor's absence to cruelly misuse the unfortunate ambassador and his wife. To give greater weight to the Embassy, Albuquerque had constructed, as he told the king some time afterwards, two gold caskets, one for his letters of credence and one for the piece of the true cross.[1]

Meanwhile the preparations for a voyage to the Red Sea had been progressing, and on February 7th, 1513, Albuquerque left Goa with 1,700 Portuguese and 1,000 natives of India in 24 ships. In Goa he left a garrison of 400 men, and in Cochin and Cananor 80 men each. Southern India could be left comparatively weak, as negotiations with the Samuri for a peace were far advanced.[2] The objects of this expedition were to explore the shores of

1 See Cartas, pp. 312—316 and p. 381. The part of his letter of Oct. 15th, 1514, in which he confesses how he had been in the habit of furbishing up the gifts of Indian princes to increase the honour of the King of Portugal is interesting.

2 Cartas, page 125.

the Red Sea as yet unvisited by a Portuguese fleet; to destroy any preparations the Egyptians might be making for a fresh invasion of India; to open up communications with the Prester John and to stop the Red Sea traders who still evaded in large numbers the Indian blockade. Since the Portuguese first rounded the Cape and interfered with the Muhamedan trade by Jedda, Aden had risen considerably in importance as the place of transhipment of Indian goods; the Portuguese, too, had learned that it and not Socotra was the gate of the Red Sea, it therefore was the first place to be attacked. After watering at Socotra, the fleet reached Aden on March 25th; Mir Amrjan was the Captain of the city, under Shaikh Hamid who was absent. As it was Albuquerque's intention to capture the town no time was wasted in preliminaries, and on the morning of March 26th the attack was delivered. The whole conception of the operations—if such a term can be applied to what was merely a confused melee—was faulty. Ladders had been brought from Cochin wide enough to admit six men abreast, but they proved too short; the water shoaled rapidly, and in wading from the boats the matchlock men's powder got wet. After landing, 100 men were sent to make a diversion higher up the hill where the wall seemed lower, but they were driven back by rocks rolled down. The rest planted their ladders against the part of the wall nearest to them and climbed up. The ladders were not only too short, but broke under the weight of the crowds, and Albuquerque, in his endeavour to mitigate the evil by telling off halberdiers to hold up the ladders with their halberds, aggravated the misfortune, for the halberdiers were smothered and the stormers spitted.[1]

[1] A curious story is told by Castanheda, interesting as D. Garcia de Noronha was afterwards Viceroy. He forced open an embrasure and ordered some men in, they refused; they were ready to follow him, but he was not their Governor to order them.

Some fifty men gained the top of the wall, and among them a priest, Diogo Mergulhâo, who held a cross raised on a spear, but the brave man had to retire with six wounds, and his cross was held under an arm pinned by two arrows. The efforts were continued for some time; many were killed inside the walls, and many, jumping from them, saved their lives at the expense of broken legs; five bannarets were lost in the city,—the total number of killed is nowhere recorded. After the Portuguese had retired in great disorder to their ships, Albuquerque and his captains had a long and anxious consultation as to whether they should attack an outlying fort whose artillery fire was causing the ships some damage. But by the time the council had decided that an attempt should be made they found the work done; the master and sailors of Manuel de Lacerda's ship had landed in a skiff, with their swords and lances, and captured the fort and 27 pieces of artillery.[1]

Failing here, Albuquerque sailed for the Red Sea. The Red Sea pilots of those days lived on an island close to Perim, and one was secured by sending forward as a decoy an Indian built ship. The passage of the first Portuguese fleet through the Straits of Babel-Mandeb was the occasion of much ceremony. On the way north Albuquerque's vessel, the Santa Maria da Serra, was nearly lost by striking on a shelf of sand, on either side of which was deep water; in gratitude for his escape from this danger he afterwards built the chapel of Nossa Senhora da Serra in Goa, where he was buried.[2] Passing Jebel Zukr, the fleet made its way to Kamaran. Kamaran Island is about 11 miles

[1] The news of the attack reached Cairo by land in 15 days. Albuquerque blamed no one for this failure. "It was a well fought out affair" is his comment.

[2] Albuquerque continued his horrible mutilations on all the people he captured in the Red Sea, except the residents of Kamaran from whom he hoped for some benefits.

long with a few villages of fishermen, some cultivation and a few cattle and sheep; at this time it belonged to the Imam of Sanaa; its chief attraction was its plentiful supply of good water. Watering was completed as quickly as possible, and then the fleet started for Jedda; but the wind failed, and after beating about fruitlessly till the end of May, it returned to Kamaran, where it stayed till the middle of July. The crews spent here a terrible time; there was very little food save shell-fish; every living thing on the island, down to the roots of the palm trees, was eaten, and the hard work of cleaning and caulking the ships in the trying climate of a Red Sea summer, combined with the bad food, caused a great mortality—500 Portuguese and nearly all the natives of India died; no prizes even could be made, for, partly through fear of the invaders and partly owing to the season of the year, there were no ships on the sea.[1] The halt was not altogether wasted, as the minute acquaintance with the Red Sea which Albuquerque's letters exhibit, proves the care he devoted to acquiring information. A man at arms, Fernao Dias, a north African, was dressed as an escaped slave and landed to find his way overland to Portugal, where he duly arrived in safety. Albuquerque is credited with having, while in the Red Sea, hit upon the idea of destroying Egypt by diverting the Nile into the Red Sea, but the idea was in no sense his own; it was a traditional scheme which had been handed down from generation to generation of Abyssinians.[2] His excitable imagination, however, did take fire at the possibility of capturing Mecca: "Jedda and Mecca," he says, "have no "men at arms, only hermits; there are plenty of horses and "plenty of men in Prester John's country. What can 3,000

[1] In Albuquerque's letters no mention is made of this time—a curious instance of *suppressio veri*.

[2] Castro Roteiro of the voyage of 1541, page 74.

"Moors do against 500 Portuguese mounted on horses? if "500 will not do, take 1,000. Mecca is so easy to destroy, "I look on it as already destroyed."[1] The imagination in Albuquerque was unduly developed.

The fleet left Kamaran on its return journey on July 15th. Perim was examined and pronounced unfit for a fortress by reason of its want of water.[2] Aden was reached on July 25th, and ten days were spent there; but the place was stronger than before, and the weakened fleet could do nothing. On August 4th the expedition started for Diu, which it reached on the 16th; Albuquerque's intention was to surprise the place, but two of his captains lost touch of the fleet, blundered into the harbour and caused an alarm, consequently the Governor's relations with Malik Aiyaz were strained. The latter refused to visit him on his ship: "He knows he could come on board," said Albuquerque, "but "he does not know if he could get off again." As Albuquerque was starting, Malik Aiyaz came out with his flotilla, and the two fleets saluted; the former was much impressed by the latter: "He always has his leg lifted ready for a kick," was his comment. A visit paid to Chaul on the way back was so far noteworthy that Albuquerque saw its importance as the site for a fortress, and it was in consequence of his opinion that one was built there some years later.

Albuquerque reached Goa in September and remained there for 18 months, the longest rest he took in the last years of his life.[3] He found much to occupy him, for his frequent absences had disorganized the internal affairs of the Portuguese in India, and the presence of a strong hand

[1] Cartas, p. 281. He calls Muhamedans "Alfenados"—the henna-dyed ones.

[2] Albuquerque calls it "Mihum"—his name for it of Vera Cruz has of course not survived.

[3] The sententious Barros, speaking of this period, has an astounding maxim: "Whoever fights has the glory of conquering his enemies, but he who governs only acquires the hatred of his subordinates."

was much needed. Before Albuquerque left for the Red Sea, negotiations had been opened with the Samuri for a peace, but during his absence the Rajas of both Cochin and Cananor, who disliked such a peace, had intrigued to prevent it. The Samuri himself was obstructive, and, as he tells us in his letters, Albuquerque incited the heir-apparent to poison his relative and sovereign. The new Samuri was a more pliable instrument—peace was signed and the fortress built. The Cochin Raja was also annoyed at the growth of Goa; the Portuguese ships there spent money which he considered should have been spent in Cochin. He joined, therefore, Antonio Real and the faction opposed to Albuquerque in urging the King of Portugal to abandon Goa; and on his return from the Red Sea, Albuquerque found a despatch awaiting him, directing that the question of the retention of that place should be considered in a council of the fidalgoes, and that it should be abandoned if the council did not consider that it was for the King's interest that it should be retained. The council voted in accordance with Albuquerque's wishes, but the despatch caused him much annoyance, The King even went out of his way to gird at him, by saying that he did not after all seem to have done much when he took Goa. Albuquerque's reply was haughty: "But I have enough to praise myself for to "tickle my own vanity, and enough to delight in to please "myself." [1] "At first," he says to the king, "I was astounded "at your order to consider the abandonment of Goa in a "public council, and when I saw the letters on which you "had based your orders I was still more astounded that "you had not burned them." [2] In the bitterness of his soul he wrote more openly to a friend—"There are men who, "knowing that I have set my heart on retaining Goa, have

[1] Cartas, p. 184.
[2] Cartas, p. 260.

"done their best to thwart me, but I tell you, sir, I do "not understand this business. I thought the King had Goa "like a stone set in a ring. I took it at his orders and his "captains signed their agreement; I took it, and strengthened "myself in it, considered it my companion and helper; I "leaned my back against it, and I trusted it freely. By it "we got a foothold in India and destroyed the dock-yard "of the Moors. Now no one can order us not to touch "the Moors, nor can the Raja of Cochin demand the life "of a Portuguese for that of a cow. It is the chief port "of India for the Deccan, for Vijayanagara, and for Europe. "In Cochin you cannot get supplies for 500 men; there is "no fish and no flesh, and fowls there are sixpence each. "In Goa 2,000 men extra are hardly noticed. In a foreign "country you cannot cut a stick without permission; and "in the bazaar, if you do not pay what you owe, or if you "touch a Moor woman or wound a man of the country, "swords are drawn at once and the fortress is besieged." [1]

The feeling produced by the tenor of the letters from Portugal, combined, perhaps, with a sense of failure in the Red Sea, and certainly with anger at the encouragement his opponents received from his sovereign, gave a painfully bitter tone to Albuquerque's letters at this time; none the less, however, he devoted all his energy to the responsibilities which his post threw on him. One of his enterprises, the conversion of the Raja of Cochin, which he undertook at the orders of the King of Portugal, and with Duarte Barbosa as interpreter, was naturally not successful. His methods as a missionary were too much like his methods as a military leader. He of course knew that the attempt was hopeless, and that if he had been successful the Christian Raja would have lost all authority over the Nairs,

[1] Cartas, p. 410.

he was consequently satisfied with the assurance of the Raja that so important a matter deserved mature consideration. [1]

To remedy the imperfect training of the matchlock-men in the use of their weapons, Sunday trials of skill were started for prizes, and each man was given half a pound of powder and half a pound of lead a month to enable him to practise. Every man was encouraged to take his pride in having the best appointed arms, and in knowing how to use them. In the evening, when the bell sounded twice, the fidalgoes had to accompany the governor in his ride, to accustom themselves to native saddles. Every morning the governor, with a stick in his hand and a straw hat on his head, rode out, accompanied by four clerks with paper and ink, who noted all orders and memorandums and got them signed at once. During these rides many complaints were disposed of summarily and to the satisfaction of the parties, which, if they had got into the ordinary channel, would have been indefinitely spun out and have become correspondingly involved. He had no stated times or seasons, but disposed of business whenever he met with it and had leisure. [2] His description of his own method will be found in a very interesting letter to the King, in which he discusses his secretary, Gaspar Pereira, who, like the clerk of many an Indian court in more recent times, would have liked "to have put the petitions in his pocket "and settled the matter behind closed doors." [3]

From May to October, Pero d'Albuquerque was in Ormuz,

[1] Cartas, p. 367.

[2] Correa, II. 395, has a curious and detailed story of one João Delgado, a ruffian who tried to poison Albuquerque. The visit to the prison when Correa was with Albuquerque is very graphically told, but the passage is too long to quote.

[3] Cartas, pp. 284 to 291, Albuquerque says that Pereira disliked "Minha domestica conversacão e trato cos cavaleiros e fidalgoes e ter companheiro delles."

whence he explored the Persian Gulf as far as Bahrein, and it was on the information which he brought back that Albuquerque determined to visit Ormuz, for he found himself, when the cargo ships were despatched, with an absolutely empty treasury and with no money to pay his men the wages they had earned. [1] In the universal peace which then obtained there were no prizes to be captured, of the hospitality of the Red Sea he had had bitter experience, and Ormuz was his only resource. This confession of his letters is of the greatest importance, for under the founder of the Portuguese rule in the East and under its most successful governor that rule was not self-supporting, possibly had his term been longer he might have made it so.

The Ormuz expedition consisted of 1,500 Portuguese besides some Malabar troops [2] and slaves, that in all amounted to almost 3,000 men, conveyed in 27 vessels, and it left Goa on February 21st, 1515, for Ormuz, which it reached on March 26th. [3] In the six and a half years that had elapsed since Albuquerque's last visit, matters had changed considerably. After the death of the then King, his brother, Saifu-d-din, had succeeded; Kwaja Atar was dead and Nuru-d-din the Minister was a Persian, old and gouty, who had called in to his help a distant relative, an able and masterful man called Rais Hamid. Hamid, after filling all subordinate posts with his own dependants, had become powerful enough to imprison Nuru-d-din; rumour had it that he meant to depose the King and seize the vacant throne, but this

[1] Cartas, p. 345.

[2] The Malabar men got 13*s* 4*d* a month each.

[3] There is a curious story by Correa, who was in the expedition, of the jest of the galleys under Sylvester the Corsican, into the spirit of which Albuquerque entered fully. (II. 406). This Sylvester was a difficult person to deal with, not only Albuquerque found it so, but also his successors. As to Albuquerque, see Cartas 301 and 375. Lopo Soares was quite unable to tame his fiery spirit. (Correa, II. 533.) He had been sent out in 1514 as capable in the management of galleys.

would seem to have been superfluous. Hamid had the assistance of Shah Ismail (1499—1525) who had raised himself by his abilities to the Persian throne, and one of the latter's envoys, Ibrahim Beg, was in Ormuz when Albuquerque arrived; it is natural therefore that Albuquerque should have come to the conclusion (which was correct) that Rais Hamid and the Shah of Persia were in league and that if he intended to act he must act quickly, or any chance of obtaining a footing in Ormuz would be gone. Albuquerque's demands were for the arrears of tribute and for possession of the site granted for a fortress at his first visit. Nuru-d-din had been released when the Portuguese fleet hove in sight, and at an interview with him the demands were agreed to, and that although part of the old site had been covered with buildings connected with the royal palace. What was almost more important, Albuquerque managed to get some private conversation with the old minister and to learn that he could count on the assistance both of him and of the king in any attempt to get rid of Rais Hamid.

Possession was obtained of the site on April 1st, and in three days it was enclosed in a stockade, with artillery mounted. This settled, Albuquerque, who never lost sight of the necessity of impressing the oriental imagination, received the Persian, Ibrahim Beg, with great pomp. This envoy returned to Persia on August 10th, and took with him a Portuguese mission, but owing to the events in Ormuz its reception was the reverse of friendly and it had to beat a hasty retreat out of Persia. Rais Hamid had not yet visited Albuquerque, but remained sullenly in his own house; rumour of course credited him with the intention of assassinating Albuquerque, and in a secret conference of Portuguese captains it was resolved to anticipate any possible action of this character on his part. The king and his minister, accompanied by Rais Hamid, were invited to visit

Albuquerque at his house in the stockade on April 18th, it being agreed that either side should be accompanied by only eight unarmed men; in spite of this agreement Albuquerque filled the rooms of the house, other than the reception room, with armed men and kept more troops ready hard by. Immediately with Albuquerque were his most trusted companions, who had coats of mail under their clothes and their daggers handy. Rais Hamid admitted first into the house alone and fully armed, was hustled with little ceremony into the presence of Albuquerque, [1] who reproached him for wearing weapons. The unfortunate man saw when too late the fate that awaited him, and caught the tag of Albuquerque's coat to beg for safety, but the word was given, and before even he could cry out Albuquerque's companions had despatched him with their daggers, cutting each others hands in their eagerness. [2]

The murder was hardly completed, and the dependants were still wrangling over the dead man's clothes, when Albuquerque advanced smilingly, met the trembling king, and congratulated him on the death of an enemy. Though music had been playing to drown the noise, the people of the town grew suspicious and tried to break into the house; they were quieted when with great difficulty the thoroughly frightened king and his minister were induced to show themselves on the flat roof of the house. The brother of the murdered man, with 700 fighting men besides women and children, occupied the royal palace: it took much diplomacy to get them embarked and started for the mainland before night. On this day, the 18th, the Portuguese were under arms from morning till evening, and were

[1] Alexander d'Ataide seized him by the hand and pulled him along.

[2] The body was hardly on the ground before the followers stripped it. Correa gives a vivid touch to the picture when he says he took the dead man's gold embroidered kerchief, which he sold for £7.

supplied with food by the servants of the king; we get a martial picture of Albuquerque himself eating his mess of rice and meat cooked together, standing with his shield pushed up his arm and his spear leaning against his shoulder. That night the king returned to his palace. Albuquerque improved the occasion by wringing a large sum of money from the king.[1]

The foundations of the fort were laid on May 3rd: the ceremony had not yet become the symbol it now has. The procession was headed by priests who prayed and sprinkled holy water and blessings; on reaching the trench, a cloth was placed on Albuquerque's shoulder, and on it a stone, which he carried to the trench and laid, with five gold coins underneath it. He was followed by the other captains each with his stone. The work was pushed on with even more than Albuquerque's usual energy: his efforts never relaxed all through the terrible heats of June and July, day by day and all day he was arranging the food of the men and the supply of materials for the work. Deprived even of fresh water for bathing, the natives of India sickened and by August nearly all were dead; 300 of the Portuguese had succumbed. Complaints were made that the doctors who were paid to look after the sick exacted money from them. When Albuquerque sent for and questioned them as to the nature of the sickness from which the men were suffering, they replied that they could not give it a name. "I will soon teach you," said the hard old man, "more than your books can ever tell you," and he set them to work at the walls all through the long hot day. "Now," he said, "you know the disease, and be careful you do not come to the galleys."

Early in August the iron constitution of Albuquerque

[1] Correa says £350,000, which is absurd. Cartas, p. 371, puts the amount at £40,000, which is possibly correct.

began to give way; he was attacked by diarrhœa, then prevalent, and his weak and spare frame had no reserve of strength to resist the disease. In spite of his uncle's request to remain, D. Garcia de Noronha started on August 29th for India, on his way to Portugal; he took with him the 15 unfortunate relatives of the King of Ormuz—sufficiently important to have been considered worthy of blinding;[1] they and their families were settled in Goa. In September the Governor got worse, and for 21 days was seen by no one but his private servants; then, to stifle the disorder that the rumour of his death might cause, he had his bed removed to a window where he could talk with his captains and watch the progress of the work. On October 20th, after nominating Pero d'Albuquerque as Captain of Ormuz, he prepared to return to India in the ship of his old Red Sea flag-captain, Diogo Fernandes de Beja, who had been badly wounded at the attack on Aden. With all his faults Albuquerque was greatly beloved by his comrades, and his last farewell of them was touching. He started on November 8th, and crossing the Arabian Sea, he learnt from a passing ship, not only that he had been superseded, but that his successor was his personal opponent, and that the men whom he had sent to Portugal in disgrace had returned to India in high employment. There was no word for him from the King even of gratitude for past services, it was his death-blow. His friends tried to amuse him by saying the King would give him high employment in Portugal: "Portugal is a small country," he replied; "what employment is there that is one-half of one-third of that of the Governor of India? I have sacrificed to one saint—the

[1] They had been blinded by passing a red-hot bowl close to the eyes. The practice seems to have ceased after the Portuguese obtained influence in Ormuz. Couto had talked with old residents in Goa who remembered some of these men begging by the roadside and asking alms as deposed kings.

King. I am out with the King because of men, and I am out with men because of the King."

He made his will, and in leaving his last wishes to his successor his old humour flashed out: "I beg he will not put up my goods to auction: I do not wish my ragged old breeches to be seen." [1] His last letter to the King was dignified and pathetic—a letter hard perhaps to have to write, but certainly harder to receive. [2] He longed with a feverish longing to see Goa before he died, and with a last effort he stood up as the ship crossed the bar, and leaned against the door frame to get yet one more view. Early on Sunday, December 16th, as the ship was casting anchor in front of Goa, he died, dressed as he wished, in the habit of the order of St. James. In the morning, seated almost upright, with his eyes half open, with the captains of the fleet around, and his royal banner which preceded him in battle unfurled before him, he was taken on shore to the chapel he had built. The grief of the people of Goa, whether Christians or not, was deep and general. "He has only gone," said the lower sort, "because God has need of him to fight battles elsewhere." His tomb for many years was a refuge where the oppressed, bringing sweet-smelling flowers, came to pray, and the jealousy of his successor was aroused by the number that visited his resting-place to pour out their complaints to him as if he had been alive. The men fresh from Portugal were unable to understand this outburst of sorrow for a man they had heard so vilified. The best epitaph, indeed, that Albuquerque can have is the grief of the city he founded.

The King of Portugal recognized too late the mistake he had made, and before the news of Albuquerque's death

[1] Lopo Soares did put up his goods to auction, but they were so poor that they redounded to the credit of the great Governor.

[2] Cartas, page 380, December 6th, 1515.

could reach him, he wrote, in March 1516, modifying his orders as to Albuquerque's return. His superstitious mind, too, paid that respect to Albuquerque's clay which he never extended to the living man. To the day of his death the King would never allow the body to be removed to Portugal: "As long as his bones are there, India is safe."[1] The people of Goa were equally superstitious, and it was only after a papal bull had been fulminated, threatening the obdurate city with dire punishment, that the body could be removed. It reached Lisbon on April 6th, 1566.

Albuquerque was 62 years of age at his death. He was the second son of Gonçalo de Albuquerque and Donna Lianor de Menezes his wife. The bar sinister came in his pedigree several times, and he could claim descent from the Royal Houses of both Portugal and France. He is described as being of medium height, well made, spare of flesh, with a long face, high colour, and a beard reaching to his waist, that in his later years was white. He was never married, and left an illegitimate son by a negress. He was like most men of his age, pitiless and cruel, but he had a keen love of justice. He kept no doorkeeper, and his door was never closed save for a short time while he slept after dinner. It was his maxim that, though the Muhamedans had been conquered, having once submitted, they should be treated with more than even justice to attach them by love.[1] Just before he started for Ormuz in 1515, two Portuguese galley captains committed a petty theft from a Muhamedan boat, the captain of Goa, however, pooh-poohed the matter, for the accused were Portuguese and captains of galleys, the complainant a mere Muhamedan. The persistent Muhamedan went straight to Albuquerque and found him just getting off his horse after his morning's

[1] This, which may seem a commonplace, must be judged by the then standards.

ride, but on hearing the story the Governor returned directly to the shore and investigated the case. Not only the two thieves, but also the masters of their galleys who had held their tongues over their captains' thefts, and the Captain of Goa himself were heavily punished.

He was full of jest and humour, some of it perhaps rather bitter. Some fifteen months before his death he was nearly cast away in Cananor, and the ship lay all night thumping on the rocks. Albuquerque tied a cloth round his waist with a long rope that his body might be recognized if he were drowned, and called out to the weeping and praying crew: "The Lisbon busybodies will say: What a great man your Indian Governor is that you must put him in a cloth and tie a rope around him lest no one should recognize him when he is dead." He, too, is the originator of what was copied by a succeeding Governor, D. Joâo de Castro. One pay-day the money ran short, and a native who came too late complained loudly that he was dying of hunger. Albuquerque pulled two hairs from his beard and gave them to him, saying: "I swear by the life I am living, what would you have? Here, take the hairs of my beard and go and pawn them." The native received the hairs and borrowed money on them, and the next pay-day the lender produced the hairs and Albuquerque released them from pawn out of his own purse.

Albuquerque's sayings and his style of writing were pithy and proverbial. His temper was quick, and sometimes he regretted in his cooler moments the acts of his passion. He was both sagacious and wily, and he was able to foil Orientals with their own weapons. The value of downright honesty in dealing with the Eastern peoples had not yet been recognized, and Albuquerque's successors, imitating his methods, but not possessing his ability, lost heavily in the game of intrigue. He, too, had limitations which many of them did not recognize, for though he certainly acted on standards of truth and honesty which are not now acknowledged, he saw clearly enough the value of both these qualities, and in this very few of his successors followed him. "I am known all over India," he tells the the King, "as a man of my word; if I send for a Muhamedan "from anywhere, he comes and demands no security. India, "sire, in my time, is governed with truth and justice, though "it is true the people of these parts speak little truth to us, "but we must not treat them in the same way." His appetite for knowledge was insatiable; besides the envoys to Continental Indian States he sent others to Siam, the Moluccas, Pegu, Java, and Persia. In 1513, after his return from the Red Sea, he sent to the King an Aden Muhamedan who could make opium: "It is only the juice of the poppy," he tells the King, "and the poppies can be grown in the Azores and Portugal."[1] He was a man with the true imperial instinct—the personality the Oriental follows blindly; clear headed, always accessible, he did his work himself: he might inadvertently be unjust, but he never allowed subordinates to rob or oppress; he knew his own mind and he never let his judgment be warped by fear or favour.

It remains to give a brief outline of Albuquerque's general policy. It is the interesting point of his connection with India, and to the English more than to any other nation, that he, first of all men, grasped the idea that by the maintenance of a preponderating sea power a country so distant as Portugal could hope to found an Empire in the East. His predecessor, Almeida, had of course recognized the necessity of supremacy at sea, but his only aim was to divert the carrying trade of the East and West into Portuguese hands. In the absence of any authentic utterance

[1] Cartas, page 174.

it is impossible to be exactly sure of Almeida's views; we can only argue on the pale reflection in the minds of writers not his contemporaries. He is said, for instance, to have strongly opposed, not only any settlement in India, but also the erection of any more fortresses. There is nothing, however, to show how he proposed to keep up the efficiency of the Indian fleet, and how the wastage of the crews was to be made good. Assuming that he had arranged for these two points, he was so far correct that experience proved that the scattering of the Portuguese forces over numerous fortresses was in later years a great source of weakness. Almeida's views do not seem to have been antagonistic to those of Albuquerque, but he grasped only half a truth and entirely missed the great conception of his successor.

To return then to the more immediate subject—Albuquerque's own policy. He aimed at a Portuguese dominion in the East, both by colonization and conquest, sufficiently preponderating to give that nation the command of all the trade between the East and West. He based his policy entirely on physical force: the power of his own nation must be incontestable as against both that of Muhamedans and Hindus, and more especially as against that of the former. He considered that alliances could not assist: if the Portuguese could command obedience they were unnecessary; if they could not, there was neither truth nor honour in the East to make the allies faithful.[1] The little band of invaders could only trust to their own right arms. Such a policy as this required, then, the maintenance of fortresses at certain strategical points which should be *places d'armes* to shelter the soldiers and protect the ships while refitting. In addition, however, there must be arrangements

[1] There are passages that show that Albuquerque saw that moral force had some value, but he did not rank it high.

to repair the terrible wastage of life, and arrangements for the gigantic trade which Albuquerque's fertile brain foresaw. To meet the wastage he proposed colonies; and the trade would need factories, not necessarily at the fortresses, but where exigency required. He does not appear to have remembered, or if he remembered, he considered it as of minor importance, that in the East his ships could not keep the sea during the south-western monsoon. For several months of the year, then, the command of the sea must be lost, not through any weakness of this fleet, but in the ordinary course of nature. The fortresses rarely commanded on land further than their own guns could carry, and the military history of the Portuguese in India contains an undue proportion of wasting defences of fortified places that drained away men and material and left no profit behind.

To understand Albuquerque's proposals it is necessary to remember that the pepper trade was a royal monopoly. It was so jealously guarded that no authority in India could enter into any agreement or make any peace that affected it.[1] It was the cause of most of the coast wars, for the Muhamedans strove by every means to load cargoes of pepper for the Red Sea, and there can be no doubt but that not many years after the time of Albuquerque all the Portuguese from the Governor downwards, traded illicitly in pepper. The prices paid by the King were those fixed when his ships first visited the coast, before competition had raised them; naturally the King got the worst stuff in the market; some sent home by Diogo Lopes de Sequiera was so bad that 33 years later it still lay in the Lisbon warehouses.[2]

1 Correa, IV. 104. The monopoly was abolished in 1570. Ar. Port. Or., Fasc. 5, No. 679.

2 See Ar. Port. Or., Fasc. 5, No. 30, of February 7th, 1520, for an order that all captains who have pepper on board that they cannot account for

As Albuquerque considered that the commerce of India could not be acquired by either peaceful methods or by alliances, he proposed to have strong fortresses at Aden, Diu, Ormuz and Goa, and factories with small forts at Cochin, Cananor and Quilon. The position of his fortresses showed the quarter (the north) from which he feared the enemy would come; still, if this enemy came in great force, he considered that the Portuguese would never be strong enough to engage him on sea and land at the same time, and that, under such circumstances, the ships must be laid up, the forts defended, and natural agencies be trusted to dispose of the enemy's fleet: he had had experience of the action of such destructive agencies in the Indian waters.

The condition of the Indian fleet did not satisfy him. "Our "ships put to sea," he says, "with water, rice and a little fish: "they return to Cochin for the monsoon, where the crews "have rice, fish and debauchery, and they die. When the "Portuguese are colonized in India, not only will the minds "of the Muhamedans be settled and they will no longer look "on us as mere tramps, but the captains will have healthy "men to hand, able to feed on the food of the country in "which they were born; and for choice I would have Goa "men—they eat wheaten bread and beef." In each fortress there would be a garrison of 500 to 1,000 men; 300 men for each factory and 1,600 for the fleet. Every captain would arrange for his own garrison and not trust entirely to Portugal. The headquarters of the government were to be at Goa, and under the Governor there were to be

are to be sent to Portugal. No. 10 of March 15, 1518, shows that 4 cwt. was allowed unquestioned. Pero Nunes, when Comptroller of Revenue, introduced great reforms. He purchased direct from the producer, and the loss fell from 30 or 40 p.c. to 7 p.c. Castanheda, VI. 72. The account of Albuquerque's policy is taken from his letters. It is difficult to give references: the letters must be read as a whole to get the general drift. The more important will be found at page 37 and following, and page 403 and following.

4 factors respectively of Ormuz, Guzerat, Cochin and Malacca. "The volume of Indian trade is," he says, "enor-"mous; silks, brocades, copper, mercury, coral etc.—it is "beyond belief. When the mouth of the Red Sea is closed "by Aden, all the north-going trade must go by Ormuz and "and the Persian Gulf where the Portuguese are supreme."

The King had suggested that Hindu and native Christian traders should be favoured at the expense of the Muhamedan, but Albuquerque brushed this aside indignantly. "Neither Hindus nor native Christians are capitalists," he says; "the "Muhamedans alone are in a big way of business. All religions "and races work together so much in India that you cannot "separate them. Guzerat banias employ Muhamedan sailors." These native traders then, with the non-official Portuguese, were to have all the local carrying trade in their hands. The King of Portugal would be the only merchant between India and Portugal, and he would sell goods for distribution, and from the profits cargoes could be bought for home-going ships. Portuguese ships would only travel between Portugal and Cochin and back, and Cochin would be the headquarters; ships starting from India could undertake the voyages to China and Bengal. The only duty of the Cochin factor would be to receive and send out goods to or from Europe or other factories. The factor, the treasurer, the captain of the fortress and the commissary would be the Council for the purchase and sale of goods. The discipline of the fortress was to be solely in the charge of the captain, and he would have full power to conquer any territory from the Muhamedans that came within the limits of his captaincy. The salaries of the Indian establishment could, he thought, be met from the so-called tributes paid by certain seaside states, the price of safe-conducts sold to trading vessels, and the income from the territory round Goa; the two first heads were blackmail pure and simple. There would be some income also from custom-houses, but it is difficult to understand what a great hamper to trade the custom-house of those days was. Officials were continually adding some new exaction which in time became incorporated in the demand. Take Indian cloth at Ormuz as one example not differing from many others. The original duty was ten per cent. ad valorem; in time there was added to this, one per cent. for the officials, and *6d* a bale also for the officials. When these extra items became recognized, importers had still to find favour by giving something over and above the demand, and in this way the duty gradually increased until it became prohibitive.

In Albuquerque's opinion officials should be appointed for 8 and not for 3 years: he was certainly right. The shorter term was barely long enough for a hungry man to fill his purse and leave all as clean swept for his successor as his predecessor had left it for him; while with the longer term there might conceivably have been some rest, and possibly the growth of a higher standard might have been promoted. Albuquerque is very definite as to the stamp of man sent out. "They are ready," he says, "with their paltry "cargo of pepper when the ships come in, but with the "riches of India before you it is nonsense to talk of pepper. "These Government officials never search for other profitable "merchandize, nor have they even the training to buy in "the cheapest market, they are not fit to purchase twopen-"nyworth of bread in the bazaar. A clerk trained in the "counting-house of Bartholomew, the Florentine, would be "more useful than all the factors the king has in India."

Such then was the plan, in some respects crude and immature, which Albuquerque wrote in confidence to his friend Duarte Galvâo. Had he merely dangled it before the eyes of the King it might have been doubtful how far it represented his real aim, for in many of his letters we trace a habit of writing for the effect of the moment. Deficient as the plan is, it is interesting as it shows that Albuquerque was no mere vulgar conqueror consumed with earth hunger and the desire of personal aggrandizement; he could look forward beyond the present to a time of peace and commerce.[1] He aimed, then, at extending his country's power, but he also saw that his country's true interest lay in peace. It was sometimes difficult even for him to resist the reiterated commands of the King of Portugal to destroy Muhamedans everywhere. He carried the peace with the Samuri in the teeth of an opposition that few would have encountered.

With the instruments at their command, generations of Albuquerques in the Indian Government could not successfully have carried out the scheme he sketched, but on that point he may well have overrated his own ability, or underrated the difficulty of dealing with his own countrymen. The condition of affairs, however, in India was never such that any commencement even of working out his idea could be made; that interpolation—strange indeed to us—that every Captain should be at liberty to carry on private war with the Muhamedans would of itself have been sufficient to prevent the realization of the rest. It is difficult to believe that Albuquerque had not grasped the fact, though certainly his countrymen never grasped it, that the Indian Muhamedan had as clear an idea of his own rights as the Portuguese had of theirs, and was as ready when an opportunity offered to defend those rights. It seems more probable that this proposal was thrown in to make the rest more palatable.

The Portuguese government in India was never properly

[1] In this he stands alone amongst, at all events, early Portuguese governors in India.

solvent. Taking the first 50 years we have seen the difficulty Albuquerque had; Nuno da Cunha paid his way by the prizes captured in the Red Sea; Estavâo da Gama expended his private fortune; of Martim Afonso de Sousa it will be sufficient to speak when the time comes; the other governors were always impecunious. The search for prizes, by which alone their budgets could be squared, kept the Portuguese in perpetual quarrels.

The colonies by which Albuquerque proposed to man his ships were to be formed by marriages between the Portuguese and the women of the country. At that time the Portuguese race, even in its home, was rapidly becoming mixed; with the Africans brought home as specimens by the early explorers, with those brought as slaves by the later, and with the inhabitants of the African islands the Portuguese had formed connections which introduced alien strains of blood. The idea therefore of half-caste colonies [1] was not as unfamiliar to that nation as it would have been to some others. Albuquerque began his experiment with the banished men, and this gave point to the sneer of the captains, that from a banished criminal and a low-caste woman nothing good could come. Albuquerque certainly felt the objection to low-caste women, for he tells the King he was careful to select the captive Muhamedan and Brahmin women as being of better breeding; [2] no one indeed was allowed to retain a woman of either of these classes as a slave except on the understanding that she was to be given up to anyone who desired to marry her. A large influx of women, however, came in with the Socotra garri-

[1] Barros was perhaps referring to fidalgoes when speaking of Gonçalo Vaz de Mello in II. 1, 3. He says he was rather looked down on for being "pardo nas cores." See Barros, II. 5, 11, for the general feeling as to these marriages.

[2] Cartas, page 338.

son when that island was abandoned in 1511, and many of them who were of a low class enough were married in Goa.[1] In every Portuguese settlement the married men rapidly became a caste to themselves with special privileges; all petty offices were reserved for them, and in Goa all the lands belonging to the King—a very large part of the area—were divided among them.[2] It has already been shown that the city of Goa was in considerable danger from the conspiracy formed through the instrumentality of these women. Of course, as their connection with their blood relations grew more distant the danger of a conspiracy of this nature lessened, though there was one of a similar character in Diu in 1546. The women were nominally, at least, Christians, but their status was little better than that of slaves. The Portuguese lost in vigour from associating with an alien race, and symptoms of decay set in quickly. Albuquerque encouraged the married men to start shops as bakers, shoemakers, tavern keepers, carpenters and tailors; but the climate and surroundings were too powerful, the work was done by slaves, and the master subsisted in sloth on their earnings. To such a pitch did this come that it was stated, and not denied, that the wives were not ashamed to profit by the earnings of their better-looking slave girls, and the husbands by those of the pirates of Sangameshwar, recruited from their slaves, who preyed on the Portuguese trade. These grave evils showed themselves in a later generation; but if Correa is correct, and he was in a position to know, Albuquerque foresaw to some extent what might happen.[3] He was disappointed to find that men married women for their money without caring how that

1 Correa, II. 177.

2 Ar. Port. Or., Fasc. 5, No. 9. Later on great difficulty was experienced when the rights of the married men of Cochin were infringed.

3 Correa, II. 375.

money had been acquired. He feared for the children of such mothers, brought up in the atmosphere of a home filled with slaves, and suggested that the King should order that all children were, between the ages of 12 and 25, to be educated in Portugal; no letter to this effect appears to be extant, but if he did suggest it, it is merely another instance of his foresight. This mixed breed, the result of these unions, never invigorated by contact with the sterner race, some of whose blood was in its veins, approximated more and more to the type of the country where it originated. That it should have been unable to hold its own with hardier races is quite consonant with experience.[1]

[1] Nothing has been said of the minute care Albuquerque's letters evince in all matters bearing on trade. It would be wearisome to recount the ample evidence the letters contain of this. See, for instance, page 166 for the proper packing of goods; page 349 for the waste of wine on board ship; pp. 267, 272, 329 for bad trading; page 199 for Goa horses etc.

CHAPTER IX

LOPO SOARES, GOVERNOR, 1515-1518—DIOGO LOPES DE SEQUIERA, GOVERNOR, 1518-1521

Lopo Soares.—The Governor sent by the King of Portugal to supersede Albuquerque was in every way his contrast. Lopo Soares had been, in 1504, the admiral of the annual fleet; he then reached India after the brilliant defence of Cochin by Duarte Pacheco, and assisted by the prestige due to that exploit, he had loaded his ships with a rich cargo. His personal courage was unquestionable, for he had, on December 31st, 1504, led the gallant attack on the Muhamedan vessels at Pandarani Kollam; unfortunately he had none of the qualities necessary to make a good governor. His staid and solemn deportment alienated those accustomed to Albuquerque's more genial manner, and his relations with the ruling chiefs, who did not conceal their distaste at the change, were not happy. It took 12 days of solemn trifling to arrange the exact ceremonial of a meeting with the Samuri—Albuquerque would have settled it with a stamp of his foot.

He was weak enough to endeavour to justify his own selection as governor by interfering in every arrangement of his great predecessor; he could only find the Orphans' Fund to meddle with, and that he wound up, says Correa, who hated him.[1] His own actions as governor were such

[1] Correa gives two curious instances of his petty spite—the instance referring to the A carved in stone on the Ormuz fortress does not appear to have

that they threw into relief the qualities of him whom he succeeded; he was weak, vain and wanting in nerve, and his solitary success consisted in building a fort among the unwarlike Singhalese. In the Red Sea and at Aden his failure was so conspicuous that it became a by-word among both Muhamedans and Portuguese alike. His internal policy was equally disastrous and resulted in the dissolution of that discipline which Albuquerque had so carefully fostered. One of Albuquerque's most stringent rules was that no Portuguese should engage in trade: Soares at once gave permission to all to do as they pleased, and the Eastern Seas were crowded with so-called traders who were but pirates under another name. No ship was safe from the cupidity of these vermin, it did not matter whether she were friend or foe, whether she had a Portuguese safe-conduct or not; if the Portuguese were the stronger, she had to yield her cargo to the spoiler and her crew to the slavery of the oar and the pump. Another result followed: as all Muhamedan ships carried pepper and spices, they began to be built larger and armed more heavily than before, and could often hold their own against their enemies. As every Portuguese, even if a peaceable trader, was thus brought into contact with interests that clashed with his own, collisions with natives of the country became more frequent, and as Soares showed little disposition to back his own men at all hazards, his influence over them decreased as much as the prestige of the Portuguese nation diminished.

Lopo Soares left Europe on April 7th, 1515, with 15

come under Correa's personal notice (II. 506). The other, which was even stranger as it referred to Albuquerque's tomb, of which Correa as employed in the Goa public works was in charge, and which, together with the Chapel of St. Catherine, Soares wished to destroy, will be found Vol. II. p. 472. Correa attributes the order about the tomb to the jealousy of Soares that people should go there to offer up petitions to the dead man.

ships, 1,500 men at arms, and new captains for all the fortresses; he also carried back Matheus, the envoy sent from Abyssinia to Portugal, and a Portuguese return embassy headed by Duarte Galvâo, an old man of 70, who had made himself an honoured name in the history of his country. The presents carried by the ambassador were estimated as worth £15,000, but Galvâo died of vexation and hardships in the Red Sea; Matheus was not landed in Abyssinia until many years later—history is silent as to the fate of the presents. When Soares reached Goa on September 8th, Albuquerque was still in Ormuz; but without waiting for his return he interfered in every detail of the administration. The trained bands were dismissed, as he considered drill in India oppressive; the horses in the stables, and the elephants that had been captured were sold off. After Albuquerque's death even his private property was dispersed by auction, but the sale redounded to the credit of the great governor rather than to that of his successor, for the animus was evident, but the goods were of little value. Disgusted with what had happened, and perhaps foreseeing the future, Albuquerque's captains, the "flower of India", left in the fleet with Garcia de Noronha.

The Governor's troubles began early. At one petty town 24 Portuguese from the ships of Simâo d'Andrade, who had distinguished himself by his extravagant expressions of joy at the death of Albuquerque,[1] were killed in a riot by the Muhamedans. The latter were apparently trying the temper of the new Governor, and at least they quickly found his measure; for at his visit soon after, he extracted no reparation, and when the chief of the town sent him three decrepit old men as guilty of the massacre—an act that savoured strongly of sarcasm—Soares politely

[1] He had sailed into Cochin harbour with his ship decked with flags when he was the bearer of the news of Albuquerque's death.

returned them. At Ormuz there was a quarrel between two Portuguese, one of whom took refuge with D. Aleixo de Menezes, the Governor's nephew; although his opponent cut him down at D. Aleixo's own table he was never brought to trial. Curiously enough the first shooting dispute on record took place at this time, when, in the rains of 1516, one Gaspar da Silva started off in a boat with some friends for a shooting picnic on the mainland behind Cochin. The natives begged him not to shoot peafowl, but he persisted, and when a wounded bird fell close to a chief's house the infuriated people drove the Portuguese to their boats, with the loss of four of their number killed.

In January 1516 a speedy vessel from Portugal brought definite news that the Egyptians were preparing a fleet in the Red Sea, to revenge the defeat at Diu in 1509, and the rest of the year was spent by the Governor in getting ready to go in search of the enemy. In all, 37 vessels were collected; they carried 1,800 men at arms attended by 2,000 fighting slaves, and there were 600 Portuguese seamen assisted by 1,000 others from the Indian coast, in addition to slaves for the oars and pumps. A start was made in February 1517: Socotra was reached on the 28th, from there the ships stretched over to Aden. The Governor of Aden, Mir Amrian, had but just repulsed a vigorous attack of the Egyptian fleet; as his walls were breached and his garrison entirely unable to meet a fresh foe, he sent the keys of the town to Lopo Soares in token of submission to the King of Portugal. This, almost the only chance the Portuguese ever had of getting possession of Aden, was rejected by the Governor without even a Council. His argument was, shortly, that the orders of the King were to find out and fight the Egyptian fleet; that to take possession of the town would only weaken and divide his force, and that on his return he could easily get the place. He apparently did not remember that the defeat suffered by the Egyptian fleet before Aden had by so much lessened their power whether for offence or defence. Another act of blind obedience to the letter of orders written many thousand miles away in complete ignorance of the facts, brought, later on, ruin to the expedition.

The history of the Egyptian fleet that had been defeated before Aden, the news of which had caused such preparations in India, must be briefly traced. After his defeat at Diu in 1509, Mir Hashim escaped to Jedda, and, finding nothing else to do, spent his energies in fortifying that town. By wood and by boat-builders brought across Egypt to Suez, a new fleet was got together by the last of the independent Mameluke Sultans, but when it was ready the command was given, not to Mir Hashim, but to one Sulaiman who had taken an opportunity to visit India and personally inspect the Portuguese fleet. Sulaiman was a Turk of Mitylene, a ship's carpenter by birth, who had acquired reputation as a corsair in the Mediterranean. In this fleet sailed one with whom the Portuguese had afterwards, when he was employed by the Sultan of Guzerat, considerable dealings. This man was, on account of his small size, known as Sifr Agha (the Cypher), he was a native of Brindisi, the son of an Albanian by an Italian woman.[1] Sulaiman left Suez early in October 1515, with 27 ships and 6,000 men,—Mamelukes, Arabians and renegades. He reached Jedda on November 4th, and left on the 19th for Kamaran, where he spent eight months in building a fort to prevent a landing by the Portuguese, and then even left in unfinished. He next attacked Aden, using as a pretext some discourtesy to Mir Hashim when a fugitive from Diu, but, defeated

[1] According to Elliot, History of India, V. p. 347, he received the title of Khudawand Khan while in India, and in Bayley's "Guzerat", p. 438, he is mentioned by this name with the addition of Rumi.

there, he returned to Jedda, where he fell out with Mir Hashim. Mir Hashim, worsted in the game of intrigue, was taken prisoner and sent to sea, where he died either naturally or by violence. When the news of the defeat of the Mameluke Sultan and the conquest of Egypt by the Ottoman Turk reached Jedda, Sulaiman sent the greater part of his fleet to Suez and only retained a few galleys.

This was the condition of affairs when Soares entered the Red Sea; with that entry his troubles began. He passed through the straits by night, with little precaution, and in a storm of no unusual violence two of his ships were lost and two were permanently separated from the fleet; in these ships was a large portion of his munitions and provisions, and in one of the wrecks was lost Jorge Galvâo, the son of Duarte Galvâo, the first of the many brothers who died in the East. The rest of the expedition made its way to Jedda, and off that town picked up a boat with eighteen escaped Christian slaves, chiefly Venetians, who had been captured at Alexandria by the simple expedient of raiding the vessels of that nationality trading there. From these Soares learnt that the town was demoralized. When he reached Jedda, however, the forces there made a considerable display; projectiles weighing over 70 pounds fired at the vessels gave the power of the artillery, and a survey of the mouth of the harbour showed that the only entrance was by a narrow and tortuous waterway, commanded at every point by cannon,—unless these were spiked any attack was out of the question. Soares remained off the entrance in inglorious inaction for 11 days, and then, amid the execrations of the old fighting men of his force, sailed away. The letter of the King's orders was again quoted: they were to fight the Egyptians at sea, and this did not include fighting them on land. The capture of the city would cost more lives than it was worth, and as the enemy's fleet had dispersed, all danger to India was at an end. Soares was soon to learn that the summer months in the Red Sea were more deadly to troops without shelter or supplies than an attack on a strongly defended town.

Owing to calms and contrary winds the return to Kamaran took several days; water failed in some ships, in all it was deficient, and many died of mere thirst. When Kamaran was reached the danger of death from thirst had passed, but the danger of death from famine grew more acute, for the stores in the ships could only supply the men with a little cooked rice once a day; naturally, when called on to work in the heat of the summer sun at demolishing the partly built fort, the men died fast. A bold attack on Jedda would have given ample supplies; now vessels sent in all directions failed to collect anything from those arid shores, and several lives were lost in vain skirmishes.

One of the first and certainly the most illustrious of the victims was Duarte Galvâo, who died on June 9th; his grave was marked by Francisco Alvarez, the priest who was with him at the end, and who, ten years later, at the close of that Abyssinian journey of which he has left us such a valuable account, reverently disinterred the bones of his old master and carried them to Portugal. Soares fell out with Matheus, the Abyssinian envoy; in spite of his orders he affected to doubt that he was a genuine Abyssinian and declined to land him at Massowah. In the miserable three months at Kamaran the expedition lost 800 Europeans and nearly all the slaves; the living were so enfeebled they could not bury the dead; in July the demoralized fleet put to sea and made for the straits. In one ship only 25 were left alive out of 130—two of the survivors murdered their captain, a nephew of the Governor, but the rest were too apathetic from their sufferings to take much notice even of such a crime.

About half the fleet stayed with Soares, and to get food attacked Zeila, but even over the arrangement of this attack the Governor and his captains squabbled. Soares fired the place and burned in it provisions that the fleet soon wanted sorely. At Aden the walls had been repaired, and Soares met with a very different reception from that of a few months before; there was no talk now of surrendering the fortress, but as a great favour he was allowed to buy some water and some provisions that did not, however, supply the daily consumption of his halt. Rebuffed here, he started to sack Berbera, but the wind was contrary, and losing patience and giving no fresh orders Soares bore up for Ormuz, leaving the other ships to follow if they pleased. But that some unexpectedly found water on the Arabian coast, few would have survived to tell the tale. Ormuz was reached about the middle of September, and when the season arrived Soares returned to India.

During his absence Goa had been involved in considerable difficulties owing to the action of the captain, a Spaniard named D. Goterre de Monroy, who had married the Governor's niece and who had been appointed deputy during his absence. The captain had been free in granting passes, and encouraged by the prevailing laxity, one Jeronimo de Sousa [1] started off to the African coast with a Government vessel to do some buccaneering. When the news of this reached Goa, another expedition, under the captain's brother, was sent to arrest him, but he went to the Maldives and began piracy on his own account.

The captain, however, was involved in most difficulty in his affairs on land. One Fernâo Caldeira had been a page of Albuquerque's and had, owing to complaints against him, been sent a prisoner to Portugal; [2] he returned, like many

[1] Jeronimo de Sousa had no difficulty in getting a pardon afterwards.

[2] He is mentioned in the account of the old scandal whose dry bones still rattle in the pages of Castanheda. III. 123—125.

others of Albuquerque's enemies, with Soares. He came out in Monroy's ship, and on the way quarrelled with his captain. Knowing the latter's revengeful temper, he left the vessel when the chance offered, and did not return to his wife and children in Goa, but lived at Ponda in the Adil Shah's territory, under the protection of the captain of the castle, Ankas Khan. Monroy could not rest without revenge, and sent his man[1] João Gomes to worm himself into Caldeira's confidence and murder him. Gomes killed Caldeira, but Ankas Khan pursued him, cut off his head, tied it to the tail of his own horse and whipped the latter over the water into Goa territory, to carry its own message. Communication with the mainland was interrupted, and Goa suffered from a failure of its supplies.

Goterre de Monroy awaited the rainy season to take his revenge on Ankas Khan. João Machado, the banished man, had been appointed by the king thanadar of the island of Goa.[2] As such his duties were to arrange for the cultivation of the island and collect dues from the cultivators, and to keep a roll-call of them and their payments in duplicate; but neither the organization of raids nor the carrying on of warlike operations was part of his business. Machado, however, was too old a free lance to be troubled by any scruple, and he agreed to make a night raid on June 1st and seize Ankas Khan. The captain's brother, Fernando de Monroy, who had returned from the Maldives with his booty, was in command of the 60 horse, Machado led the foot. The raid was a ludicrous failure. The force stayed squabbling so long outside Ponda that their approach

[1] "Cousa sua" of Correa.

[2] Ar. Port. Or., Fasc. 5, No. 1, dated February 4th, 1515, contains the order of his appointment. For the duties of a thanadar—who was not the official now known by that name—see Ar. Port. Or., Fasc. 5, No. 19 of March 30th, 1519.

was discovered: the Muhamedans bolted, and then the two bodies into which the Portuguese had divided, ran from each other. The Muhamedans recovered from their panic first, pursued the Portuguese and killed some fifty of them, including Joâo Machado; of the country troops that went with them, about 100 were killed, and all the party threw away its arms. The whole frontier was of course at once in a blaze, and Goa a beleaguered city until the ships of the year arrived in September. Goterre de Monroy, who was responsible for the troubles, made an excellent defence against the army of the Adil Shah that had been sent to support his lieutenant.

In the fleet of 1517 came a new official, Fernâo Alçaçova, the Comptroller of Revenue, whose powers were very extensive in all matters of revenue. The intention of the King of Portugal was obvious: he considered that the time had come when the work in India should be devolved on two separate establishments. We are so accustomed to see the command of the Army separated from the management of the revenue, that it is not easy for us to understand the anger that this change created in India. [1] To the Comptroller were made over by the King's orders all the factors and writers in the settlements; no captain of a fortress could spend any money, and any factor who made a payment on the order of a captain was held personally responsible. [2] Had Soares been loyal the change, great as it was, could have been introduced, but he was not; outwardly he professed entire obedience to the King's orders—privately he directed the officials to obstruct the new Comptroller. Alcaçova found his position untenable, and went back to Portugal in the return voyage of the ships in which he had come out.

[1] See Cartas, p. 19. Albuquerque originally suggested the appointment of a Comptroller.

[2] For Alcaçova's instructions see Ar. Port. Or., Fasc. 5, Nos. 2, 3, 4, 5.

As only a year of his term remained, Soares devoted his energies to preparing an expedition to Ceylon. The rains of 1518 were spent in Cochin, where his judgment and discretion in dealing with the brawls that came before him in no way belied his former reputation.[1] In the middle of September the expedition started, and, after a fight with the local forces, a fort was built on a point of land at Colombo. This fort was at the best but a flimsy structure, and about 1520 the Captain rebuilt a great part of it with stone and lime.

Soares left India unregretted; he was famed for his sudden outbursts of passion, partly due perhaps to gout, and after his failure in the Red Sea all respect for him vanished. He was dry in speech, pompous in manner, and his justice was never tempered with mercy. He had no intimates; presents from foreign ambassadors he tolerated as the custom of the country, but no one dared to offer him a personal gift, or even a banquet; no one could sit or even cover his head in a house where he was, without special permission—rarely given. It was his rule that the Governor must be excelled by no one in matters of food and drink, and he had the best arranged table that had been seen in India. He ate at one table with those of sufficient rank to enjoy the honour; the two other tables were presided over by his steward and the captain of his guard. On his return to Portugal he was coldly received at Court, and retired to his private estate at Torres Vedras, where he lived with his daughter, refusing to leave it even to reply to the accusations of Fernâo d'Alcaçova.

Diogo Lopes de Sequiera.—Diogo Lopes de Sequiera, who succeeded Lopo Soares, had, in 1508, been sent to

[1] See Castanheda, IV. 33, for a story of his injudicious treatment of a private quarrel.

discover Malacca: his failure there was notorious, and in that voyage he so seriously disobliged Albuquerque that he did not even dare to visit Cochin to supply his necessities on the return from the further East. He left Portugal on March 27th, 1518, and reached Goa on September 8th.[1] From there he pushed on to Cochin in the hope of intercepting Lopo Soares before he started for Ceylon; his messenger indeed reached Cochin a few hours after Soares started, and there is no doubt but that the latter knew of the arrival of his successor and eluded him in order to score one success before his departure. Soares gave over charge and left India on January 20th. The orders of Diogo Lopes included building a fort in Diu; the exploration of Massowah, and the landing there of Matheus, the Abyssinian envoy, and of D. Rodrigo de Lima, the Portuguese Ambassador; and the erecting new forts in the Maldives, Sumatra, the Moluccas and Chaul.

By the end of the rains of 1519 the preparations for the Red Sea expedition were far advanced, and, as the ships of the year had not arrived, orders were sent to Mozambique to direct the vessels to proceed straight to Ormuz. On February 15th, 1520, Diogo Lopes started for the Red Sea with 24 sail, carrying 1,800 Europeans and 800 fighting slaves. His flag-ship was wrecked between Aden and Babel Mandeb, and the Governor and the crew escaped with little more than their lives. The fleet worked part of the way up to Jedda, but the winds were contrary, and as soon as it was ascertained that there was neither an Egyptian nor a Turkish fleet in the Red Sea, a course was steered for Massowah. Matheus, who was found to be, after all the discussion, a genuine envoy, was landed, and

[1] The only recorded event of the voyage was the attack of a sword-fish on the ship of D. João de Lima. See Barros, III. 3, 1, for a long dissertation on this then almost unknown fish.

the Portuguese ambassador with his suite started inland on April 20th.[1] The first meeting with the Abyssinians was a cruel disenchantment for the Portuguese. For many years they had eagerly looked forward to opening a communication with a mighty emperor of their own faith, who would assist them against their hereditary foe, the Muhamedan. Where all was unknown the imagination had filled in the details as fancy dictated.[2]

His business concluded at Massowah, Diogo Lopes hurried from the Red Sea lest the fate of the fleets of Albuquerque and Lopo Soares should overtake him. At Ormuz he met the Portuguese fleet of 1519, under the command of Jorge d'Albuquerque, who had been Captain of Malacca and who was returning to the same appointment.[3]

The island of Diu, which for many years occupied an important place in Indo-Portuguese politics, was not a mart whence the merchandize for Europe could be shipped; its importance in Portuguese eyes was that it was a stronghold where, as long as it continued in Muhamedan hands, the Turks could always find a refuge. The stamped cloths of Guzerat, however, off whose coast the island lies, had an extensive sale all over the East, and when, a few years later, there was war over the Portuguese demand for the cession of Diu, the latter people felt severely the stoppage of the supply of these cloths, which were used as currency in many places beyond Malacca. Diogo Lopes visited Diu on his way from Ormuz to India, and there can be no

1 Alvarez has left an account of the doings of this embassy, which has been published by the Hakluyt Society—"A book rather virtuous than learned, composed carefully as far as his wit allowed," sneers Barros, III..4, 3.

2 The note of disappointment appears in Correa's description of the people (not, of course, Abyssinians) who met Diogo Lopes at Massowah. Correa, II. 584.

3 Dr. Pero Nunez, the new Comptroller of Revenue in the place of Alcaçova, came in this fleet and went direct to India.

doubt that he would then, if he could, have taken possession of the town; but Malik Aiyaz, whether he was prepared or not, showed a bold front.[1] The Portuguese council of war would not fight, and Diogo Lopes, after tasting the hospitality of Malik Aiyaz and listening to his protestations of impotency as the mere slave of the Sultan of Guzerat, sailed to Goa.

The talk of Diogo Lopes while at Diu had been indiscreet, and Malik Aiyaz employed Sid Ali, the one-eyed envoy[2] who had done him good service before, to follow him to Goa. His reports revealed such danger that no pains were spared to strengthen the fortifications of Diu and replenish the magazines; the mouth of the harbour, too, was guarded by a chain, and fresh guns were mounted. When Diogo Lopes, therefore, arrived again before Diu on February 9th, 1521, with 42 vessels carrying 2,000 Europeans and 1,800 local troops, these preparations made such an impression on his council of war that it again refused to fight, and the Governor, after landing an envoy for the Sultan of Guzerat, sailed on to Ormuz. There had been a factor in Diu since the days of Albuquerque, and to remove one difficulty, Fernandes de Beja, who had been Albuquerque's flag-captain in the Red Sea, was left to get him off. He was successful, but the evasion was looked on as an act of hostility, and the Diu flotilla under Agha Muhamad poured out of the harbour to attack the Portuguese ships. The Portuguese found that they had to deal with an enemy who could give shrewd blows, whose artillery, although it was only of iron, was quickly served, and whose powder was of surprising strength. De Beja's vessels cut their cables and escaped as best

[1] Barros says that he was not prepared, and that Diogo Lopes was deceived.

[2] Albuquerque considered him "an evil man who knows Portugal well." Cartas, p. 333.

they could; they reached Ormuz on May 25th—ten days after the Governor.

The vast fleet that Diogo Lopes had collected was now perforce dispersed to its different destinations. Jorge d'Albuquerque sailed in command of the ships for the furthest East; under him were Antonio de Brito and Jorge de Brito, who were to build a fort in the Moluccas, and Rafael Coutinho bound for China. Of this fleet it was said that of the 1,000 souls on board not 100 ever returned to India. [1] The King of Ormuz, when pressed for his tribute, pleaded his long-standing quarrel with Mukarram, the ruler of El Hasa, on the Arabian coast, over the ownership of Bahrein, which was valuable for its pearl fishery. Mukarram had agreed to pay tribute for the island, but no instalment could be recovered without an armed expedition, and as one of these was just starting, Diogo Lopes agreed to assist by sending his nephew, Antonio Correa, with 400 Portuguese. Antonio and his brother Aires had, when boys, been saved from the Calicut massacre in 1500, when their father was killed; and Antonio had already given proof of his courage and ability in Malacca. The force started on June 15th, but the ships did not keep together, and Antonio reached the Island of Bahrein with only 250 Portuguese in company. The heat was terrific, and although the opposing force far outnumbered his own, Correa determined to attack. His boldness met with its due reward; Mukarram was killed and his army defeated. The dashing exploit was rewarded with a bi-lingual inscription in Ormuz, erected by the governor, and an augmentation of Correa's arms granted by the King of Portugal.

On August 20th Diogo Lopes despatched Fernandes de Beja with four ships to cruise off the Guzerat coast and

[1] Barros, III. 4. 10.

blockade Diu. While one of them was plundering a Red Sea ship off Diu it fell calm. Agha Muhamad's flotilla of light boats was on the alert, dashed out, saved the captured ship, and with the fire of its heavy guns, sank the Portuguese ship, 25 of whose crew were taken prisoners. Before the breeze sprang up the other three vessels were separately attacked; all were roughly handled, and De Beja's own was only saved from sinking by a piece of leather nailed over a shot hole between wind and water. When there was wind enough the battered ships made the best of their way to the opposite coast to refit. Hurrying back to warn Diogo Lopes, De Beja found him off Diu with his fleet weakened by disaster.

As soon as his arrangements at Ormuz permitted, Diogo Lopes had followed De Beja with the rest of the fleet; his latest plan—for he frequently changed—was to plant a fort at Muzafarabad, 20 miles from Diu, and thence harry the coast. As he discussed his plans and intentions openly, there were spies enough round him to carry the information to Malik Aiyaz. Among his ships was one commanded by Aires Correa, which carried most of the stores needed for the expedition. Some recently captured Muhamedans, who preferred death to slavery, set her on fire, the magazine caught and all on board perished. The coast of Guzerat was on the alert and more strongly fortified than ever, and Diogo Lopes again gave up all attempt at building a fortress, not only in Diu, but also in Muzafarabad.

After his first failure at Diu, Diogo Lopes had turned his thoughts to Chaul, which Albuquerque had suggested as the right place for a fort. Chaul has now sunk into insignificance, but for some centuries it was an important place of trade. One of the Governor's earliest acts had been to send Christovâo de Sousa to the town, but, although supported by a large body of matchlockmen, he was thrashed out of the place by the townsmen with bows and arrows. It belonged to Burhan Nizam Shah, and to him Diogo Lopes sent an envoy, Fernâo Coelho, and obtained the necessary permission to erect a fort. After his last failure at Diu, Diogo Lopes went on to Chaul to take advantage of the grant,[1] he was, however, closely followed by Agha Muhamad and his flotilla sent to impede his design. Agha Muhamad's appearance off the harbour caused a panic among the Portuguese, and it was with difficulty that the Governor, who was unpopular because he was unsuccessful, and whose term of office was on the point of expiring, could induce some ships to accompany him over the bar. The eagerness of the captains was not increased when they saw one of their own ships, commanded by Pero da Silva, which was returning from Ormuz and running in before the sea breeze, sunk before their eyes with all on board, and they in shore impotent to help. Desultory fighting continued for nearly a month; the Portuguese sank a few of the enemy, but in their turn they were badly mauled by their nimble antagonists; at the end of that time the supply of powder ran short and they were reduced to the defensive. When Diogo Lopes heard of the arrival of his successor, he prepared to return to Cochin, and made De Beja commander of the sea forces; but before he could leave, De Beja himself was killed, and his ship only saved from capture by the confusion caused among its assailants by Agha Muhamad accidentally falling overboard. De Beja was succeeded by Antonio Correa, and on December 27th Diogo Lopes proceeded south. Correa had to defend himself both by sea and land, and was only saved from serious disaster by the gallantry of the garrison, less than 30 in number, of an isolated battery who held their ground

[1] The fort was also known as Rewandanda. Chaul was the more usual name.

after their commander and gunner were killed, until reinforcements could arrive. Correa was relieved in time to accompany Diogo Lopes to Europe. They sailed on January 22nd, 1522. During his term as Governor, Diogo Lopes had amassed considerable wealth and, if scandal speaks truly, not always by the most honest means; one particularly black act stands on record, the more important for its after effects. Kuti Ali was a wealthy Muhamedan of Tanur who imitated European ways, furnished his house with chairs and tables, and gave banquets to the Portuguese; he entered into partnership with Diogo Lopes—the Governor, and another Portuguese, to run a cargo of pepper to the Red Sea. When it was loaded Diogo Lopes confiscated the whole as contraband and appropriated even the vessel. From this date Kuti Ali became a corsair, and joined Ali Ibrahim, that other victim of Portuguese injustice, in harrying the trade of the Malabar coast. Diogo Lopes had to disgorge in Portugal a part of his ill-gotten gains to silence the underlings of a venal court, by these means he retained the remainder. He never succeeded in anything he undertook,—always excepting the amassing of wealth.

As an official Diogo Lopes was a man of some energy. There are extant several of his orders affecting Goa, and these may be considered with the orders of the King of Portugal, granting privileges to the citizens and conferring municipal rights on the city. The grant of land to the residents of Goa who by their marriage were considered to have done the King good service, is dated March 13th, 1518.[1] Under it all the royal properties in Goa, consisting of cultivated lands and palm groves, chiefly the property of Muhamedans who had absconded, were conveyed absolutely to the married residents,—two-thirds to be divided

[1] Ar. Port. Or., Fasc. 5, No. 9.

among those married and settled at the time of the grant, one-third to be divided among men who should settle after the grant was made. Three classes of the community were formed—fidalgoes who took three shares, cavaliers and esquires two shares, and common persons one share. Pending the division of the reserved one-third, its income was to be expended on beautifying the city; the grantees had no powers of alienation. Almost all municipal offices were reserved for the married men, and all food-stuffs for the city were freed from taxation.[1] The rule as to presents was very similar to that now in force in British India.[2] The Goa municipality was founded on the lines of that of Lisbon, so much so indeed that the officials in Portugal did not take the trouble to grant a separate charter to Goa, but sent a copy of the Lisbon one; the aldermen were elected annually by votes, and provision was made that certain mechanical trades should be represented. The Goa municipality used to receive at intervals letters of goodwill from the King of Portugal,—it also showed a patriotic self-sacrifice at certain important crises in the the history of Portuguese India, and the Governors never appealed to it in vain for pecuniary assistance; some of its petitions to the king are valuable as an exposure of the more crying evils under which the residents suffered, but the municipal body was an exotic, and in time even the right to elect to petty offices in their gift, though it remained theoretically in their hands, was always exercised

[1] Ar. Port. Or., Fasc. 2, Nos. 2 to 9 and Nos. 11 to 14 contain different privileges of Goa and its citizens. In Fasc. 5, No. 10, are many interesting provisions as to the fees to be levied at the fords into Goa, and as to the arrangements for paying men their salaries etc. Fifty government horses were to be kept for defence, and every resident who kept one was to be paid 2 pardâos a month, that is about 16 shillings Of late years the cost of keeping a horse was estimated at 16 rupees, it is probably more now.

[2] Ar. Port. Or., Fasc. 5, No. 24, Nov. 20th, 1519.

in accordance with a royal *congé d'élire*. The lowest depth was perhaps reached when, in the middle of the 16th century, that body was ordered to elect to a small office the person whom the existing holder might select, either his heir or else the person whom his daughter might choose to marry. [1]

[1] For constitution of the municipality see Ar. Port. Or., Fasc. 2, No. 1 of March 2nd, 1518. The constitution of Lisbon sent as a model, No. 10, Nov. 29th, 1519. Fasc. 1, No. 15 of April 1st, 1550, gave the power of nomination above referred to to a certain holder of an office.

CHAPTER X

D. DUARTE DE MENEZES, GOVERNOR, 1521-1524—D. VASCO DA GAMA, VICEROY, 1524—D. HENRIQUE DE MENEZES, GOVERNOR, 1524-1526—LOPO VAZ DE SAMPAYO, GOVERNOR, 1526-1529—APPENDIX I. THE SUCCESSIONS—APPENDIX II. REVENUE SETTLEMENTS OF THE GOA VILLAGES

D. Duarte de Menezes.—D. Duarte de Menezes, the new governor, accompanied by his brother, D. Luiz de Menezes, reached Goa in September 1521. He had won his reputation in the wars of Northern Africa, but in his character licentiousness and covetousness were so predominant that even in quiet times he would have cut a contemptible figure. Unfortunately for himself he had to deal with troubles arising partly from the misdeeds of his predecessors, and partly from the mistakes of the home authorities. Emmanuel, King of Portugal, died on December 13th, 1521, and although the news did not reach India for nine months, still as the change of governors occurred about the same time, the two events may be considered contemporaneous.[1] One of the earliest acts of the new governor was to send his brother to Chaul, but his task there was easy; the quarrel between the Portuguese and Guzerat was regarded by Malik Aiyaz as a personal one with Diogo Lopes, and on the latter's departure, although

[1] For a vivid account of the reception of the news of the King's death at Goa, see Corea, II. 730.

no definite peace was concluded, the former's boats under Agha Muhamad were withdrawn. Malik Aiyaz himself died in 1523.

It was fortunate for the Portuguese that the war with Diu had died down, for troubles had fallen upon them in Ormuz, to understand which it is necessary to go back some years. Albuquerque had, in 1515, fixed the annual tribute at £5,000, and to show that this sum could be easily paid—which his captains had denied—he sent to Portugal in 1508 a detailed statement of the income and expenditure of the country. Judging from the character of Albuquerque's own letters, it may be safely said that without perhaps intending to misrepresent facts, this statement would have received from his sanguine mind the tinge necessary to prove his case. Anyway, against his statement must be set the hard fact that between 1508 and 1517 the full amount of the tribute had never been paid, the reply to this was that a large part of the income was intercepted by the Ormuz officials. Whatever may be the truth, this amount of tribute had not been collected when, in 1517, a sea captain increased it with a light heart to rather over £8,000. When the arrears accumulated the attention of the King of Portugal was directed, not to the exactions of his officers, but solely to the fact that the money had not been paid; he laid all the treaties and agreements with the King of Ormuz before a council of learned theologians who, guided by the precepts of the canon law, decided that the King of Portugal was the sovereign of the state of Ormuz.

Under this ruling Diogo Lopes was instructed to take possession of the whole custom-house arrangements of the town. That Governor, however, supported by the advice of the best Indian officials, hesitated to carry out this violent measure until in the ships of 1520 came, not only reiterated orders, but also a whole staff of officials on the scale of the Lisbon establishment, he therefore had no choice but to obey orders. The change was effected, and the feeling it excited was deep and universal. Diogo Lopes, however, on his departure left at Ormuz a smaller number of soldiers even than the regulations required, and when the Captain, who knew the danger, represented to the Governor that his force in the face of eventualities, was far too small, he was roughly told that if he did not like to stay there were plenty of others willing.

There seemed no hope left for the people of Ormuz save in an armed rising, for the taking of their custom-house was but the culminating act of a series which included the forcible conversion of several persons to Christianity. The King of Ormuz was then Toran Shah, but the real power lay in the hands of the chief minister, Sharfu-d-din. The conspiracy had been brewing for a long time, and the proposal to kill the Portuguese was openly discussed in the Ormuz bazaar, but the Portuguese, either ignorant or careless, took no precaution. A large part of the colony continued to sleep in the native town, even the artillery was not mounted on the walls of the fort, and so far from a proper supply of water being kept, one of the cisterns was filled with wood. On the night of November 30th, 1521, a sudden attack was made on the Portuguese, and out of 300 men, women and children 120 were killed; the survivors escaped to the fort where munitions were scarce, and where the big guns, even if on the walls, could not be fired lest the crazy water tanks should burst.

The Portuguese, however, succeeded in beating off the attempts at storming, and on January 19th, 1522, the King and his people abandoned their homes to found a new settlement in the island of Kishm—a course which showed their despair and their bitter hatred of the Portuguese.

Both Portuguese and Muhamedans suffered much from hunger and thirst, and scandal said that when the Captain's brother brought a ship-load of provisions the trading instinct was so strongly developed in him, that he allowed the Muhamedans in Kishm, as they were ready to pay the highest price, to have the first choice of his cargo.

When D. Luis reached Ormuz on April 20th, pressure was put on him to attack Kishm. This he refused on the reasonable ground that if the people were driven out of Kishm, Ormuz would still be no better off; he had, however, recourse to an ignoble intrigue. Rais Sharfu-d-din had found that Toran Shah, the titular king, if he had no will of his own, still had to be humoured, he therefore assassinated him and made another "melancholy little kinglet,"[1] Muhamad Shah, a son of Albuquerque's early opponent, and still a mere boy. D. Luis employed one Rais Shamsher, a relative of Sharfu-d-din, to assassinate the latter and his son-in-law Shahabu-d-din; the price agreed on was £3,000 and the wazirship of Ormuz. This bargain was kept secret even from the Captain of the fortress, and as the presence of D. Luis in Ormuz kept Sharfu-d-din on the alert, he left. Shamsher then murdered Shahabu-d-din, but Sharfu-d-din managed to escape with all his treasure to Ormuz, where the Captain, knowing nothing of the secret diplomacy, imprisoned him; the puppet king and his new minister returned to Ormuz.

D. Duarte de Menezes left Goa for Ormuz in February 1523, and on his way there a shameful incident occurred. Two of his galleys commanded by Bastião de Noronha, and Luiz de Noronha—brothers—pursued one day a Muhamedan ship from Ranir, near Surat, and by sun-down had reduced her with artillery fire to a sinking condition, they

[1] Triste reyzinho. Correa, II. 744.

lay off the ship for the night and all on board went to sleep. The Muhamedans, finding their ship foundering, approached her to that of Bastiâo de Noronha, and by a sudden attack drove the Portuguese overboard. The fugitives scrambled into the sister ship, but they were too demoralized to attempt to recover their own vessel which the Muhamedans took safely to Diu; the brothers went on with their shame to Ormuz. This was but one instance of tne decay in spirit that accompanied the decrease in public morality. D. Duarte found Sharfu-d-din still in prison. A bribe of £40,000 taken by the Governor, and a treaty dated July 15th, 1523, on the part of the nominal king, agreeing to a tribute of £20,000 a year, an increase of 150 per cent, put Sharfu-d-din in power and sent Shamsher to his death.[1]

The Portuguese historians, usually so diffuse, are significantly silent as to many events that occurred during the time of D. Duarte; fortunately they are not all silent on the same events. They all, however, dilate on the discovery of the tomb of the Apostle Thomas at a spot near where Madras now stands; the narrative of Correa is singularly naive, and as he was an eye-witness of some of the earlier transactions, singularly valuable. It leaves a feeling of wonder that in such an entire absence of evidence the identification of an event historical or otherwise should be thought complete.[2] It was in connection with this tomb that Manuel de Frias had been sent, in 1522, by the the Governor as factor to the Coromandel coast; the important act, however, which has caused Frias' name to

[1] He is said to have been thrown overboard from the Governor's ship with the chamber of a falcon tied to his neck.

[2] Correa speaks of an English Duke George as having been there in 1502 or 1503. This was of course vouched for by tradition. See Correa, II. 721—726.

be remembered was his assumption of a protectorate, in 1524, over the Ceylon pearl fisheries—an act which brought much misery to the unfortunate fishermen, and which subsequently led to the mission of Xavier and the Jesuits on that coast.

War had for some time been simmering with the Samuri. The nerveless administration of the corrupt crew that held the reins of Portuguese government was not even accorded the respect that is given to a hardy buccaneer. Cargoes were continually and openly run to the Red Sea, and the flotilla of Wali Hussain insulted the Portuguese fort at Calicut with impunity; men of position of that nationality could not even go through the streets of that town with any safety. The captain of the fort was Joâo de Lima, one of Albuquerque's captains at the capture of Goa; at this time, if not altogether crazed, he was certainly so on the subject of the natives of India; everyone who came near him was an assassin, and when—no unusual thing in that latitude—several cobras were found in the fort, he was persuaded they had been put there to bite him. Hostilities that had been long pending actually broke out after a riot arising out of the capture of some women, but although the fort was besieged it was not at first hard pressed.

D. Vasco da Gama.—The Government in Portugal had at last become aware of the confusion into which Indian affairs had fallen, and the King, D. Joâo III., selected as his first Viceroy Vasco da Gama, now a man of 64 years of age. He came out with all his old prejudices unchanged and with powers extensive enough to carry out any changes he might consider necessary. He reached the Indian coast in September, and died on Christmas Day 1524; during this short interval he laboured hard to stem the tide of corruption that was carrying every Portuguese in India with it. Whether he would have succeeded had he lived, is more than doubtful. D. Vasco da Gama lived long enough to order back to Portugal his predecessor, D. Duarte, as a prisoner. His conduct to him was characterized at the time as unnecessarily severe, but he knew that he was delaying his return merely in the hope of getting another term of office on his death, and he knew that D. Duarte was carrying off his ill-gotten gains, and had baffled all his attempts to intercept them.[1]

If in nothing else, Vasco da Gama introduced an important reform into ship-building, for he first began to build flotillas of light boats to meet the more agile craft of the coast. Some of his measures were certainly harsh. He ordered that all hospitals, which were also poorhouses, should be closed, as he considered they were refuges for lazy men. Many of his crews died of sickness and some had to beg in the streets, a sight then new, though afterwards common enough. From every fortress he touched at he brought away all save the married men; and in Cochin his coming caused such dread that all the Muhamedans left, and many Portuguese emigrated to the Coromandel coast. He was buried in Cochin, and in 1538 his remains were carried to Portugal.

D. Henrique de Menezes.—On the opening of the successions[2] the new Governor was found to be D. Henrique de Menezes, the Captain of Goa, a handsome and courteous man of 45 years of age, essentially a fighting man with no experience of administration. He was not avaricious, but he was suspicious, weak and obstinate, his obstinacy once

[1] For the story of his chest of treasures in charge of Bastião Pires the Vicar-General, and the ox's skull that marked where it was buried, see Correa, II. 841.

[2] See Appendix to this Chapter.

involved him in a quarrel which, but for the extraordinary loyalty of the Raja of Cochin, might have led to very serious consequences,[1] he was therefore ill-fitted to be Governor. The interest of his term centres round the Malabar War, and mainly round the defence of the Calicut fort.

Dr. Pero Nunez, after doing excellent service as Comptroller of Revenue, left India in 1524 on the arrival of his successor Afonso Mexia. Mexia was a sufficiently remarkable man to merit a few words, the more especially as the prominent position he gained under Henrique de Menezes, combined with a private quarrel with Pero Mascarenhas, led him to take in 1526 a certain course of action and assume a responsibility that caused dangerous dissensions in Portuguese India. As seen in the light of his orders and instructions as Comptroller of Revenue, Mexia is the very type of an active intelligent official satisfied with nothing less than a personal examination of every point over which his supervision extended. If copper has to be made into money, he has some coined before him to ascertain the cost; if biscuits, he personally tests the number that can be made from a given quantity of flour; if the question be hospitals, he enquires how many loaves and of what size should on the average be given daily to each inmate. Earthenware cooking vessels in coasting boats are too costly as they are easily broken, and they must be replaced by copper. He was one of the ablest and most honest officials that ever worked in Portuguese India, and to him more than anyone else it is due that Nuno da Cunha received charge of such well-found establishments as he did. His body of revenue rules for the management of the 31 villages into which the island

[1] For a detailed account see Correa, II. 921, and following Correa was then a petty official in Cochin. For another curious instance see Correa, II. 955.

of Goa was divided, is a document of great interest for an Indian Revenue official even now. It gives a picture of a village community, such as there are many, differing of course in details, at the present day, drawn up when Akbar's great finance minister, Todar Mal, was still a child.[1] Mexia certainly derogates from the solemnity of one of his official papers by perpetrating a joke, but this only makes him the more human. He is explaining to the Commissariat clerk how to get oxen slaughtered in the cheapest way. The butcher is to receive certain parts: "Your profit," he continues, "will be only the tongues, that with them you may tell the King how valuable your services are."[2] In 1531 Mexia was sent to Portugal a prisoner, and his property confiscated.

The more liberal policy of Albuquerque had resulted in a revival of Muhamedan trade,—a revival which the cunning of his successors turned to their own profit. Vasco da Gama definitely embarked on war to the knife with all the trade interests which he considered opposed to the Portuguese, and his successor followed the same line. In one of his visits to a creek to destroy some shipping, a curious incident occurred. The Arel of Porakkat was present as an ally of the Portuguese, but for some reason the Governor thought him lukewarm and fired a shot at him to wake him up; the shot broke his leg and turned a friend into a bitter enemy who joined the party of the Samuri.

Exasperated at the attacks on their boats, all the Muhamedans on the coast joined in the siege of the Calicut fort. The war had been carried on in a half-hearted way

[1] The paper is so intere ting that I give a full abstract of it at the end of this chapter. It was bas d on enquiries begun before Mexia's time. It is the earliest description, at : l events by a European, of a village community.

[2] Ar. Port. Or., Fasc. 5, Nos. 5 and 53 to 58—all of August and September 1526—are the orders referred to here.

for some months, but the serious attack was made during the monsoon of 1525, when landing on the unprotected coast was difficult. Owing chiefly to the skill of a Sicilian renegade who had been in the Turkish siege of Rhodes,[1] the Portuguese were hard pressed. In October the relieving force reached Calicut, the Samuri's troops were driven from the neighbourhood of the fort; but, as under the changed policy no fort was needed in Calicut territory and no peace desired, the place was abandoned after an unsuccessful attempt to blow it up.

The Governor, D. Henrique de Menezes, was ill at the relief of Calicut; soon after he became worse, and died at Cananor on February 2nd, 1526. He died poor: the whole term of his government had been one long fight with the Muhamedans of the Malabar coast.

Lopo Vaz de Sampayo.—On February 2nd, the day of Henrique de Menezes' death, the second succession[2] was opened in Cananor, and by it Pero Mascarenhas was named as the new Governor. Pero Mascarenhas, who was at this time Captain of Malacca, had commanded the trained bands at the attack on Benasterim when his bravery had won him the signal mark of favour from Albuquerque which aroused the envy of the other captains. As he was so far from India it would take a year for the news to reach him and for him to return, meanwhile the threatened Turkish attack still hung like a cloud over India, and hostilities with Guzerat and the Samuri were actually in progress. It was impossible for the Portuguese settlements to be left without a head, and it was difficult to decide how a temporary Governor should be appointed. After

[1] This was the siege of 1522, when Rhodes was captured by Sulaiman II. after the heroic defence of Villiers de L'isle Adam.

[2] The first had been opened on the death of Vasco da Gama.

two days' discussion it was agreed by the majority that the next succession should be opened after all present had taken an oath to obey Mascarenhas when he returned. In the next succession was the name of Lopo Vaz de Sampayo, Captain of Cochin. In these debates Afonso Mexia had taken a prominent part; he had had a violent quarrel with Mascarenhas over the loading of a ship, and he had written privately to the King of Portugal complaints of Mascarenhas that were to bring forth fruit later; at the same time it is impossible to find any fault with the decision of the council which followed the advice he had given. It was imperative to appoint a ruler, and one with the royal sanction would be more likely to win respect than one appointed without it. Lopo Vaz, before taking over charge, swore to obey Mascarenhas on his return.

On the arrival, however, at Goa of the ships of 1526, the difficulties of the situation were much increased by the action of Mexia. At that time Lopo Vaz was at Ormuz, and in his absence Mexia, as next senior officer, received from the ships a new batch of successions which the King of Portugal had sent out in supersession of those previously despatched, but which were dated two months after the death of Henrique de Menezes, though before the King knew of that event. These orders had clearly been made inoperative by the death of the Governor whose succession they were intended to regulate, because the former orders had already been acted on before the fact that they had been cancelled was known in India. Afonso Mexia, however, who probably gave a shrewd guess that the name of Mascarenhas had, owing to his complaints, been omitted, or else fresh orders were not needed, opened the new successions without even the formality of a council. As he expected, Mascarenhas was not under these new orders governor, but Lopo Vaz. Lopo Vaz, though he did not authorize the opening of the papers, accepted the situation, took charge of the government and ordered the exclusion of Mascarenhas by force if he tried to land in India. It is impossible to acquit Mexia of desiring to injure a personal enemy in adopting that interpretation of the situation which best suited his own interests.

Mexia carried out the Governor's orders in Cochin by a levy *en masse* of the settlers, and when Mascarenhas reached there at the end of February 1527, he was repelled by force and several of his followers were wounded. Mascarenhas himself, as did his old master, Albuquerque, when similarly situated, ostentatiously avoided the use of any weapons. He left Cochin amid a cloud of affidavits, and reached Goa bar on March 16th, whence he was sent a prisoner in irons to Cananor, but this did not close the controversy. During the monsoon months, two influential men, Christovâo de Sousa, Captain of Chaul, and Simâo de Menezes, Captain of Cananor, declared in favour of Mascarenhas, and the latter went so far as to release him from captivity. In Goa, also, his party grew, and there was nearly a riot on August the 9th when Hector da Silveira and 16 other fidalgoes were imprisoned as partizans of Mascarenhas. In all the settlements, save perhaps Cochin, the poorer sort were also in his favour, and the cooler heads saw that matters could go little further without civil war.

Christovâo de Sousa, who acted throughout the negotiations with rare disinterestedness, arranged with Antonio de Miranda, who inclined to the party of Lopo Vaz, that a body of arbitrators should be nominated by either side to determine which of the claimants should—considering only the good of India—be Governor, leaving the question of right to the King of Portugal. Lopo Vaz and Pero Mascarenhas awaited at Cochin—each in his ship—the decision of the arbitrators. The court was carefully packed to favour Lopo Vaz, and on December 21st gave its decision accordingly. Subsequently, on Mexia and Lopo Vaz the hand of the King fell heavily for their share in this dispute. It could not be otherwise, as the difficulty was partly due to the faulty orders of the King and his councillors. Both were sent prisoners to Portugal. Mascarenhas recovered £9,000 for unreceived salary from Lopo Vaz as a private debt; the latter was two years in prison before he was sentenced, he was then adjudged to receive no pay during his term of office, fined £4,000 and banished to Africa. The fine was, however, remitted, and the banishment only lasted a short time.

Lopo Vaz, who, in consequence of the decision of the arbitrators, became undisputed governor, was one of Albuquerque's captains. He came out first in 1510, he was present at the capture of Goa and in several actions round that town, he accompanied Albuquerque to the Red Sea, had been frequently wounded, and had more than once been the voyage to Portugal: if he was never particularly distinguished he had never disgraced himself. He was a capable and provident Governor and gained over several of his opponents by his tact, but he was never followed by the fidalgoes with any enthusiasm.

One of the interesting events of his term was the return, late in 1526, of D. Roderigo de Lima and his suite from Abyssinia, where they had been since 1520, they brought back with them an Abyssinian envoy for Portugal. But the main interest of the period centres round Diu, where hostilities again became acute. The Diu flotilla of small boats was as effective as ever, and the defence of Henrique de Macedo's vessel against 33 of them, in an engagement lasting for eight hours, was a famous one. A representation of it was for many years painted annually in the verandah of the Church Das Chagas in Goa. Another ship of the same fleet, commanded by Lopo de Mesquita, fell in with a heavily armed Malabari vessel. After the captain and his brother, Diogo de Mesquita, followed by thirty fighting men, had boarded her; their own ship—injured in the fight and crushed in the tumble of the sea by its heavy opponent —broke the grappling rope and sank. Though left alone in the face of 200 enemies, the boarders carried the Malabar vessel, only to find her apparently ready to founder. The only boat would hold but few men, so the captain sent her off with his brother Diogo, a few of the Portuguese, and such of the more valuable cargo as they could at the moment lay their hands on, to make the best of their way to shore. Lopo de Mesquita, with the rest of the Portuguese, managed to bring their prize safely into port, but Diogo and his boat were snapped up by the flotilla. The captured Portuguese remained prisoners for several years, and to this we are indebted for much of our knowledge of the events of this time in Guzerat; for Diogo de Mesquita wrote an account of his captivity which has not indeed come down to us, but from which Correa derived the materials of his history.

In Diu, Malik Ishak had succeeded his father Malik Aiyaz, but he had none of the latter's ability; his position was unstable, and he coquetted with the Portuguese. Had the fidalgoes followed Lopo Vaz, they might have secured a footing in Diu at this time, but they refused, and the Sultan of Guzerat superseded Malik Ishak.[1] Lopo Vaz was not only thwarted in his design on Diu, but also, from the same cause, in his intention of visiting the Red Sea; the fidalgoes were jealous at the promotion of one they considered merely their equal. On October 16th, not

[1] See Bayley's "Guzerat," p. 336, for the account of these events from the Indian side.

being able to undertake any more important enterprise, he attacked the stronghold of the petty chieftain, the Arel of Porakkat, who since the rough treatment of Henrique de Menezes, had done the Portuguese all the damage that lay in his power. His headquarters were burned, but twelve years later, his predatory habits rendered another expedition necessary.

It was on the return from this that Lopo Vaz heard that Nuno da Cunha was on the way to supersede him. Delayed on the voyage, the latter did not cross the Indian Ocean in 1528, but ran north to Ormuz. He reached India on October 24th, 1529.

Lopo Vaz left the fortresses well provided and in good repair, and a very efficient fleet for his successor.

APPENDIX I

Opening the Successions

Successions were first sent out when Vasco da Gama came out as Viceroy. There was kept in India with some high official a sealed bag, marked—"This bag is not to be opened until the death of..." naming the Viceroy or Governor in whose succession the package had been sent. In the bag were several sealed envelopes each with the royal signature. On one was written—"First succession: not to be opened until the death of..." naming the same person as on the outside of the bag. Another was endorsed—Second succession: not to be opened until the death of the person, named in the first succession, and so on. On the death of a Viceroy or Governor, and before the funeral, in the presence of the corpse, and usually in the church, the bag was brought, its seals examined by those present, and an attesting document drawn up and signed; the required envelope was withdrawn from the bag, which was again sealed, and a similar attesting document drawn up as to the condition of the envelope which was then opened, and the name contained was that of the new Governor. If the person named was dead, or in Portugal, and in later times if he were not between Diu and Cape Comorin, a fresh succession was opened with similar precautions.

APPENDIX II

Abstract of the Rules and Customs of the Village Headmen and Cultivators of the Island of Goa [1]

In all the villages in this island there are a certain number of headmen [2] in some more, in some less, according to custom. The origin of these headmen is lost in antiquity, but they are descended from those who brought the land under cultivation. [3] Each village is bound to pay the revenue assessed on it, which revenue the headmen and writer of the village [4] shall distribute among the cultivators and those owning heritable rights in the village, according to custom.

After paying the Government dues, the balance of the collection if there be any, or the deficiency in the revenue if there be any, is distributed among those persons who, according to custom, should receive such profits or pay such loss. Loss due to war is remitted. Certain gardens, palm groves and rice lands pay a fixed assessment and the owners are not liable for loss, as are the owners of other lands; there are other lands again which the headmen can give free of any rent. Should any village be so destroyed

[1] Ar. Port. Or., Fasc. 5, No. 58. For the present condition of these communities see Fronseca's Goa, p. 20.

[2] "Gancar" is the word used. They are called "lambardars" in Northern India.

[3] The names of the villages are given, and in the list 8 are called principal, the rest are subordinate.

[4] The writer of the village is, in Northern India, the "patwari." It is not stated how the revenue of each village was calculated, probably by customary rates on the actual cultivation.

that it cannot pay its revenue, the headmen and inhabitants must inform the chief thanadar and the writer of the island,[1] who shall visit the spot, and finding that the loss is as stated, they shall call together the headmen of the 8 chief villages. The headmen of the other villages may come, but the business lies with those of the eight. When they are all met, and the said chief thanadar and the writer of the island are present, the headmen of the destroyed village may make it over to the headmen of the 8, whc are bound to take it, and in the presence of the officials put it up to auction and lease it to the highest bidder. The balance of loss on the lease as compared with the revenue shall be either spread over the 8 villages, or over the whole island on those properties which are bound to make good such losses in such a way that the revenue shall be paid in full in any case. The lessees shall be bound to improve their village, and this shall be one of the conditions of their lease. The headmen of the leased village do not by reason of this lease lose their rights, but shall again receive possession if they apply at its termination. As the office of village headman is hereditary it is not lost through any misconduct, nor is the writership, which is equally hereditary. Men holding these posts shall suffer in their persons and purses for any crime; should they be executed their heirs succeed. Cases of little importance can be settled by the chief thanadar taking counsel of some headmen. The worst cases go before the Governor of India, or the Captain of Goa, or the Comptroller of Revenue if it affects his jurisdiction. Village writers are appointed first by the headmen; they are not removable for any fault, and the office is hereditary. Headmen can arrange for the cultivation of waste by leases at any rate of rent they

[1] Kanungoe of Northern India.

please up to 25 years, but after that time lands must pay the customary rent. The usual rate is for each strip of 12 paces broad, (the distance between two palm trees) up to 100 trees in length, at five tangas of 4 barganim the tanga (about 6*s* 8*d*). Betel plantation lands are let in plots of 5 cubits square (that is from one plant to another) up to 100; if irrigated from a well the 100 plots pay 4 barganims, if from running water 6 barganims. Gardens and plantations like these descend from father to son, and the holders cannot be dispossessed unless there be any special custom to the contrary. The writer of the island must be present at all meetings of the chief headmen with the officials, to make notes of the proceedings and resolve doubts. The village writers in the same way must attend all meetings of their particular village. Headmen can make grants to the village officials, such as the Brahmin of the temple, the village writer, the watchman, rent collector, washerman, shoemaker, carpenter, blacksmith, and the sweeper and the dancing girls of the temple. When once given these grants cannot be resumed, nor can others be made; but when a grantee dies without heirs, a new appointment may be made and a grant can be made to non-residents. When an assembly is ordered all the headmen must be represented, but the village headmen of a village may attend by proxy. No assembly can be held unless all the headmen that should be there are represented. One headman may not sell his property without the consent of all the headmen of that village. No sale can take place without the signatures of the seller and all his heirs. Should any headman abscond to avoid paying his revenue, there shall be a meeting of the headmen, who shall fix a term within which the headman must return, and failing that, his heirs must take up the inheritance. Should they refuse, it may be given to any one who will take it and pay all the outstandings. Should a headman abscond for debt or for any other reason, and his heirs refuse to take up the property, then the immovable property shall go to the headmen, who shall be responsible for all arrears of revenue, and the movable shall escheat to the king. The rice lands which are not in separate ownership shall, according to the custom of the village, be let annually by auction, and should there be in any village a rule that outsiders may bid at these auctions, it must be carried out. The headmen are bound to supply forced labour [1] to clean the walls of the city from all jungle growth. In disputes as to real property the only competent evidence is that of written documents and the book of the village: should there be none and the book of the village be lost, the possessor shall be put to his oath in the Temple of Uzu(?). Disputes as to debts to be decided in the same temple. No loan of over 50 tangas (£3 *7s*) to be made save in writing. Money can be lent at interest to receive one barganim for every six tangas and no more. [2] Arrears of interest shall never exceed the principal. The following are not competent witnesses: youths under 16—a drunkard—a blind, dumb, or deaf man—a pimp—a day labourer—a gardener—a gambler—a son of a prostitute—a man declared infamous by law—a man with an enmity to another as against his enemy. These can all give evidence in petty cases. On the death of a man without a son, even though his father be living, his property falls to the King unless he and his father are joint owners. If a man have four sons or more or less, his property cannot be divided amongst them against his wish; if he agrees, all sons shall share equally, but they must maintain their father. If any son,

1 "Begarins."

2 If this be annual interest, it is about 4%; if monthly, just 50%

after partition, turn Muhamedan or jogi,[1] the King shall take his property. When a man whose property falls to the King, dies, the headmen of the village are bound to inform the officials before he is buried, or burned as the case may be. When such property is revenue paying, and has to be sold, residents of the village and relatives shall have a right of preëmption, this right shall be exercised within five days of the sale. In the case of movable property there is no right of preëmption. Inheritance is from father to son and grandson downwards and to fathers and grandfathers upwards. Besides these only brothers can inherit—daughters never. Thieves shall be punished according to law, and stolen property restored to its former owner. Treasure trove shall belong to the King. If a man be married to two wives and have four sons from one and one from the other, or whatever the number may be, the heritage is to be divided in half, the one son of one wife getting as much as the four sons of the other.[2] Girls shall not inherit. No official is allowed to take bribes or to hold land or to engage in trade within the limits of his jurisdiction. Headmen shall not levy any cesses for themselves or for the captains or other officials, under heavy punishment. Whoever smuggles shall pay eleven times the duty, if found out. The chief thanadar and the writers shall be fed when they visit the village, according to custom. If any peon be sent in the public service he shall be paid for every day he is delayed in the village, two measures of rice and one real ($^1/_4 d$) for betel. At any festival where betel, sweetmeats etc. are distributed the chief headman of every village shall receive it and

1 "Which are as ciganos are among us."

2 This method of division is known, among other names, as *jorubhant* or division by wives, in the N. W. P. The other method is *bhaibhant* or division by brothers. By No. 72 of the same vol. of Ar. Port. Or. the provision in the text was modified and either form of inheritance was allowed, according to local custom.

after that the other headmen, according to custom. When any list of names has to be prepared the same order shall be followed. When the headmen are collected, the chief headman of the village of Neura shall proclaim what has been agreed in council and ask for dissentients. The village of Taleigâo, by right of preëminence, begins rice cutting, and the headmen have to present a bundle annually at the chief altar of the Cathedral, and the Factor and Vicar shall spend 4 pardâos on necklaces to put round their necks. In each village the chief headman shall begin the sowing and the reaping, and the same order shall be followed in annually thatching the roofs of the houses with palm leaves. After the principal headman has begun there is no defined order. Dancing girls shall go first to the house of the chief headman; if there are two equal the girls can choose which they please. When two headmen equal in rank have to take betel, they shall stand together with their arms crossed left over right; and if one says his honour is greater as he took the betel in his right hand, the other can say that his honour was greater as his left hand was above the other's right.[1] When two men are equal they can sell their right to any other, or, to save dispute, the writer of the village can receive the betel. No one can use a torch, palanquin or umbrella without a royal license, unless he has inherited such a right. There are two kinds of these rights, one in which the man is allowed to pay the bearers and buy the oil himself, the other where the government pays for these; and again there may be a right only to have one of these three articles.

[1] This is unintelligible as an Eastern would not receive in his left hand.

CHAPTER XI

NUNO DA CUNHA, GOVERNOR, 1529—1538

WHEN the news reached the King of Portugal of the disputes in India on the opening of the successions, after the death of D. Henrique de Menezes, he selected as the new governor Nuno da Cunha, the son of Tristâo da Cunha. Nuno da Cunha, who was born in 1487, had already been in India with his father; he was at the capture of the Socotra fort in 1507, and was knighted after the fight on the Malabar coast in November of the same year; his father was still alive, and in fact survived the son, and only died in 1540. The new Governor was ordered more particularly to build a fortress in Diu, but he was also to build another somewhere in the territory of the Samuri. He took with him his brothers Simâo and Pero Vaz da Cunha, and his fleet consisted of 11 vessels, carrying 3,000 men. The voyage out was most unfortunate, both of his brothers died before they reached India, sickness swept away a large part of the crews, and 4 vessels, including the flag-ship, were lost.

The Tagus was left on April 18th, and as early as May 6th one of the vessels was sunk by a collision, with the loss of 150 persons. Castanheda, the historian, sailed in this fleet with his uncle, but their ship was a bad sailer and was left by her companions off the Guinea coast. The captain, put on his mettle by the desertion, shifted the cargo till her sailing improved, and then watched her course day and night; she and one other were the only ships that reached India that year from Portugal; they arrived, however, with many of their crews dead. At the end of October, while Nuno da Cunha's vessel and two others were at anchor off the Madagascar coast, the sea rose without any gale, the rotten cables of the flag-ship parted one after the other, and the vessel was wrecked; the crew, who saved little more than their lives, were huddled on board the other two ships. Eventually, the remains of the fleet collected at Malindi, too late to cross to India that year. Malindi is an open and rather dangerous roadstead. The crews wanted employment, and the Shaikh of Mombasa, near by where the harbour was better, showed no eagerness to receive them; the place was therefore attacked and sacked. The crews were sickly from the long voyage; the only food in Mombasa, rice and millet, was unsuitable, and 400 men, including Pero Vaz da Cunha, the Governor's brother, died. After some months stay, at the end of March 1529, the town was fired, and the remains of the expedition left for Ormuz, which was reached on May 19th.

At Ormuz, Sharfu-d-din was in power and more satisfied than ever that money was the great lever to influence the Portuguese. Nuno da Cunha, however, had hardly reached Ormuz when a curious incident occurred. Manuel de Macedo, who had taken Sharfu-d-din to Goa at the end of 1527, had carried to Portugal strange stories of the doings of his countrymen in India, and of the wealth of some of the native chiefs, more especially of Sharfu-d-din. The King apparently feared lest all this wealth should go to his subjects, and consequently adopted the extraordinary course of sending Macedo back to Ormuz on a special mission to take Sharfu-d-din prisoner and bring him to Portugal, and that without reference to the Governor and in entire disregard of how it affected his plans. Nuno da Cunha was naturally angry, but Sharfu-d-din himself remained calm. "If I can take my money," he said, "I have no fear," and he was right. He was for a short time detained in prison, curiously enough in the same that contained Lopo Vaz, but afterwards he was at large, and eventually, in 1545, was sent back to India and became as powerful in Ormuz as ever. Nominally as a punishment for the murder of one Rais Hamid, who had been minister while Sharfu-d-din was a prisoner in Goa, the Governor on August 27th, 1529, issued an order to the captain of the fortress to collect annually in future £ 33,000 as tribute instead of £ 20,000. [1]

The deportation of Sharfu-d-din had one unexpected result. Among the most powerful of his relations was Bahau-d-din, the Governor of Bahrein, and although in no sense a rebel, he resisted all attempts to exact a higher tribute from him. On September 8th, 1529, Nuno da Cunha despatched 300 men under his brother Simâo da Cunha to bring him to terms. Simâo, when he reached Bahrein on September 20th, found that Bahau-d-din had hung out a white and a red flag, and had left the Portuguese to take their choice of peace or war; but although the Bahrein garrison was only too anxious for peace, the Portuguese fidalgoes were opposed to any arrangement. The invaders landed and prepared to breach the walls; but it was the sickly season, and before long there were only 35 men left fit for duty, there was therefore nothing to be done but to retreat. Ropes were tied to the feet of the sick, and they were dragged to the boats. For supplies and refreshments they had to depend on their magnanimous opponent, and but for native sailors their ships could not have left the harbour. Simâo da Cunha died of grief, and only a small remnant of the force returned to Ormuz.

[1] This order is given in Botelho Tombo, p. 85.

After carefully weeding out all opponents in Ormuz, Nuno da Cunha left that place on September 15th, reached Goa, where he was received with considerable pomp, on October 24th, and assumed office on November 25th. Few Governors of Portuguese India ever took over charge of the military and naval forces in such an excellent condition as did Nuno da Cunha from Lopo Vaz, [1] and it was owing to this that he was able to at once harry the coast in a way that no other Governor had ever attempted.

Diu was, however, the centre of interest during Nuno da Cunha's whole term. Early in 1530 to be nearer it the head-quarters of government were moved north from Cochin to Goa, which from this date became in name, as it had ever since its capture been in reality, the capital of Portuguese India. Diu was at this time in the kingdom of Sultan Bahadar, a grandson of that Sultan Mahmud Bigarha who ruled Guzerat when the Portuguese first reached India. Sultan Mahmud had died in 1511, and Sultan Bahadar secured the throne on his father's death in 1526, after a struggle with his brothers. Malik Ishák who had succeeded his father Malik Aiyaz as Governor of Diu, was in 1530 a fugitive in the Rajput country, where he was soon afterwards killed by order of Sultan Bahadar; his place in Diu was taken by his brother Malik Toghan. To prepare for Diu, every available Portuguese was called in; ships were even sent to the Coromandel coast with free pardons to all offenders, to sweep in recruits. The government arsenals and dock-yards worked their full time, and private individuals were tempted to embark their fortunes by the promise of the command—at government rates of pay—of whatever class of ship they provided. Correa tells us that he fell also into the prevailing "foolishness" and

[1] The credit of this was due to Afonso Mexia more than to any other person.

built a lateen-rigged vessel at a cost to himself of £150, and now, he adds, "in my old age the King will not allow me to forestall my allowance to buy myself a shirt." Castanheda, the historian, was also with this fleet. Da Cunha did not confine himself to force, for he also employed diplomacy. A Persian merchant, "Coge Percolim",[1] was sent to work on the fears and cupidity of Malik Toghan, and, as far as can be gathered, with some success; for it would seem that the imposing force of Da Cunha was only to give a colour of good faith to a pre-arranged surrender.

The Governor left Goa on January 6th, 1531. His capital was almost deserted and the force collected was imposing; for, including those of sutlers, there were 400 vessels in Bombay harbour, one of the most beautiful in the world. The scene aroused the enthusiasm of Correa, but the Muhamedan spectators were critical; when they saw that Nuno da Cunha, though in good health, required a page boy to prop him while he rode, they said: "This is not the man to take Diu." They were right; the Governor was physically not what he had been when 24 years before he had raced Afonso de Noronha for the honour of place at Socotra fort. After a stay of several precious days in Bombay he went to Daman, where, standing on a cask-head, a herald went through the form of proclaiming defiance to the Sultan of Guzerat with whom they had been fighting for many years. There was at least no hypocrisy: the King of Portugal, it was said, as ruler of the sea wanted Diu, and he meant to have it.

There was on the Guzerat coast, some 8 leagues east of Diu, a rocky islet, separated from the mainland by a narrow channel, called by the Portuguese from the tragedy

[1] Orta mentions him frequently in Colloquios as a very learned man. He calls him "Coge Perculim". The Mirát-i-Sikandari puts this expedition in 1533, confusing it with Nuno da Cunha's second visit.—Bayley's Gujarat, p. 368.

soon to be enacted there, the Island of the Dead.[1] It was strong by nature, and a small garrison of 800 men with 1,000 labourers was busy fortifying it. The possession of this island would in no way assist the Portuguese design on Diu any more than the loss of the men there would weaken the Diu garrison, and in a council there were many who opposed an attack. The Governor and the majority who hoped to terrorise their opponents carried the day. On the arrival of the fleet the garrison offered to surrender on condition that they should go free with their wives, children and private property, but to these terms the Governor refused to accede; they must all be enslaved. To the honour of the Portuguese he stood alone in this determination.

Either side spent the day in preparing for the fight. As the island was surrounded by the Portuguese vessels escape to the mainland was impossible. The garrison knew that all resistance to the overwhelming force brought against them was in vain, and rather than that their wives and children should fall into the hands of the hated Portuguese they killed them. An eye-witness tells us that he saw on a rock by the water's edge one man with four women. He rowed in shore to capture the women, but the man drew his dagger and cut the throats of two before he was brought down by a musket shot. Seeing no other chance of death the other two women threw themselves into the sea, and though they were picked up, they eventually succeeded in attaining their end, and drowned themselves rather than be slaves. The next day the place was stormed; the resistance was stubborn. Muhamedans forced their way along the shafts of the Portuguese lances to get home one stroke before

[1] The Indian name is given by the Portuguese as "Bete", which is generic. There are 3 small islets—Shial Bet, Sawai Bet and Bhensla Rock—some 26 or 28 miles E. of Di the tragedy probably occurred on one of these.

they died. Everything living on the island was killed. The Portuguese lost 150 killed and wounded, and among the former Hector da Silveira, a man they could ill afford. Eight days were spent at this islet, where the Governor awaited in vain the coming of the Jew and the Persian—his two emissaries in Diu; they had been prevented from leaving the town by the arrival there, 6 days before Nuno da Cunha's attack on this islet, of reinforcements from the Red Sea. The delays of the Portuguese had lost Diu.

To explain these events it is necessary to go back somewhat. Sulaiman, who commanded in the Red Sea, had from 1517, the time of Lopo Soares' visit, remained on in Jedda, awaiting reinforcements from the Ottoman Turk. About 1529 these came in the shape of certain vessels commanded by one Haidari. The new comer fell out with Sulaiman, and killed him, but Sulaiman's death was revenged by his nephew Mustafa, who killed Haidari. Mustafa did not at once leave the Red Sea; for some months he besieged Aden, whence he was driven by the rumoured approach of the Portuguese fleet. Having failed here, and fearing the vengeance of the Turk for the death of Haidari, he started for India. In one ship he put his harem and the pick of the artillery, and into another, commanded by Sifr Agha, he put his treasure, which was considerable; his force consisted of 600 Turks and 1,300 Arabs. The arrival of these ships in Diu harbour changed the whole aspect of affairs. Mustafa took the charge of the defence from the nerveless hands of Malik Toghan. He mounted his artillery—far superior to anything made in India—where it was most needed; he mined the entrances to the city and distributed to the best advantage the defending forces. As the Portuguese were coming to an anchor before Diu, on February 11th, 1531, Mustafa gave them a taste of the power of his artillery by three well-aimed shots from a "basilisk", that threw up where they struck "a jet like a whale spouting," and compelled Da Cunha's ship to shift her berth.

A recognizance made in person by the Governor convinced him that an attack on the sea face was hopeless; batteries commanded every approach to the chain that guarded the harbour: a land attack might have been more hopeful, but there were not enough men to defend the ships if sufficient force were landed. Something had, however, to be done, and the plan, if plan there were, was to breach one of the forts near the chain, break the chain, attack the Turkish ships, and master an isolated fort standing in the harbour. The next day selected ships battered the forts at a distance of some 50 yards with 40-pounder guns, firing double charges, until all these guns burst; but the ships received much more damage than they inflicted, and in the evening they were withdrawn. The loss of the Portuguese has not been recorded; it must have been heavy. The panic at the failure was such that, when the Muhamedans fired a salute in honour of their victory, the crews abandoned their most crippled ships and with difficulty were induced to return, and had the enemy's flotilla dared to come out several of them must have been captured. When damages had been repaired the fleet sailed away in considerable disorder—a defeated force. Sultan Bahadar of Guzerat recognized in Mustafa the preserver of Diu; he gave him the title of Rumi Khan and made him Captain of Broach. The burning of Goga and the prosecution of the coast war did not compensate the Portuguese for the check they had received. The Governor returned to Goa on March 15th.

Before continuing the story of Diu, there are a few miscellaneous matters to be brought forward. Deprived of its sea-borne supplies by the Portuguese flotillas, the country of the Samuri was suffering the horrors of famine, but the Portuguese had no intention of granting that ruler easily the peace of which he was desirous. They began instead an intrigue with his subordinate, the Raja of Tanur, and bought from him for £300 the site for a fort at Chaliyam.[1] The place was chosen with judgment, for it was in the Samuri's country, and a small river navigable for boats to the Ghats, gave them access to a large stretch of territory. The Raja of Tanur hoped that, as the result of this sale, he would be able, like the Raja of Cochin, to use the Portuguese to shake off the suzerainty of the Samuri. In feverish haste, lest the Samuri should come by land, the fortress was finished by March 1532, and an old man, Diogo Pereira, with 25 years' experience of the coast and such a knowledge of the language that he did not want an interpreter, was made captain.

It was during the course of 1532 that Nuno da Cunha became involved in a dispute with one of his chief subordinates, the details of which throw an interesting sidelight on the life of the period.[2] Antonio de Macedo was the chief judicial officer in Goa; in civil matters his orders were final, but in criminal they had to be countersigned by the Governor; his reputation stood high. To one part of his duties he strongly objected, and that was to leave his judicial work to ride before the Governor, with his wand in his hand, "like a porter", and this disinclination was the beginning of bad blood. The Governor showed his distaste to the judge's company by keeping Macedo waiting when he came on duty, and by other slights by which men in power indirectly manifest their annoyance. One Sunday while the respectable people were at church, a tipstaff arrested a man in the street; the man had no connection

[1] The present railway station of Beypur stands nearly on the site of this fort.

[2] They also perhaps to some extent explain the treatment the king reserved for Nuno da Cunha when his term as governor ended; he condoned here an offence against the royal person.

with Diogo da Silveira, the governor's brother-in-law, but passing his house he called out—"Help! Diogo da Silveira." The master was at mass, but his servants and negroes ran out, beat the tipstaff, broke his wand and rescued the man. News reached Macedo, who, collecting what townspeople he could, demanded the prisoner in the name of the King from Silveira's bailiff. The man was insolent and there was a dispute; but before the quarrel had gone far the subject of it came out to look on at the fun, and was promptly arrested. Macedo returned to his house to await events.

When Silveira heard what had occurred he left the church beside himself with rage, and came down the street abusing his servants for not plucking out the beard of that Judas, Macedo; he did not even spare in his fury the King of Portugal himself. To prevent further mischief Nuno da Cunha confined Silveira to his house, and, apparently not knowing how far he had gone in his abuse, directed Macedo to report on the whole matter. When Silveira's rage had cooled he was very anxious to apologise; the governor also tried to smooth matters over, but Macedo was obdurate. Words had been spoken against the King; the serious charge could only be determined in Portugal, and Silveira would probably lose his head. When Macedo found that Silveira was released from his arrest, and also given a command at sea, he sent a magistrate and notary to order him to proceed to Portugal in the next ships to answer the charge of treason. The Governor was furious and destroyed the record.

When Afonso Mexia was leaving India he, under the royal orders, made over the successions to Macedo, who, to keep them dry, put them among the books in his library.[1]

[1] "Bartolo" is the author specially mentioned. Presumably Bartolomeu, the Sicilian, who died in 1476, many of whose works on canon law were printed between 1517 and 1545, is referred to. See Migne Encyclopedie Theologique, *s.v.*

The Governor now sent for them, and as Macedo refused to give them up save under another royal order, the former lost his temper, sent a posse of men and had all the latter's papers ransacked. No successions were found, but the notes of a slanderous report against Nuno da Cunha were found. To force him to give up the successions Macedo was put into irons and kept in solitary confinement. At this he did not complain, for anyway his life was safe in prison; out of doors he might have been killed in a sham street row or shot from behind a wall, and no enquiry made. When, however, he was thrown into the filthy prison of Goa, among the common criminals, his fortitude gave way and he gave up the successions. He returned to Portugal in the ships of the year, but the king refused to hear the charge until Nuno da Cunha returned; and as he died eventually on the way home, it was never gone into fully, but Macedo recovered some £4,500 arrears of pay from the Governor's heirs after his death.

Ismail Adil Shah of Bijapur, from whom Albuquerque had conquered Goa, did not die until 1534, but the intrigues for his succession were already afoot in 1532. He had two sons, Mulu Adil Shah and Ibrahim Adil Shah, both equally worthless, who in turn succeeded him; but there was a strong party in the state who favoured his brother, Mir Ali, a man of whom we shall hear much later on. At the head of this party was a powerful noble, originally a slave, called Yusaf of Lar,[1] who had received the title of Assad Khan and had made Belgaum his headquarters. The land on the mainland at the back of Goa was within his jurisdiction, and to purchase the assistance of the Portuguese he allowed them to occupy Salsette and Bardes, they agreeing to support Mir Ali. The country thus acquired was

[1] So I read Çufolarim Castanheda, VIII. 53.

assessed to bring in £16,000 a year, but the Portuguese overstepped their bounds by building a fort in Rachol. After the death of Ismail, Mir Ali for a time fell into the background, (he was but a pawn in the game) and Assad Khan joined his master Ibrahim Adil Shah against the Portuguese; pressure was thus brought to bear to make them restore the two districts. A desultory war continued for some years with varying success. In one of the fights the Captain of Goa was killed; and in the rains of 1536 Goa itself was hard pressed, and the spirit of the garrison sank so low that they had to be driven to the front, and in the face of the enemy preferred being taken prisoners to fighting. When Nuno da Cunha, however, in 1538, blew up the Rachol fort, the war ended with the temporary evacuation of the two districts of Salsette and Bardes. It was not till a few years later that the Portuguese finally obtained possession of them.

In 1528 one Martim Afonso de Mello Jusarte was sent on a voyage to the far East: his voyages were among the abortive attempts of the Portuguese to gain a footing in Bengal. Wrecked after crossing the bay, he, with some companions, made his way in a boat up the Pegu coast, intending to go to Chittagong. The sufferings of the ship-wrecked men from hunger and thirst were very great, and several were accidentally poisoned by eating wild beans; but their thirst they lessened by the old expedient of sucking a bullet, and their hunger they appeased by a lucky find of turtle eggs which they cooked in a rusty helmet. Deceived by some fishermen, they found themselves, not in Chittagong, but in Chakiria, to the south of it, the capital of Khuda Bakhsh Khan, a petty chieftain subordinate to Bengal. Khuda Bakhsh Khan imprisoned them, but promised them their liberty if they would fight his enemies; when they had helped him, however, he broke his word.

An attempt to escape resulted in a closer confinement and the sacrifice before their eyes of one of their number, Gonçalo Vaz de Mello. Eventually Martim Afonso was ransomed for £1,500, through the good offices of Khwaja Shahabu-d-din, a merchant of Chittagong, and was sent with his relative, Khwaja Shakr Ulla, to India, where he arrived in 1530.

When therefore Shahabu-d-din got into trouble with Nasrat, Sultan of Bengal, and wrote to ask the assistance of the Portuguese, Martim Afonso was naturally selected for the command of a friendly trading expedition. An account of his experiences will show the difficulties the Portuguese met with in opening up intercourse with a land-locked country, like Bengal, not depending on seaborne trade for its necessaries. He had five ships: one, the San Rafael with 150 men, belonged to Government; the rest were private property; the cargoes were joint-stock ventures. The ships reached Chittagong in safety and were well received by the governor of the town.[1] The custom dues were very high (rather over 30 per cent.), but when the Portuguese began to smuggle freely no notice was taken. An experienced trader told the Commander this was suspicious and boded no good: "The sauce the Bengalis serve us will be bitter to the taste," said he; but his warnings were disregarded. Some Portuguese were sent up country to the Sultan at Gour, with valuable presents worth some £1,200; it was characteristic that part consisted of cases of sweet waters robbed from a Muhamedan vessel, with the names of the original owners still attached.[2]

The natives of the country were venal and servile, and

[1] A Portuguese description of Bengalis calls them "False and thieves; people who get up quarrels as an excuse for robbery."

[2] They had come from the Sufiturk, a ship of 800 tons richly laden—captured at Shahr on the Arabian coast.

the Portuguese took full advantage of these qualities. Nothing appeared on the surface, but in reality all offences were treasured up against them, and when orders came from the Sultan to arrest them and confiscate their goods, attentions were redoubled. Martim Afonso and his captains must honour the Governor's poor house with their presence at a banquet. They were so confident as to go with their swords only. During the banquet, which was in a courtyard surrounded by walls, the Governor complained of sudden illness and left. The doors were closed, and the Portuguese caught like "fowls in a coop." The walls were lined with archers who fired among them and killed several, until, from the safe vantage ground of an aperture overlooking the room, the Governor counselled the survivors to surrender. There was no other course for them to adopt. Of the other Portuguese on shore some were killed, some escaped to the ships, and property valued at £100,000 was confiscated. Nearly all the fidalgoes had been netted by the Governor; but a few who had preferred a hog-hunt to the banquet, escaped. The prisoners were taken to Gour with every mark of indignity, and were nearly starved on a very inadequate allowance. An attempt was made a few years later to ransom them, but the sum demanded, £15,000, was refused as exorbitant, and Chittagong was burned in revenge. All save four were released in 1537, just before Sher Shah captured Gour and killed Sultan Mahmud; the death of that monarch gave liberty to the rest.

Nuno da Cunha had never through all the other questions that demanded his attention lost sight of Diu. He had failed in war, and now tried diplomacy alone. Malik Toghan, who was still in command there, kept the governor's numerous spies and secret envoys in play sufficiently to prevent their losing all hope of ultimate success. The accredited envoy to Sultan Badahar was the governor's secretary, Simâo Ferreira, but his efforts were neutralized by his interpreter Joâo de Santiago.

The history of this adventurer is curious enough to merit a few words. Born in Africa, he was enslaved by the Portuguese in early youth. They made him a Christian; and his master, a caulker, taught him his trade. Together they more than once performed the Indian voyage; and when his owner died in Goa and left him free he did not begin the world with quite an empty purse. He started next as a travelling purchaser of precious stones, and being naturally quick, picked up an acquaintance with several languages, and, if scandal did not speak falsely, was as ready, if it served his turn, to worship in a Hindu temple or a Muhamedan Mosque as in a Christian Church. When he found that Southern India could no longer hold him he drifted to Ormuz, where for some time he stood in high favour with the king; but the Portuguese had before long to interpose to save him from death. He lived after this quietly at Goa until the governor's secretary selected him as his interpreter. He not only balked his employers at Diu by his intrigues, but managed to secure the good graces of Sultan Bahadar and hardly waited till Simâo Ferreira was out of the country to take service with him. He received the title of Frangi Khan and for the next few years he played a certain part in Guzerat history.[1]

Simâo Ferreira so far succeeded that he arranged a meeting between Sultan Bahadar and Nuno da Cunha, who therefore left Goa in October 1533. His expenses had

[1] For his death see page 249. Apparently he is referred to under the name Sakta, which is possibly a corruption of Santiago, and as such should read Satgo in the Indian historians—at least Sakta was converted by Bahadar to the Muhamedan faith and called Firang Khan.—Bayley, "Gujarat," p. 391.

been again enormous, for Goa had been ransacked to give splendour to his fleet. But by the time he got to Diu Bahadar's mood had changed; he would not fix a day for the interview. The most picturesque incident of this visit to Diu was the challenge to mortal combat given by Manuel de Macedo, in Bahadar's open darbar, to Rumi Khan. The ostensible reason was that Rumi Khan had tried to supplant Malik Toghán at Diu. The challenge was accepted, and the fight was to have been on the sea, either in his own boat alone, but Manuel de Macedo waited in vain a whole day for Rumi Khan.

Though Bahadar would not meet Nuno da Cunha personally, he sent to him an envoy—Khwaja Shaikh Iwaz—offering a grant of Bassein and some territory round it estimated to bring in £30,000 annually, if he could only get peace. Pressed by Humayun, the Emperor of Delhi, on the north, and by the Portuguese on the south, the harassed monarch saw no other way of escape. With characteristic oriental diplomacy, however, Badahar was not offering them something that was altogether his own. Bassein was in the fief of his subordinate Imadu-l-Mulk, who in 1541, after peace with Guzerat had been concluded, gave the Portuguese considerable trouble with his claims. The conditions which Bahadar had, however, to accept were hard. All Guzerat ships for the Red Sea were to put into Bassein to get their passes from the captain, and no ship of war was to be built in Guzerat. All horses from Ormuz were to be brought to Bassein, but after the first 60 Bahadar was to pay full duty.[1] Possession was given to the Portuguese by

[1] The treaty will be found in full in Botelho Tombo, p. 134. There were other conditions as to payments to mosques; release of the 4 Portuguese, Diogo de Mesquita and others still in captivity. At the same time there are difficulties in the chronology. The historians say that Nuno da Cunha left Diu in a rage in January 1534. They give no date for the

beat of drum; the villagers came forward with roots and plants, products of the soil, to give them symbolical entry on their new territory.

To understand subsequent events it is necessary to trace the quarrel between Sultan Bahadar and Humayun, the Emperor of Delhi, which belongs rather to the general history of India; it had, however, great influence on the fortunes of the Portuguese, and it is further interesting as one of the few instances in which the same events are related by both Indian and Portuguese historians; the result of a comparison of both authorities inspires great confidence in their accuracy. [1] Sultan Bahadar of Guzerat had given an asylum to Mirza Zaman, a relative of Humayun, who had fled from Northern India after an attempt to murder his emperor. An embassy sent to demand his extradition returned with a scoffing reply. War followed, but Bahadar conducted his campaign with little skill. He wasted his

treaty, but put it later. In Botelho the treaty is dated December 1543, in figures which admit of no error; as Da Cunha had been dead for 4 years then, this must be wrong. Botelho himself puts the date as December 1533 and says it was made as Da Cunha had advanced against Guzerat at the head of a large force. I have followed Botelho.

[1] This is of course before clerical influence had infected the Portuguese histories. As an instance of agreement I may mention the account of Bahadar's council held at Mandeshwar in 1535, though this is a very severe test for both. Correa's account is in III. 598 and 599. The account in the Tabakat-i-Akbari will be found in Elliot, V. p. 191. The latter history was written at Delhi in 1593. Correa's account was written before 1566 in southern India, was taken to Portugal before the Tabakat was written, and not published till 1858. They could not either have copied the other. They may have quoted from the same authority, but this is hardly likely. What went on in an obscure council in distant Rajputana could not have been much talked of, and Correa would not see a native account. In Correa the "Capitâo Velho" and the "regedor" want to fight in the open. The Tabakat agrees and gives the name of the "Capitâo Velho" as Sadrkhan. In both, Rumi Khan counselled waiting in the entrenchments, and Bahadar followed his advice. Correa gives Diogo de Mesquita, who was in Guzerat, as his authority. Many other points on which the accounts agree could be given.

strength in the siege of Chitor, a city of Rajputana, which he took and sacked, after the besieged had burned their wives, children and goods, and devoted themselves to death. The possession of this city in no way affected Humayun, and while Bahadar was engaged in the siege a large but unsupported force under Tatar Khan Lodi, which he had sent towards Agra in the hopes of rousing possible malcontents, was cut off and destroyed by the Moghals. When Humayun advanced against Bahadar the latter awaited him in an entrenched camp at Mandeshwar. The two armies came into touch in March 1535. Sultan Bahadar acting on the advice of Rumi Khan, tamely remained in his entrenchments and made no fight in the open.[1] Humayun, on the other hand, was in no hurry to attack entrenchments flanked by a tank on the one side and a river on the other, and defended by powerful artillery. The active and warlike Moghals cut off all supplies from the camp, and by the end of April its condition was desperate. On the night of April 23rd, without making any show of fighting, and without attempting to save his army, Bahadar, followed by four or five horsemen, fled to Champaner.

The day after Bahadar's flight, the confusion in the Guzerat camp proclaimed the news; the slaughter was terrible, the spoil immense. Rumi Khan deserted to Humayun, whom for some years he served faithfully as an artillery officer; but he was eventually poisoned by his new master. Bahadar, in his flight, passed through his treasure-house, Champaner, whence he despatched Diogo de Mesquita and the other Portuguese prisoners to beg help from the Governor at Goa; he then continued his flight to Diu.

[1] According to the Indian accounts Bahadar promised Rumi Khan the Governorship of Chitor, but when it was taken by his exertions, refused to fulfil his promise. Rumi Khan's treacherous advice and desertion were the consequence. Bayley, "Gujarat," p. 583.

The Moghals sacked Ahmadabad, but their most brilliant feat of arms was the capture of Champaner. This place was surrounded by two sets of ramparts, the outer enclosing a village was difficult, the inner enclosing the hill fort almost impregnable. It had occupied Mahmud Shah Bigarha in a siege of twelve years' duration from June 1482 before he captured it. On this occasion the Moghals, guided by some villagers who supplied the town with butter and wood, discovered an approach somewhat less precipitous than elsewhere. By driving iron spikes into the rock a sort of ladder was constructed, up which the storming party of 300 men climbed; Humayun himself was the 41st to ascend. The plateau of rock on which the fort stood, was gained by night, and next morning, not without suspicion of collusion, Ikhtiar Khan, the commander, capitulated, the spoil almost exceeds belief. The only bright spot now on Bahadar's horizon was that, in the name of his sister's son, still a child, an army was collected which—working round to the rear of the Moghals—recaptured some territory and recovered many prisoners of Mandeshwar, including 22 Portuguese and Frenchmen, the remnant of the 70 who began the campaign with him.

As the south-west monsoon was blowing when Mesquita and his companions reached Chaul, neither the Governor, who was at Goa, nor Martim Afonso de Sousa, who was at Chaul, could at once go to Bahadar's help, and Bahadar, almost beside himself with terror, and desiring perhaps not to throw himself unreservedly into the hands of the Portuguese, sent an envoy to Egypt on September 8th, 1535, with rich presents to buy the help of the Ottoman Turk. [1] The turn which affairs had taken aroused jealousies

[1] Turkish accounts put the value of one girdle alone at 30 million aspers, or about £50,000. Bird's "Gujarat," p. 245, note. Portuguese accounts put the total value at 2½ millions, but omit the currency.

between the governor and Martim Afonso de Sousa, the commander at sea; the former ordered the latter on no account to proceed to Diu, while he sent there privately Simâo Ferreira, his own secretary. Martim Afonso evaded the governor's order, and he and the secretary were disagreeably surprised when they met off Diu bar on September 21st.

Martim Afonso at once got permission to build a fortress and began work; an urgent letter from Bahadar to Nuno da Cunha, dated September 28th, brought the latter to Diu, and a peace was signed on October 5th, 1535,[1] confirming the grant of the site for a fortress, which included the small fort in the harbour. The King of Portugal was to have no claim to any of the customs' receipts; but the curious and noteworthy clause of the peace is that in which both agree to prevent religious proselytizing. Nuno da Cunha was annoyed with Martim Afonso for having forestalled him, and still more annoyed when he found that he had already sent a Jew and an Armenian overland with information to the King of Portugal. A yet more unpleasant experience of the same nature awaited him.

In the time of Almeida, Antonio Real was Captain of Cochin and he is often mentioned in Albuquerque's letters, against whom he persistently intrigued. He had by one Yria Pereira—a Portuguese woman—a bastard son, Diogo Botelho. The mother brought up her son very carefully and educated him as a pilot; he showed considerable aptitude for cartography and was the favourite pupil of a Dominican friar then in Cochin. He made some important corrections in existing maps and took them to Portugal to show the King. Encouraged by his reception, he asked for the captaincy of a fort, and was met with the crushing rejoinder that cap-

[1] The original documents will be found in Botelho Tombo, p. 217 and following.

tains of fortresses were not made out of pilots. From a hasty remark it was inferred that he would transfer his knowledge to some other country, and as the example of Magalhaens was recent, Botelho expiated his momentary passion within the walls of a jail. In 1524 when Vasco da Gama went to India for the last time, he sought and obtained permission to take Botelho as a banished man; Botelho, however, was too ambitious to accept the situation quietly. During the eleven years he had been in India he had scraped together some money, and when the news reached Cochin, where he then was, that there would certainly be a fort in Diu, he obtained a foist, ran north to Chaul, and thence crossed to Diu in a smaller boat. There Botelho took the measurements and plans of the fortress that was being built, obtained a copy of the treaty and returned to Chaul. On November 1st he left Chaul with some 8 poverty-stricken Portuguese and 20 slaves, and stood across to the African coast; all his companions agreed to stand by him. Nuno da Cunha had in the meanwhile been getting ready a vessel of 250 tons in which to send Simâo Ferreira, his secretary, to Europe with the good news. The disappearance of Botelho roused suspicion; it was thought he was making for some foreign country, and Ferreira had orders, if he caught him, to kill him at sight and burn his boat. Botelho, with his 12 days' start, was never caught, but in a mutiny of the slaves three of his Portuguese were killed, and of the 6 left, two were ill and two wounded—Botelho himself, the only navigator on board, could not, owing to his wound, speak for a fortnight, and directed the course by signs. In Fayal, Botelho was recognized as a banished man, but he escaped capture by his audacity.[1] The King forgave his

[1] An officer feigned to have forgotten the Christian name of one Botelho who was banished, and asked Diogo if he knew. Diogo disarmed suspicion

escapade in leaving India without permission in recognition of his zeal, but more than this he did not get, and his boat was burned lest men should know that the voyage from India could be performed in so small a vessel.

From the moment that work was begun on Diu fort in October until the following March when it was finished, all high and low worked with a will. "The Portuguese fight like heroes and work like *begaris*" (forced labourers), said Nuno da Cunha to Sultan Bahadar. All ranks were animated by the hope that this fortress would close the last port open to the Turks in India. The fidalgoes spent their substance in providing food for the poorer sort; of these nobles, Garcia de Sa, afterwards Governor of India, was among the most respected, and the bastion on which he worked was as well known by his name as by its own more proper appellation, the Santiago bastion. In the fort and the outlying work in the harbour there was accommodated a garrison of 900 men with 60 pieces of artillery, many matchlocks and abundant supplies. Manuel de Sousa, a comparatively young man, was appointed captain.

Hardly was the ink of the treaty dry before the Governor felt how impossible it would be for him to carry out his promise to assist Bahadar by land as well as by sea. Not that anything fresh had occurred since the peace was signed—the objections that existed after it was signed had always existed. All the Portuguese in India could not drive out the Moghals from Guzerat, even to undertake a campaign under the orders of a general like Bahadar would be to send them to certain destruction; further, once the Moghals driven from his borders—if they were ever driven—Bahadar would be independent of Portuguese help and not desirous of their presence in Diu. Something, however,

by frankly saying he was the man. Botelho was made Captain of Cananor in 1550, but he died of a dropsy within the year.—Couto, VI. 8. 1.

had to be done, and as his share of the work of expelling the Moghals in exchange for the fortress of Diu, Nuno da Cunha sent to Bahadar Martim Afonso de Sousa with 50 horse and 100 matchlockmen; the result was naturally a ludicrous failure, and Bahadar had to return to Diu somewhat disconcerted. No better success attended Manuel de Macedo who went to defend Broach: a bombastic letter from the Moghals stampeded the Broach merchants, who bribed their defender to let them run away comfortably. When the Moghals approached, Macedo retreated, and Broach, Ranir and Surat were looted and burned

There came, however, soon after this a change over the face of affairs, though not through any action of the Portuguese. Bahadar, with his own troops, defeated detachments of Moghals in scattered engagements; and Humayun himself was recalled to Northern India by urgent advices from Delhi. Bahadar's feelings must have been bitter indeed at seeing his country cleared from the tide of invasion by his own exertions and by extraneous circumstances, while those whom he had bribed with Bassein and with Diu had stood aside and done nothing to help him. Bahadar asked permission of the Portuguese to build a wall to cut off the fortress from the city of Diu, and when this was refused he was angered, and said openly that he had been deceived and that the Portuguese had broken their word.

The Portuguese in Diu lived from the first on the worst possible terms with their neighbours in the city. Although the Captain forbade any Portuguese, under the penalty of a heavy fine, from going more than a stone's throw from the walls, there were many riots, and several Portuguese were killed; the position was indeed almost impossible. We have only the Portuguese accounts, and it is incredible that all the provocations came from one side only. Continual infractions also of the treaty—or else what Bahadar considered as such—occurred; his own ships, for instance, were not allowed to leave his own port of Diu. Possibly smarting under his injuries, Bahadar may have tried to weave a combination of Muhamedan powers against the Portuguese, but he drank heavily, was subject to sudden and uncontrollable impulses not governed by reason,[1] and was therefore unfitted for any calculation that needed a cool head.

That he deeply regretted the treaties he had made with the Portuguese there can be no doubt; there is no ground for asserting that he ever infringed those treaties. He may possibly have meditated assassinating the Governor if he had a chance,[2] but there can be no doubt but that the idea of assassinating him was always present to the Portuguese mind; fabulous stories of his wealth were current among them, and they looked on him not as a human being but as a galleon to be robbed. His conduct did not display either the fear of a would-be assassin, or the timidity of one who thought his life was in danger. Accompanied by a very few attendants he came and went freely in the Portuguese fort, and of one such visit, on November 13th, 1536, we have two accounts. Bahadar, with Sifr Agha and a few others, came to the fort, without warning, at 8 in the evening; he was then very drunk. When word was brought to Manuel de Sousa that the Sultan was

[1] In this both Indian and Portuguese accounts agree. Orta Colloquios gives unimpeachable authority (Martim Afonso de Sousa) for his statement that he was addicted to "bhang."

[2] Indian historians assert this as well as Portuguese. Nuno da Cunha was warned from an Indian source that this was intended. Most likely these rumours were founded only on the ravings of a drunken man, carried and magnified by intriguers. There are other traces that busybodies were making mischief between Bahadar and the Portuguese. One night the Captain of the fort was secretly told that Bahadar intended in the morning to invite him to an interview and assassinate him. The invitation duly came; the Captain, like a brave man, went alone, but nothing happened. See also the account in Correa, III. 754. Bahadar's drunken talk seems to be mutilated Hindustani abuse.

at the gate, the alarm was sounded, and with a blare of trumpets the garrison fell in in two ranks, with lighted torches. The gates were thrown open, and the sight of the soldiers drawn up for him to pass through their ranks, and the glitter of the torches on their arms, sobered, if it did not frighten, the Sultan. He passed down the line and was shown over the fort, and was told in courtly phrase that all was his, but the fumes of the wine had left him: "Faith, my friend," he replied, "the fort is your King's and the houses are your own." When they saw Bahadar leaving the fort unmolested, the Portuguese were furious with the Captain for his "weakness of heart;" the governor took the same view, and the Captain received from him a severe reprimand. To do Correa justice, he had some qualms over the matter: "In some parts an act of this kind "would be a breach of faith," he says, "but not in India where "it is customary. We were not allowed to take such a "chance by reason of our sins," he sighs. There is grim humour in a religion which regards the divine permission to commit a cowardly and treacherous act as a reward of virtue.

There happened, while Nuno da Cunha had been preparing to visit Diu, to come to Goa an embassy from Sultan Bahadar, consisting of Shaikh Iwaz—who had been on similar embassies before—and Nur Muhamad Khalil, a more formal envoy who was supposed to be deep in his master's secrets. For this envoy Nuno da Cunha set a trap, Shaikh Iwaz assisting him. "Coge Percolim"—the Persian who had been Nuno da Cunha's emissary in Diu, Shaikh Iwaz and Nur Mahamad Khalil met at a friendly dinner.[1] The Governor was careful that the wines were well chosen, and that a trusty Portuguese was concealed where he could

[1] Indian and Portuguese histories agree in this anecdote.

overhear all the talk. When they had all well drunk, "Coge Percolim" began by arrangement to abuse the Portuguese, and Nur Muhamad was induced to reveal his master's plans.

The Governor had, on hearing the rumour that Sultan Bahadar meditated assassination, determined to take any opportunity that offered of making him prisoner. The air was electrical. Sultan Bahadar was a great hunter, and he sent some recently killed antelope to the Portuguese. When the latter noticed that each animal had lost some part, one a head and another a foot, they inferred that the present had a symbolical meaning, which was that the Portuguese were to be treated as these creatures had been.[1] The sapient Joâo Rodriguez, the chief physician, went so far as to say that the inspection of the recently torn flesh told him that poison had been introduced into the animals' flesh to kill those who partook of it. The hungry soldiers were not to be balked of their meal, and though the flesh should by order have been thrown into the sea, they ate it, and it is hardly necessary to say, with no ill effects. This tension of the atmosphere must be remembered; it was the result of years of anxious longing and of present half-contented desire, and it explains to some extent the tragedy that was soon to happen.

Early in January 1537 Nuno da Cunha reached Diu. He feigned sickness to avoid going on shore to meet Sultan Bahadar, and as an excuse for refusing the invitation to a banquet under cover of which there lurked, he considered, a sinister design. Sultan Bahadar was out hunting when

[1] All Portuguese writers mention this present of game. One adds also that it was another present—that of 40 skinny fowls, with their heads cut off, after his drunken visit in November—that brought home to the Captain of the fortress the mistake he had made in not capturing Bahadar. The state of mind that looked on these presents as insults is now difficult to follow.

Nuno da Cunha's fleet cast anchor, and Manuel de Sousa, the Captain of Diu, was at once sent to him with the Governor's regrets that the state of his health would not allow him to come in person. No sooner had Manuel de Sousa left to return, after delivering his message, than Sultan Bahadar was seized with one of his sudden impulses, and ordered his boat to be got ready to row out to see Nuno da Cunha. Besides the boatmen, Bahadar took with him in his foist, 2 pages and 7 companions:—Sifr Agha, the Italian renegade who had come to Diu with Mustafa; the latter's two sons-in-law, Asit Khan, surnamed the Tiger of the World, and Kara Hussain;[1] Langar Khan and Amin Hussian, two young Guzerat nobles; João de Santiago, the interpreter; and another Muhamedan.[2] Of his pages, one carried his sword and another his bow and arrows.

Bahadar was, of course, not expected; he was not recognized until near the ship, and then all was hurry. Nuno da Cunha got hastily under a heap of bedclothes, and the crew were still buckling on their swords when he passed over the deck, alone and unsuspicious of evil, into the Governor's room. He stayed there a very short time; possibly he felt, when too late, that Nuno da Cunha's ship was not the place for him: the anxious tension was evident. The fidalgoes, knowing what happened after Bahadar's visit to the fort in November, were waiting for the Governor's

[1] Kara Hussain was also a European renegade who married the widow of the Tiger of the World. In 1563, when Couto was in Broach, he was Captain there, and they used to read the Italian poets—Ariosto, Petrarch and Dante—together, so he was a man of some education. Indian accounts say that Bahadar's visit was intended to remove any suspicion from Nuno da Cunha's mind.

[2] One authority gives the name of the seventh companion as Rumi Khan, the son of Sifr Agha. Sifr Agha had a son who afterwards received this title, but he does not seem to have been in the foist. The Mirát-i-Sikandari gives the names of the two young nobles as in the text, and adds 4 other names which cannot be identified. The author was not a contemporary.

orders; but at the critical moment Nuno da Cunha's nerve failed him, and he kept his eyes sullenly fixed on the deck. The arrival of a messenger from them, sent to ask for definite instructions, seems to have aroused Bahadar's suspicion; he got up, looked into the verandah to see if men were hidden there, and then going to his boat, ordered his men to row quickly to the shore. With the departure of Bahadar, Nuno da Cunha's presence of mind returned. He called to Manuel de Sousa and ordered him to at once follow the Sultan's boat, and tell him that in the hurry he had forgotten to give him a message from the King of Portugal, and ask him to await his (the Governor's) arrival in the fortress. With Manuel de Sousa went Diogo de Mesquita and Antonio Correa.

This sudden departure of Manuel de Sousa added considerably to the growing excitement, and another order of the Governor, to all the fidalgoes, to follow Manuel de Sousa and do as he bade them (they were not told what orders he had received) only added to the effect. Nuno da Cunha's ship lay a league from the shore, and the Sultan's boat had got some distance before Manuel de Sousa started at about 4 p.m.; it would have got further, but the Sultan had stopped to let Sifr Agha get into the boat rather than leave him behind.[1] Bahadar also appears to have slackened speed when he saw Manuel de Sousa's boat following him, with de Sousa in the bows, waving to him. When he reached the Sultan's boat De Sousa gave the Governor's message, and at Santiago's suggestion he stepped from his own boat into the Sultan's, but incautiously, and fell into the water. Bahadar's boatmen pulled him out, while Bahadar himself sat laughing at the figure he cut. Meanwhile the other boatloads of overwrought men, with

[1] Sifr Agha appears to have been in another part of the ship while Bahadar was with Nuno da Cunha.

naked weapons in their hands, were coming up in a bubble of excitement, ready to take the disturbance as a deliberate attack on the Captain of Diu.

Who struck the first blow it is impossible to say; but the arrow fired by the page, at the Sultan's orders, from the Sultan's bow, into the air, proclaimed to all that war had broken out. [1] Manuel de Sousa was one of the first victims. The Portuguese poured into the King's foist; one was shot with an arrow by the King's page, one was literally cleft by the Tiger of the World; another Portuguese twined his arms round the Tiger, and though he received 20 wounds in the terrible scuffle, never left his hold till the Tiger was dead. Diogo de Mesquita went straight for Sultan Bahadar and wounded him with a sword-thrust. [2] Bahadar jumped overboard, and either to save their own lives or his, his followers imitated him. Bahadar caught hold of an oar, but the Portuguese were killing all whom they could reach, and he was brained by a sailor for the sake of a gold dagger he wore; as the body was never recovered it was only by this booty that his fate was known. Of his companions, Sifr Agha (wounded) and Kara Hussain alone escaped; Santiago swam to the fort and

1 All accounts agree as to the arrow. This appears to have been a recognized way of declaring war. See Castanheda, II. 16, where it is mentioned with reference to Vijayanagara. For another instance of this in Malabar see Correa, IV. 708. Similarly the gift of an arrow from the royal quiver was a security of peace. See also Bayley, "Gujarat," p. 389. Humayun's quiver bound round a minstrel's loins invested him with the power of releasing prisoners.

2 In connection with this attack of Diogo de Mesquita there is a curious point. In the account in the Akbar Nama—Elliot, VI. 18, it is said that Bahadar was attacked by a European "Kazi"; all the Portuguese accounts say that Mesquita was the man who wounded Bahadar. "Mesquita" is the Portuguese for a mosque, and "Casis," pronounced almost exactly like Kazi, is the Indo-Portuguese for a priest. I suggest that the two facts are connected, and that possibly Mesquita's nickname was Kazi or Casi. He was well known to the Guzeratis; for his history see page 212. Bahadar was 31 years old at the time of his death.

called out for help, but the guard stoned him to death. A few boats pulled off from the shore, and some 14 Portuguese in all were killed, and 25 or 30 wounded, in the melee. The general fear and horror at this great crime were so great that, but for the exertions of Sifr Agha, wounded as he was, the town would have been entirely deserted; later the Portuguese badly repaid the invaluable services he rendered them at this time.

Nuno da Cunha appropriated the enormous mass of war material he found collected in the arsenals, but although Bahadar's palaces were carefully searched, only a very small quantity of treasure was brought to the public exchequer. Sultan Bahadar was beloved by his people, for he had the one great virtue that in an oriental state condones all vices—he allowed no tyrant but himself.[1] There were some even among the Portuguese who saw the murder of Bahadar in its true light. When Martim Afonso de Sousa and the Comptroller of the Revenue reached Diu ten days after the event, they did not hesitate to express their opinion; but the Governor sent off Isaac of Cairo[2] overland to Portugal, and the messenger received a pension for the good news he brought. Sifr Agha was put in charge of the city and Antonio da Silveira, the Governor's brother-in-law, made captain of the fort. Sultan Bahadar left no son, and the Portuguese coquetted with Mirza Muhamad Zaman, the Moghal who had been the immediate occasion of Humayun's attack on Bahadar, and who now was a pretender to the Guzerat throne. They indeed entered into a formal treaty with him,[3] by which, in return for their moral support and the inclusion of his name in the "Khutbah" in the Diu Mosque, he granted them Mangalor

[1] See Correa, IV. 452. Bayley allows him no virtue, "Gujarat," p. 63.

[2] Garcia de Orta mentions this man as noted for his learning. See Colloquios, pp. 131 Y. and 164 Y.

[3] See treaty in Botelho Tombo, p. 224, dated March 27th, 1537.

and Daman, and a strip of country along the coast, $2^1/_2$ kos broad. Miran Muhamad Shah Farruki, the son of Bahadar's sister, received, however, so much support that Mirza Muhamad Zaman had to fly, and his followers who desired the security which the town of Diu could alone afford them, had to fee the Portuguese with their all before they could be admitted within its gates. Mirza Muhamad Zaman himself returned to Humayun's court, and was forgiven, but was soon after accidentally drowned.

Before completing the history of the connection of Nuno da Cunha with Diu, there are some matters in other parts of India to be brought forward. In the 9th century Perumal, the last King of Malabar, turned Muhamedan, and after dividing his kingdom among numerous chieftains, left India for Arabia. His memory in Malabar was still kept green; in Cranganor, his capital, wooden shoes and water were always ready for his use, and on a certain night there was a great assembly at a temple in his honour. The Raja of Cranganor was a subordinate of the Samuri's, but with the example of Cochin before his eyes he was always ready to seek any means of rendering himself independent. In this intention he was sustained by the Raja of Cochin until the latter found that, if he were successful, the Portuguese would have a factory at Cranganor and seriously diminish the Cochin trade profits. When Perumal's festival was at hand in 1536, and the Samuri expressed his intention of attending it, Cranganor, after casting a longing look at Cochin, who refused assistance, had perforce to submit.

The Samuri, however, having succeeded in this one matter, determined on another which brought him into contact with Cochin itself. He determined to perform those ceremonies at the sacred stone which his predecessor had removed in 1503 from Cochin to Eddapalli, which would enable him to claim lordship over the Southern Malabar States. As the Raja of Cochin was particularly desirous that this should be prevented, the Portuguese, though their hands were full elsewhere, sent a force to his assistance. The stone was brought back from Eddapalli to its old resting-place in Cochin; but, unfortunately for the future peace of the country, the small payments made to certain Malabar chiefs were stopped by the Portuguese, this detached them from the party of the Cochin Raja and was some years later productive of trouble.

Kunji Ali and his family who were employed by the Samuri, continued to be a thorn in the side of the Portuguese. In 1534 they had seized a brigantine off Quilon and killed all the Portuguese in her; they then rounded Cape Comorin and were with difficulty prevented from capturing the forty Portuguese at Negapatam. An expedition was, however, hurrying up the coast after them, and they had barely time to fortify themselves in a creek near Canhameira, when it was upon them. Kunji Ali's fleet was destroyed and he only escaped in disguise to Calicut. A more serious raid was that of 1537. Kunji Ali with his brother Ali Ibrahim Marakkar, and brother-in-law, Ahmad Marakkar, collected a number of foists in Panane. Ali Ibrahim with 47 foists avoided the strict blockade of Martim Afonso de Sousa, and after doing considerable damage to Portuguese trading vessels, rounded Cape Comorin. His object was to assist that one of the two factions in Ceylon that was opposed to the Portuguese, but beyond sacking Tuticorin nothing much was done. Hearing of the approach of the Portuguese, Ali Ibrahim fortified himself on the mainland, at Vedalai in the Gulf of Manaar. Martim Afonso de Sousa was baffled in his first attempt to round Cape Comorin by contrary winds, and a boat expedition which he organized failed for want of supplies; but in a third attempt he succeeded in coming to terms with the enemy. 600 Portuguese attacked the position held by 8,000 Muhamedans and defeated them, capturing their camp and its spoils, and burning or securing all their ships. The Portuguese acknowledged only to a loss of ten killed and 70 wounded Of the Muhamedans, 800 are said to have been killed, but their greatest loss was their admiral, Ali Ibrahim, who died on his overland journey to Calicut. This action was important as it allowed the Portuguese to devote all their attention to Diu, with no fear of any enemy in the rear. Martim Afonso de Sousa returned to Cochin in February 1538.

The troubles of Ormuz were chronic. The old puppet king died in 1534, and his successor, a boy of 8, was poisoned by his uncle, a Goa refugee, who was a mere tool of the Portuguese. By 1537, owing to the reiterated complaints against the Captain, D. Pedro de Castello Branco, the Governor had to remove him from his office. Correa's account of the proceedings which followed this exhibition of administrative vigour, may be quoted:[1] "D. Pedro "threw himself into working out his release, and as he had "much money he produced so many false witnesses to "contradict the evidence which condemned him, that he "upset it all, and they drew up a record divided into 4 "parts, each of 4 reams of paper, which I saw, and as "there was none to accuse him and show up the contradic- "tions, for the King's proctor likes to sleep his sleep "undisturbed and to make money, justice was lost sight "of, and D. Pedro was sent back to rob what remained "and to destroy those who had given evidence against him. "But our Lord ordered it so that this D. Pedro was robbed "on the coast by French pirates, who left him nothing and "robbed the ship, for which some of those who were going

[1] He did not return to Ormuz till 1540, but the story is ended here in order not to break the narrative.

"to Lisbon in the same ship, complained that they had "been ruined for D. Pedro's sins."[1]

After Nuno da Cunha returned from Diu to Goa in February 1537, Guzerat remained in a very disturbed state.[2] Diu was not regularly besieged, but a Guzerat force, under Ali Khan, stationed on the outskirts of the town, cut off the supply of provisions. A truce was made in July 1537, but no definite peace was concluded. On February 13th, 1538, Nuno da Cunha again reached Diu, and although nothing certain was known as to the approach of the Turks, he hurried forward the work necessary for the safety of the fort. While thus occupied there came from Ormuz a ship with a Venetian, one Duarte Catanho, on board. He had lived 20 years with the Turks, but professed to be still a Christian. He had brought certain goods for sale overland from the Red Sea to the Persian Gulf, as the Red Sea ports were closed to prevent any information reaching India of the Turkish fleet collecting in Suez. The news this man brought created extraordinary excitement among the Portuguese, and the Captain of Diu was not alone in the opinion that he ought to be poisoned: even in after years men were found to have the same opinion, for Catanho was observant, kept his ears and his eyes open, and carried with him to Europe much information which the Portuguese would have preferred to keep to themselves.[3]

The preparation of a fleet at Suez had for some years been actively in progress. The town of Shahr, in the Hadramaut, some 350 miles east of Aden, was a favourite resort

[1] Correa, III. 842.

[2] The internal disorders in Guzerat were due to a succession of puppet sovereigns with little power.

[3] Catanho went to Europe in 1538, and was for some years a channel of communication between the King of Portugal and Turkey. At length he fell under the suspicion of the former, and was imprisoned.

of those Portuguese pirates who drove their trade at the mouth of the Red Sea. These men, not only used the harbour for a refuge, but even robbed the very boats of Shahr itself. The local Shaikh, in 1535, paid off old scores by capturing a number of these freebooters, and curried favour with the Turks by sending them to Suez. At Suez the more intelligent were reserved as pilots for the fleet destined for India, and the balance sent as galley slaves to the Mediterranean, where they spread among the other miserables of their class the news of the Red Sea preparations. When therefore some of these galleys were captured by Doria, in 1536, he sent the information he had gained from the slaves to Portugal. Isaac of Cairo, when he carried the news of Bahadar's death, however, assured the King of Portugal that that event had caused the Turk to suspend his preparations, and consequently no reinforcements were sent to India; but this suspension, if it ever occurred, must have been very temporary, and the news brought by Catanho was in fact correct. It was confirmed in a curious way. Sifr Agha, whom the Portuguese had put in charge of Diu city, first secretly sent away his wife and children, and then followed himself, on April 27th, 1538.[1] Sifr Agha's flight caused a stampede among the banias, which the Captain in vain tried to stop by hanging some of them. It was not long before the meaning of his departure was known, for on June 24th he returned with Ali Khan and 19,000 men and laid siege to Diu fort. Before long the Portuguese found that their force was too small to defend their extended position, and on August 9th they retreated from the city; a retreat that was conducted in some disorder and confusion, and in which

[1] Sifr Agha was well received by the Sultan of Guzerat and made Governor of Surat, of which place he completed the fort commenced by Mustafa Rumi Khan. Sifr Agha's son also received the title of Rumi Khan from the Sultan at a later date.

there was considerable loss in artillery and munitions. The following day the close siege of the fort and of the outlying Gogala bastion began. This preliminary attack by Sifr Agha was very fortunate for the Portuguese; it showed them the weak spots in their defence, and during the delay caused by a slight wound received by Sifr Agha they had time to complete their preparations. At the commencement of the siege there were in the fort 800 Portuguese soldiers; 600 fighting slaves; 200 Goa craftsmen, and a large number of women, children and ordinary slaves: in all about 3,000 persons.

Before going further it is necessary to bring forward the history of the Turkish fleet now coming to Diu. Before Safár Khan, the envoy of Sultan Bahadar, could reach Constantinople, the death of that monarch was known there; but the Sultan of Turkey, flattered by the thought of getting a footing in India, determined to undertake an expedition. He supplied the troops and appointed to the command Sulaiman Pasha of Cairo, who had to provide the ships. Sulaiman Pasha was a eunuch, a Greek by birth, advanced in years, unwieldy from corpulence, and with all the defects of his unfortunate class. By methods familiar to oriental statescraft he gathered 72 vessels in Suez, and he supplied the fleet with artificers by the simple device of sweeping up the crews of the Venetian vessels peaceably trading in Alexandria. His armed force consisted of 1,500 Janissaries, 2,000 Turks and 3,000 other soldiers. Suez was left on June 22nd; the passage of the fleet was a terror to all the Red Sea ports, but at Aden, which was reached on August 3rd, the Pasha's hand fell heaviest. Shaikh Amr ibn Daud received him with demonstrations of pleasure, but there were certain events which Sulaiman did not forget: he remembered how one of his predecessors, angered at the conduct of this Shaikh, had sent him 100 bows, 10,000 arrows, and a cwt. of balsam, a symbolical present meaning that with the arrows he would slay him and with the balsam embalm him.[1] The unfortunate Shaikh was enticed into the flag-ship, and incontinently hanged from the yard-arm. Aden was sacked, and in the sack Mir Amrjan, who for many years had been governor under the Shaikh, was killed.

Diu was reached on September 4th, 1538. While crossing from Aden the fleet scattered in a storm, and four of the versels were wrecked on different points of Western India; it was through these wrecks that the Portuguese first learned that the fleet they dreaded was in Indian waters. Swift boats sped north and south, and warned the settlements to be ready. Sulaiman's orders were to seek out and fight the Portuguese fleet; fortunately for that nation he disobeyed his orders, and besieged Diu, which was at that time the most strongly fortified place held by the Portuguese in India. Had Sulaiman brought the Portuguese fleet to action he could have destroyed it in detail; had he even selected any port other than Diu he could have—at the cost of little trouble to himself—secured a base for operations at their expense; and even were Diu captured the defeat would not be decisive. The power of the Turks lay in their formidable artillery; their metal was heavier than that of the Portuguese, and their gunners were exceptionally well trained; in an action at sea this superiority should have given them the victory. In matchlockmen the Portuguese with their handier and more quickly loaded weapons considered themselves superior. The composition of the Turkish fleet was not homogeneous, for besides 1,500 Christian slaves from all parts of Europe who rowed on the benches of the galleys, a Venetian, Francisco, commanded ten galleys and 800 free Christian soldiers. Discipline, as far as it was maintained at all, was main-

[1] Albuquerque Cartas, p. 95. There is an account of this voyage in Ramusio, written by a Venetian who was in the Turkish fleet.

tained by the most summary methods; we hear of several hundred soldiers and sailors being hanged for one mutiny.

The weak point in the formidable combined attack that now threatened Diu was the want of solidarity between the parts of which it was composed; the only common bond between Turks and Indians was hatred of the Portuguese. Ali Khan, as commanding the Guzerat forces, wanted the Portuguese expelled to recover Diu island for the Guzerat sovereigns, consequently he refused to allow the name of the Ottoman Turk to be included in the Khutbah read in the Diu City Mosques. Sifr Agha, on the other hand, was ready to allow anything so long as his own power in Diu was assured. Sulaiman Pasha intended to establish Turkish rule with himself as head of the administration. A wreck of one of the Turkish ships strewed a cargo of saddles on the Guzerat coast, and from these the Guzeratis inferred that a sea campaign was not the only warlike operation the Turks contemplated; a land campaign could only be directed against their own or some other Muhamedan state. The fate of the Shaikh of Aden was a warning too recent to be disregarded, and the lawless conduct of the Janissaries who were landed on September 5th, was the clenching proof. Ali Khan with the forces under his command, though they did not leave the neighbourhood of Diu, withdrew from active co-operation in the siege. Sulaiman Pasha landed some heavy artillery for Sifr Agha to place in position, and passed on with the galleys to Jafirabad, on the Ranai river, to refit.

Sulaiman Pasha returned to Diu on September 24th, by which time it had become generally known that on September 11th, D. Garcia de Noronha, nephew of the great Albuquerque, had reached Goa bar as viceroy, and had superseded Nuno da Cunha. Nuno da Cunha, who was never promoted to a higher rank than that of Governor, felt deeply the slight put on him by his supersession at such a critical moment by an almost untried man; while the other residents in India were disgusted to find that at such a time they had to follow a man whom they did not know and who did not know them; subsequent events justified their resentment. Nuno da Cunha's feelings also were exasperated by the treatment he received from his successor, for he was not allowed to return home in a king's, or even in a contractor's, ship; he had to hire a private vessel. The progress of the quarrel may be traced in Nuno da Cunha's own letters.[1] In the last of these, written just before he left India, the varnish of politeness even had disappeared. Some of his complaints almost rise to dignity; much is the mere outpouring of an angry man. "My mother bore me," rails the veteran, "to be a great captain, and not your lascar."[2]

With his body enfeebled by his long service and his mind disturbed by these annoyances, Nuno da Cunha was seized, soon after he sailed, with an illness which, fortunately for himself, proved fatal. By his own special orders he was buried at sea with two chambers of a falcon tied to his feet, and equally by his orders, the king was paid for the two used,—the king deserved the scorn of the order. At Terceira the ship was boarded by a royal officer with a set of irons, and orders to bring the late governor home in them. Failing even the body of their master, his servants were imprisoned and not released for many months. The belief in Nuno da Cunha's wealth had set envious tongues wagging, and even Garcia de Noronha had not thought it beneath him to send home a speedy vessel with information intended to damage his predecessor's character. The king of Portugal demeaned himself to open Nuno da Cunha's private letters, to search the house of his widow, and to

1 Barros, IV. 10 c. 20 and 21.

2 "Lascar" here means a common soldier.

appropriate what he found there. Nuno da Cunha was licentious in private life, and cunning rather than able; he was successful in carrying out what he undertook, and yet it is impossible to trace in any event of his time a guiding hand. He did not create opportunities—he availed himself of those that offered.

CHAPTER XII

D. GARCIA DE NORONHA, VICEROY, 1538-1540. D. ESTAVÂO DA GAMA, GOVERNOR, 1540-1542

D. Garcia de Noronha—D. Garcia de Noronha, who was selected as the third Viceroy of India,—a dignity to which his illustrious uncle Albuquerque never attained—was a man of 60 years of age, the grandson of an archbishop of Lisbon, poor with a large family to be provided for. He had already been in India with his uncle. To man the 11 ships of his fleet extraordinary expedients were adopted, for so scarce were men in Portugal that outlaws had to be tempted in and prisoners released by a pardon, general to all offenders save those against religion and the king. Those condemned to death were sent to India in perpetual banishment, and those condemned to imprisonment for longer or shorter periods: there is on record the case of one Manuel de Mendoça who had been sentenced to banishment for nine years, and was allowed to keep his term by taking his two brothers with him for three years, this thrice three years being accounted equal to one punishment of nine. Even by these means the force collected was of such inferior quality that they were described as a lot of tattered boys without beards, and men fit for nothing in the world, who had not a sword among them. [1]

There had been before this time Roman Catholic Bishops

[1] D. João de Castro made his first voyage to India in this fleet.

in India; the names of Duarte Nunes titular bishop of Laodicea, who came out in 1515; D. Diogo, who came out in 1520; D. Martinho, in 1523, and D. Fernando Vaqueiro, (who died at Ormuz in 1535,) in 1532, are on record; but in this fleet there came D. Joâo d'Albuquerque, the first Bishop of Goa, which had been made a bishopric by a Bull of Pope Paul III, of November 3rd, 1534. He assumed jurisdiction, not only over followers of the Romish, but also over those of the Nestorian Church. The church of St. Catherine was made a cathedral. On the arrival of the new Viceroy at Goa, on September 11th, he found some seventy or eighty vessels in the harbour which had been collected for the relief of Diu, to the siege of which we must now return.

The fortress of Diu stands on the eastern end of the island of that name, while the western side is occupied by the town. On the further side of the creek that makes Diu an island stands the suburb of Gogala, which, from the events of Almeida's time, was known to the Portuguese as Villa dos Rumes. Here the Portuguese had an outwork. From a rock in mid-channel rose an isolated fort that guarded the entrance. On the northern side of the fortress, where alone the enemy could bring troops to bear with effect, the two eastern bastions were known as Garcia de Sa's (nearest the creek) and St. Thomas. The Gogala outwork was held by a weak force of 70 or 80 men; the fortress and the isolated fort were held in strength. On September 28th the Turkish galleys returned, after careening, from Jafirabad, and passed slowly in single file, led by Yusaf Ahmad, the second in command, their sails showing in quarters white and red, in front of the fort, discharging their artillery. The fortress replied, but the garrison suffered from their own firing far more severely than from that of the enemy; through a mistake committed when Bahadar's munitions were brought into the fort, the finer matchlock powder had got mixed with the coarser artillery powder and burst the guns, killing several of those serving them. In this siege the inefficiency of the Turkish galleys was very marked; it is intelligible that they would not care to attack stone walls, but they did not even keep the blockade, and boats were continually passing to and fro.

The brunt of the first attack fell on the Gogala outwork; it capitulated after it had been battered into a shapeless mass. Under the capitulations the garrison were to be allowed to enter the fort, but after the surrender Sulaiman coolly broke them, saying the Portuguese would be better outside the fortress than inside where he should be sure to kill them; they were sent to the galleys. After the capture of the outwork a regular summons and defiance were exchanged; manners have altered, and the language then thought heroic would now render the user liable to a fine in a police court. By Oct. 4th the Turks had erected and armed 6 batteries, at distances varying from 60 to 150 paces from the land face of the fort, and some of the guns they mounted threw cast iron balls of 60 to 100 lbs. weight. This powerful artillery completely mastered that of the Portuguese.

On October 5th fire was opened on Garcia de Sa's bastion, and it was not long before the wall was breached, the fight raged daily over this breach during all October. Driven to construct inner lines of defence as each wall was in turn battered down, at the end the Portuguese only held about a third of the original bastion, but from it they were never dislodged. The breach was narrow, and at the foot the defenders lighted a large fire as an extra impediment to stormers; some of the most noteworthy incidents of this great defence gather round this fire. The Portuguese over their low breast-wall kept it together with long hooks; the enemy on their side used hooks to scatter it. Ever and again two opposing hooks would grapple and then came a grim struggle, either side trying to pull the other into the flames. At the same time not a day passed but an attempt was made to storm the breach, and often more than one; the besieged were thus kept always on the alert by the fresh troops the besiegers could from their numbers bring against them.

Stories of individual adventure and heroism abound. There is the story of Fonseca, who held the breach, fighting on with his left hand after his right had been shattered by a musket ball; of Joâo Gil, the small captain's boy, who followed the huge Muhamedan into the water almost out of his depth and who still could not reach him, and was nonplussed until he heard his master's voice: "The point, John, the point"; of Penteado who left the breach to get his wound dressed by the surgeon, but finding the waiting for his turn long, returned to the fight to be again sent back with a severer wound; but before the surgeon even saw him the roar of the breach again drew him, and this third time he had to be carried with his fresh wound out of the press; and of the man unknown, who, in the heat of the fight, found his bullets expended and fired a loose tooth at the enemy rather than miss a chance of doing him harm.

The women and children equalled the men in devotion and excelled them in ferocity. They expended their ferocity on unfortunate prisoners and slaves; in their devotion, however, they undertook all the fetching and carrying of wood, water, earth, stones, building of walls, tending of sick, and everything that could relieve the soldiers from all save actual fighting, but even in the thick of the struggle they were found carrying water and food and binding up wounds. D. Isabel de Veiga and Anna Fernandes the wife of the surgeon, hobbling on her stick, are handed down to us as those who organized the women.[1] From time to time small reinforcements were thrown into the fort, but the water was bad and the garrison suffered much from scurvy, and when the final attack was repulsed on November 4th there were only 40 men fit for duty, but very few serviceable arms, and the only powder available for powder pots, the chief defensive weapon of the Portuguese, was that drawn from the charges of the big guns.

The protracted defence of the Portuguese had accentuated the differences between the Turks and the Guzeratis. Owing to their own excesses the strangers could not even get the necessary supplies, and all attempts to enlist the sympathies of the southern Muhamedan states on behalf of the Turks had signally failed. Sulaiman Pasha withdrew his artillery, embarked, and was out of sight on the morning of November 6th. At the last his movements had been accelerated by the approach of a convoy of foists with supplies from Goa, which his fears converted into the Viceroy's relieving force. He left behind him 400 wounded men, and his homeward voyage was marked by cruelties as gross as those which stained his outward one. On the departure of the Turks the Guzerati forces removed from the neighbourhood. The relieving force was, however, only a smal body under Antonio da Silva, which was welcomed by the garrison; but before long there began a bitter feud as to whether the defence had driven away the enemy and thus raised the siege, or whether that result was due to the relieving force. Whichever view we take, this defence of Diu ranks very high among sieges, and the people of Portugal my look back on it with pride.

The news of the retreat of the Turks was received at

[1] Isabel de Veiga's name appears in Barros. His grandson married her grand-daughter.

Goa with angry mutterings. By bringing in outlaws with pardons and by raising a forced loan among the Portuguese,[1] Garcia de Noronha had collected 180 vessels and 5,000 fighting men, but the leader had no stomach for the fight. The rank and file were correct in their view, the Guzerat trouble was only postponed, and a notable opportunity had been thrown away through timidity and irresolution. Antonio da Silveira, the hero of the siege, was well received in Portugal, and the fame of his defence spread throughout Europe. Antonio himself was at one time spoken of as a possible Governor of India, but he was a spendthrift, and this reputation spoiled his chance; he ran through his own fortune and his wife's, and died poor.

On November 20th the Viceroy started for Diu with a fleet of 90 sail.[2] He proceeded north at a leisurely pace, anchoring every night, and only reached Diu in January 1539, and then with only part of his fleet, for nearly half of the vessels had been scattered or lost in a great storm. The ruins of the fortress were as the Turks had left them, and the first task of the Viceroy was to rebuild the place, which was made stronger even than before. Communications were opened with the Sultan of Guzerat, and peace was signed with him on March 11th, 1539.[3] Under its terms, a wall of 4 cubits high was to be erected between the fortress and the town; the custom-house receipts were to be pooled, and one-third[4] was to be paid to the Portuguese. Although this peace was concluded, the relations of the Portuguese with the Muhamedans, especially with those left behind by

[1] Correa thought that in 1550, when he wrote, the whole of the forced loan had not been paid off, and such a loan was never attempted again. It became complicated with the question of compensation to the masters for the price of fighting slaves killed.

[2] João de Castro has left a log of this voyage which was printed in 1843.

[3] See treaty in Botelho Tombo, p. 229.

[4] Altered to one-half in time of Estavão da Gama.—Botelho Tombo, p. 232.

the Turks, remained very bad; an extraordinary instance is the hog-hunting story in Correa.[1]

All the combinations to which the Samuri had trusted to enable him to resist the growing power of the Portuguese having failed, he was compelled to sue for peace, and to get it had to yield all the points in dispute. In exchange he was allowed to send certain merchandise on favourable terms to Europe and receive other goods in exchange; but he never enjoyed the most favourable of these stipulations—that, namely, referring to pepper, for as it affected a royal monopoly it had to be referred to the King of Portugal, who refused to ratify it.

During all this time matters in India had been going from bad to worse. The Viceroy had—as he said—come to India to get the reward of his 50 years' service. He paid no salaries, as he expected Government servants to live out of their offices. Everything that he could sell he sold—offices, voyages, or pardons; and even when he had sold to one man he was quite ready to sell the same thing at a higher price to the next, and not return the first his money. All through the rains of 1539 he hardly left his house; after the rains were over his health grew gradually worse, yet indoors or out, ill or well, his one thought was to make money, that, at his advanced age and in his state of health, he could never enjoy.[2] Yet if avarice was a blot on his character it was not the only one. One night, early in April 1540, there was a street row in Goa and swords were drawn, one man was slain across the Viceroy's threshold. Though the actual murderer escaped, his companion,

[1] Correa, IV. 89.

[2] D. Christovâo da Gama in a letter to the King, of Nov. 18th, 1540, speaks in the highest terms of Joâo de Castro, who kept everything straight in spite of the "comdysâo forte" of D. Garcia. See Francisco de S. Luiz edition of Andrade's life of Joâo de Castro, p. 313.

a new Christian, Francisco de Veiga, was captured. The Viceroy's house had been desecrated; it was treason to have struck the blow, and the man must be hanged without process or trial. In vain the Bishop and the chief officials pointed out the injustice and begged for a reprieve. With his hands so feeble that his servants had to guide the pen, the Viceroy ordered his immediate execution, and never left gazing out of the window till he saw the man hanged there before him. That night (April 3rd) he died. When the successions were opened Estavâo da Gama, second son of D. Vasco da Gama, who had just returned from a term of service as Captain of Malacca, was found to be the new Governor.

D. Estavâo da Gama.—Estavâo da Gama, at the time of his elevation a man of from 35 to 37 years of age, first went to India with his father in 1524. He had been Captain of Malacca for five years, during which time he had amassed considerable wealth, and fearful lest his new dignity should tempt slanderers to blacken his good name, he had an inventory of his property taken by State officials, both when he took over and when he gave over charge of his office; it was found that his term as Governor had cost him £12,000 from his private purse. He was a contrast to his predecessor, physically and morally; he was below the middle height, the other was exceptionally tall; he was liberal, just and prudent, the other was the embodiment of avarice and cruelty. He found the dockyards depleted, and to carry out the royal orders to visit Suez and burn the galleys there he had to equip a fresh fleet. He placed the chief fortresses in a condition to repel any sudden attack, and he determined, should the Turks not return to India before October, to search them out in the Red Sea.

The gravest anxiety of the Governor was, however, due to the state of Goa itself. In this year the great famine that had been threatening the whole East for some years reached its culminating point, and by this famine Goa, though not in the most affected tract, suffered. On the Coromandel coast, where it was most severe, man ate man, and in the Portuguese settlement of Negapatam 15 or 20 dead bodies—mere skeletons—were found every day. It is told that men and women drowned themselves in troops rather than any longer face the miseries of the world.[1] The famine extended even to the east coast of the Red Sea; the Turkish galleys could not be fitted out, and the Turks left in Aden deserted that place for the east coast of Africa, where they assisted the Shaikh of Zeila against the Abyssinians. Although Goa was not in the worst part of the famine tract, still the effects of the scarcity had been intensified by the acts of Garcia de Noronha, who had refused or neglected to pay the government servants their salaries. It was as a result of this famine that, in 1543, there was such an outbreak of cholera in Goa that the tolling of the bell was for the time discontinued, and two churches were made parish churches to meet the extra work of the funerals.[2]

All through 1539 the condition of Goa city had been very bad; seven hundred of its small population died of disease in 4 months, while robberies and murders were of nearly daily occurrence. In 1540 matters grew still worse. A man taken under the Governor's protection was followed by his adversary in a private quarrel, that had its origin

[1] D. Joâo de Castro's letter to D. Luis, of Oct. 30th, 1540, Investigador Portuguez, Vol. XVI. p. 279. He estimates that two-thirds of the population of the Vijayanagara state died.

[2] See very remarkable description, Correa, IV. 288.

in a low slum of the city, and killed almost in the Governor's house.[1]

Gonçalo Vaz Coutinho, a fidalgo of some note, was confined with several other persons of position as great malefactors as himself, in the Goa jail. By the help of a slave girl of great beauty Coutinho won over a subordinate official, and on a fixed day, when all the friends of the prisoners were waiting outside to help, the doors were flung open, and in broad daylight the prisoners marched down to the water's edge. There were so many that all could not crowd into the one boat provided, but, some inside, some swimming beside it, all crossed to the mainland and escaped, no one much trying to stop them. Coutinho expected his pardon, but it never came, and he died a renegade in the service of the Adil Shah whose troops he commanded against his own countrymen.

One of the difficulties of dealing with this state of affairs lay in the clan spirit of the Portuguese. If an offender could in any way claim the protection of a fidalgo, punishment was out of the question. An attempt of the Governor to bring the fidalgoes to a better course of action did result in some temporary improvement, but the feeling of clan sympathy was too deep to be eradicated at once. Thus in the expedition of Estavâo da Gama to Suez, at a point between Suakin and the mouth of the Gulf of Suez, where the fleet stopped for water, two soldiers fought a duel and one was left for dead. His adversary ran to the boat of his captain, and this boat, accompanied by all those of his friends, drew off and anchored some distance out to protect the man from the consequences of his act. As the wounded man recovered, however, the incident ended here. These

[1] The murderer and a companion became pirates on the African coast. Martim Afonso de Sousa, when he passed Mozambique, gave the companion his pardon and took him back to India.

disorders were not confined to Goa. In the rains of 1539 150 soldiers mutinied in Diu, took possession of one of the bastions and turned its guns against their own fortress; until they were bribed they refused to return to their duty. [1]

The preparations for the Red Sea expedition continued during the rains, and the crews were selected with unusual care, for the Governor in person sat at the table to superintend the payment of advances. A fleet of 72 sail was got ready, and its departure was preceded by a sermon from the Bishop and by a procession to the beach. Sped by the episcopal benediction, it started on January 1st, 1541. Of this expedition D. Joâo de Castro has left us a most valuable log. [2] On February 11th the whole fleet, save one ship lost in crossing the Arabian Sea, arrived in safety at Massowah, where the seaboard was held by Muhamedan tribes, whose chief fled at the approach of the Portuguese. A message was sent after him to supply two pilots to Suez and pay £5,000, or his country would be destroyed; but as the Chief had not £20 in his possession, no country to destroy, and no pilots for Suez, the Portuguese had to be content with two pilots for Suakin. The sea beyond Massowah was as yet untraversed by Portuguese ships.

On February 20th Estavâo da Gama, leaving the large vessels under Manuel da Gama to await his return, started for Suakin. When D. Christovâo da Gama with the advanced guard reached there on Feb. 22nd, he surrounded the island, but found the town already deserted. Suakin struck the Portuguese by its size and apparent prosperity. De Castro considered that it equalled if it did not exceed all other ports in the security of the harbour, the facilities for

[1] "I would have seen them dead, and the site of the fortress sown with salt," says D. Joâo de Castro.—Letter to D. Luis, October 30th, 1540, Investigador Portuguez, Vol. XVI. p. 279.

[2] Printed in 1833.

loading and unloading cargoes, and the natural strength of the site. The harbour was closed all round, difficult of access, the bottom mud, with a depth of from five to seven fathoms, with little tide. The city covered the whole of the island, and ships could lie all round with their bows on shore, and be loaded or unloaded over a plank;[1] its commerce was with all the then known world. The Chief of the City was a merchant, and the force necessary to keep the peace consisted of 40 Turks paid by the traders. The Sultan of Turkey took half the customs' dues. The Governor arrived on March 1st to find his brother attempting to exact a ransom from the town. On the 8th, the camp to which the townspeople had fled on the approach of the fleet was captured without much resistance, and such was the enormous amount of spoil that the Portuguese fell out among themselves. The city and ships were burned, and on March 10th, leaving the destruction they had caused behind them, the adventurers went on their way. The delay was fatal to the success of the expedition, for information sent up the coast alarmed the whole littoral and reached Suez in time to allow a defensive force to be collected.[2]

Up to the end of March progress had been so slow that it was clear that to reach Suez at all a still further selection must be made. Sixteen of the lightest vessels and two hundred and fifty men were chosen to go on, the balance, much to their discontent—a discontent which a speech in the Governor's very best manner did little to allay—had to return to Massowah. On April 14th Da Gama reached Kosseir, described as the most miserable spot on the earth, with no living green thing, a place that derived its sole importance from being the nearest point on the Red Sea

[1] Roteiro, p. 95.
[2] They tracked two camels and some men along the shore.—Roteiro, p. 174.

to the Nile;[1] here the expedition found some provisions to replenish their stocks. Leaving on the 18th, they crossed from Shadwan to Tor on the 21st. The town of Tor was spared in honour of the Church and Monastery of St. Catherine, both belonging to the Greek Church, whose followers then formed an important part of the population of that coast. The Christians of Tor were singularly suspicious of their fellow Christians the Portuguese. Fearing lest they should attempt to carry off their most cherished possession, the body of their saint, from Mount Sinai, they told an elaborate tale. With much grief and emotion they related the long persecution of the surrounding Arabs, which had driven them four months before to carry the body of Saint Catherine in solemn procession to Cairo, where they had deposited it in safety. The whole tale was fiction.[2] On their return the Portuguese did not revisit Tor, but put in some miles to the south, and got water from shallow brackish wells, dug on the shore. So important an event, however, was the arrival at Tor considered, that many cavaliers sought the honour of knighthood there, and by the special order of Estavâo da Gama it was recorded on his tombstone at Vidigueira, as the one action of his life worthy of remembrance, that he had made knights at the foot of Mount Sinai.

Leaving Tor on April 22nd, Suez was sighted on April 26th. Suez at that time consisted of many ruins and some thirty or forty straw huts; the only drinking water was obtained from brackish wells seven miles distant. Since the arrival of the Portuguese in India its importance as a commercial port had almost disappeared, but the presence

[1] Roteiro, p. 187. De Castro grows philosophical over it and says the inhabitants were probably annoyed at the Portuguese for burning their miserable hovels, and considered themselves in exile amid the riches of the Nile valley.

[2] Roteiro, p. 200.

there of the galleys had during recent years given the place the appearance of some activity. When the Portuguese advanced on April 27th they found that there were fifty galleys drawn up on either side of a tongue of land, the sea approach was guarded by a heavy battery, and a canal, cut across the root of the tongue, protected them on the land side. [1] The enemy showed in such overwhelming force that no attempt even was made to land. On April 28th, fearing lest the Muhamedans should turn the tables on them and attack them, the small force of Portuguese sped down the Gulf of Suez before the north wind.

When the discomfited expedition returned to Massowah early in June, the Governor found that matters had not been going on well during his absence. The climate was insalubrious, and among the numerous sick many had died; there was little food and that bad, even men with money in their hands could buy little on that inhospitable shore. João Bermudes, [2] the so-called Abyssinian patriarch, who was returning after his visit to Portugal, talked glibly of

[1] Roteiro, p. 214.

[2] The enigmatical person called João Bermudes deserves a mention. He left Portugal, still a youth, in 1515, with Lopo Soares, and entered Abyssinia as a surgeon, in the train of D. Rodrigo de Lima, in 1520. He did not return with the embassy. He published an account of his life in 1565 (reprinted 1875), in which there are chronological difficulties. He says that on the death of the Abuna Mark, the Emperor of Abyssinia elected him patriarch, with all due ceremonies, and sent him by Jerusalem and Constantinople to Rome; that the Turks detained him and cut off part of his tongue, but that eventually he reached Rome, where Paul III recognised his election and consecrated him. He reached Portugal in 1535 or 1536, and was in this fleet. He does not appear to have been recognised as patriarch by all the Abyssinians, and he escaped from that country in 1559, returned to Portugal after trying life on St. Helena for a year, where escaped slaves prevented his being a hermit, and died in Portugal an old man in 1570. In his old age he had no papers to show sceptics, and his memory appears to have been defective; but strangest of all, João III of Portugal, writing on March 13th, 1546, (Academy edition of Vida de João de Castro, p. 443) says that he knows that Bermudes is a priest, but naught of the powers he claimed to have got from the Pope.

the fertility beyond the mountains and the warm welcome the Portuguese would meet with there. The summary hanging of five deserters did not turn the famished Portuguese; they formed a body of a hundred men, well armed and with a flag and some musical instruments; an attempt by Manuel da Gama to stop them cost him his life. But the first night's march of the ill-found men, ignorant of the necessaries of African travel, found them worn out with a thirst there was nothing to quench. They fell an easy prey to the Muhamedans, and of the whole number only two, who escaped death by shamming it, ever returned. This catastrophe deprived the Portuguese of a hope, but did not reconcile them to their lot.

The condition of the Abyssinian kingdom was at this time nearly desperate. Hostilities had continued for about ten years between the Muhamedan chief of Zeila and the Abyssinians, and the latter, unable to face the matchlocks of the Muhamedans, had been defeated in several pitched battles. The Royal Family was at length driven to the refuge of an inaccessible mountain stronghold known as that of the Jews. Urgent calls for help were awaiting Estavâo da Gama's return to Massowah. It was determined to land the Governor's younger brother, Christovâo da Gama, with four hundred men, to proceed to the help of the Abyssinians, and the brothers parted for the last time on July 7th.

Leaving out of account the enterprise and love ot adventure, the expedition to the Red Sea considered merely with reference to its object of destroying the Turkish galleys, was badly executed. As the force was too small to overcome even a moderate resistance, the only chance of success lay in a quick dash; the approach to Suez was, however, advertised and delayed by sacking every town on the road. The expedition of D. Christovâo da Gama to the assistance of the Abyssinians, forcing its way among unknown savages and cut off from all chance of support, shows certainly those daring qualities that led the Portuguese to discover the sea route to India, but it also shows the defects that brought ruin on their power. The only immediate result, beyond extending geographical knowledge, of this raid to Suez, for it was no more, was to cover the Red Sea with Turkish galleys to keep out the Portuguese and to intercept any help for D. Christovâo da Gama.

The story of the unfortunate Abyssinian expedition may be shortly told. Hopeless though the enterprise was from the first, the motives that actuated those engaged in it were at least sullied by no sordid taint. The leader had many of the lovable qualities of his uncle, Paulo da Gama, who died on his return from the first voyage to India. Brave to temerity he was the first when the fight was over to help bind up the wounds of his men. Were the work never so hard he was always there to share the labours of the common soldier. After his death his followers would elect no other leader—they were still the soldiers of Christovâo da Gama, and as such they fought and conquered. Until August 8th, 1542, he was successful in his encounters, but on that day he was attacked by an overwhelming force. With many of his men dead, his camp captured, a wound in his leg and his right arm broken, escape was impossible; he spent that night in a thicket, but was taken the next day, tortured and killed. Nine months later (Feb. 1545) the remnant of the expedition—150 strong—in company with the King of Abyssinia, attacked the Muhamedans and routed them with the loss of their chief. As a consequence of this victory the Abyssinians recovered their country. In January 1544 Miguel de Castanhoso, the historian of the expedition,[1]

[1] Castanhoso's narrative has been reprinted by the Lisbon Academy, in the Collecçao de Opusculos Reimpressos. As illustrating Portuguese judicial

returned to India, and five others were carried to India at different times by passing vessels. One of these latter, known as Diogo Dias of the Preste, returned in 1553 to Abyssinia with a priest, sent to enquire into the desire of the Ethiopian Christians to join the Romish Church. At that time 93 Portuguese were still alive, settled and married in the country.

Estavâo da Gama passed Aden on July 25th, and made for Goa before the full force of the south-west monsoon. Some of the weaker ships bore up for the Arabian coast; a few vessels were lost, but the rest made Goa on August 8th. The fleet that carried Martim Afonso de Sousa, the new Governor, left Portugal in 1541, but did not reach India the same year. Martim Afonso de Sousa's selection was the result of an intrigue of several months' duration, but he was not a new man to India, as he had commanded at sea there during several years of Nuno da Cunha's term. His fleet had been stripped to send reinforcements to Africa, but it is noteworthy as he brought out three Jesuits, Francis Xavier, Father Paul of Camerino, and Mancias, a Portuguese not yet ordained. At Mozambique where the fleet arrived too late to cross, precautions were taken lest news of his approach should reach India; Alvaro d'Ataide, the brother of Estavâo da Gama, was even removed from his ship and imprisoned.

Martim Afonso de Sousa started from Mozambique for India in a handy ship on March 15th, 1542, leaving the heavier vessels to follow later, and reached Goa on May

methods, it is told that Diogo de Reynoso, who brought back Castanhoso, was, on his return, tried for going into the Red Sea against orders, and condemned to death. He pleaded ordination, but it was rejected for want of proof; he then pleaded that he was under age, and it was allowed and he was pardoned. The fact was that the condemnation was a farce to satisfy the Turks with whom the Portuguese were trying to patch up a peace, one condition of which was that they would not enter the Red Sea.

6th. The new Governor's conduct was extraordinary in the extreme,—not only did he arrange for a secret arrival, but he also, without warning, sent agents to seize all books of accounts, and keys of treasure chests, rather as if he were in pursuit of a fraudulent bank clerk than as if he were a new governor taking over charge from a retiring one. It was fortunate that Estavâo da Gama was a man of great prudence, and that the King of Portugal had, by a special patent, provided him with the powers of a goverhor to be exercised within the Castle of Panjim, or there might have been a repetition of the scandals that had disgraced other occasions of the change of government. Da Gama remained in Panjim, refusing to be drawn into any discussions as to Indian affairs, and refusing even to intercede for the release of his brother Alvaro d'Ataide, who was for no cause whatever imprisoned for several months. After his return to Europe, as the King was offended at his refusing to marry a wife of his choosing, he left Portugal and lived and died unmarried in Venice. After his death his body was removed to his old home at Vidigueira.

CHAPTER XIII

Martim Afonso de Sousa, Governor, 1542-1545. Simão Botelho, Comptroller of Revenue

Martim Afonso de Sousa.—In Martim Afonso de Sousa Portuguese India had one of the worst governors that up to that date had afflicted it. The government, if such it could be called, became little more than an organization for robbery. De Sousa either began with some rudimentary ideas of justice, or, what is more probable as the orders are isolated, adopted some from his predecessors. By the old law, when a native of the country died without sons, even if he had daughters all his property movable and immovable reverted to the King. The Governor, soon after he reached India, ordered that in such cases the immovable property should follow the old rule, but that the movable should be divided among the daughters. Later, however, thinking that he had been too liberal, he qualified this by deciding that all movable property over £16 in value was immovable property, which did not leave much to be thankful for. In another order he abolished a cess "Coshi Varado;" we are not given his second thoughts on this, but any way the cess was not one he collected.[1] Rumours of

[1] Khushiburd—gift to cause contentment. For the orders referred to see Ar. Port. Or., Fasc. 5, Nos. 76, 77, 78; see also No. 799 of October 16th, 1579, and No. 842 of July 18th, 1584—by the former of the two last orders the cess was in a time of great need reimposed, not only in Goa, but also in Salsette, by the latter it was finally abolished.

the appearance of the Turks were still current, and to some extent affected the policy of the Governor, but during his time, at least, they never actually came.

The first town which De Sousa attacked was Bhatkal, belonging to the friendly power of Vijayanagara, under the pretence that some corsairs had taken shelter there. The townspeople offered every satisfaction, but the negotiations dragged. There were some guards in the town, with whom the shore-going men of the fleet had constant quarrels. At last one of the Portuguese was killed, trying to take violently some cloth from a shop; riots followed in which several more Portuguese were killed, and that night the inhabitants abandoned the place to its fate. The next morning the Governor and his men sacked it as if it were an enemy's town conquered in war; the very Portuguese factor who lived there had difficulty in saving his own property. When, however, the Governor's immediate following began to rob the other Portuguese of that which they had robbed, there ensued a furious fight with swords and pikes. The Governor did his best, but though he belaboured both sides equally with his stick and his tongue, he could not quell the disturbance before all the property was spoiled and wasted. The Bhatkal men took heart of grace at this sight and returned; the soldiers,—the original robbers, who had now been robbed—refused to stay; there was a disgraceful panic, and many of the Portuguese were killed, and more drowned, trying to get on board the boats. Skirmishing continued for 8 days longer till the unfortunate townspeople had nothing more to lose. This was the treatment of the town of a Hindu ally.

In his treatment of Ormuz, De Sousa perhaps considered that he was following out a line of policy settled by his predecessors, though he certainly improved on their methods. At the point to which the story has been told, (1529)

Nuno da Cunha had just raised the annual tribute to £33,000. In the 12 years that had elapsed since that time the King had not, as it was perhaps known that he would not, succeeded in paying the whole demand in any one year, and the balance against him amounted to over £140,000. In 1541 the unfortunate King of Ormuz had been deported to Goa for the nominal reason that he was out of his mind; the proof that he had given of it was that he had tried to become acquainted with the true state of his finances; for between his own minister and the Captain of the fortress but little of the income reached either himself or the King of Portugal.

Arrived at Goa the King was loud in his complaints of the conduct of the Captain, and as these complaints were supported by others from Ormuz itself, De Sousa despatched his secretary to make enquiries. There was a satisfactory sum of money to be received by the Governor, and a satisfactory report of the Captain's conduct to be read from the secretary. The unfortunate King had to cede the Ormuz custom-house and all its income, and consent to receive a pittance in return. The order embodying this is dated February 27th, 1543.[1] The Portuguese made a clean sweep of all sources of revenue, including even the local tavern for the sale of country liquor, this last spoliation touched the King more than all else. The tavern had been opened at the coming of the Portuguese; Albuquerque left one Gaspar Pires, as an interpreter with the King, and gave him as a source of livelihood the tavern, then worth some £60 a year. When the tavern—still known as Gaspar's house—got more valuable, the Kings of Ormuz gave the interpreters their £60 a year in money and bestowed the tavern on any person whom they designed specially to

[1] Botelho, so full on all similar arrangements, is curiously silent on this—was he perhaps ashamed of it? Couto, V. 9. 5, preserves it for us.

honour. It was worth, when the Portuguese took it, some £1,600 a year.

The King of Ormuz certainly carried his complaint to the King of Portugal, but the relief he received was ludicrously inadequate. The King of Portugal's orders entirely affected subordinates, they ruled that the houses of his brother of Ormuz must not be forcibly occupied, that rent must always be paid when a house was taken, and that no demands were to be made for presents when a private visit was paid to him. It is interesting, as showing previous practice, that it was necessary to say that, in future, pigs should not be allowed to wander about the King's palace. These orders are only noteworthy as showing that the complaints did reach the King of Portugal, and that he is directly responsible that the evils complained of were not redressed.[1] Soon after the concession of the custom-house had been wrung from the King, he died and a boy was raised to the dangerous dignity; that the King was poisoned appears to have been notorious, but no enquiry was made.

The Governor's next exploit ranks high even among those of Martim Afonso de Sousa. The bewildered historians have supposed royal orders to account for it, but those orders have never been produced or quoted. The Conjeveram temples stand some 40 miles inland from Madras, and were at the time of which we are writing, in the territory of the Raja of Vijayanagara. They were visited regularly by the Rajas themselves, and there was a fair, partly religious and partly mercantile, of the character common all over India, held at the full moon of the month of August.[2] Kanci, as it is called in the sacred writings,[3] is one of the 7 holy

[1] Ar. Port. Or., Fasc. 5, Nos. 81, 82, 84.
[2] More accurately at the Puranmasi of Bhadon.
[3] Conjeveram is Kanci puram.

places of India, ranking with Benares, Mathura, Hardwar, Ajudhya, Dwarka and Ujain. The Portuguese calculated the attendance at the fair as 3 or 4 millions.[1] This number was perhaps exaggerated, but at that time the Muhamedans had not penetrated to the south of India, and the attendance was probably large, at the present day it averages half a million. Enriched by this annual stream of pilgrims, and endowed by the munificence of the Hindu Rajas of Vijayanagara, the wealth of the temples, two of the largest of which had been built only 35 years before, in 1509, was very great.

It is possible that rumours of the wealth of these temples had reached Portugal, it is certain that they must have reached Martim Afonso de Sousa when he held the command on the Coromandel Coast in the time of Nuno da Cunha, and although they were in the territory of, and venerated by, an ally, De Sousa, in the rains of 1543, organized an expedition to rob them.[2] As such an attack would rouse the whole coast, preparations were made to carry off the relics of St. Thomas, and the Portuguese, mostly outlaws, that trafficked to the east of Cape Comorin. The fleet which sailed early in September was scattered and delayed by a storm, and although its destination was supposed to be a profound secret, enough had leaked out to make the Raja of Vijayanagara uneasy. When, therefore, the Portuguese rounded Cape Comorin they found so large a force collected that any attack was out of the question. As

[1] Correa is nothing if not descriptive. He says he had attended the fair; that every pilgrim had to have his head shaved. The barbers sat under some large trees, and the heaps of hair hid them. These heaps sold for £200 a year, to make false hair. The heap of money the pilgrims left soon grew as high as 10 measures of wheat.—Correa, IV. 301.

[2] Though not excusing this expedition, some explanation may possibly be found for its conception in the order of the King of Portugal, in 1540. to destroy all Hindu temples in the island of Goa.

a bandit who had not been glorified by success, De Sousa returned with his force to Kayankulam.

On this coast, between Cochin and Quilon, the Portuguese had been settled for over 40 years, and they depended upon the goodwill of the residents for the supply of the merchandise which was the bait that drew them to the East. This did not prevent De Sousa from leading an expedition to attack the temple of "Tebelicare," a few miles inland, which local information reported to be full of gold. There were two *jangadas* attached to his temple, but one with almost all the guards had gone to the south when the movements of the Portuguese first attracted attention. An offer of £12,000 down failed to turn the Governor from his intention, and before nightfall the temple was reached. The building was of the common design, surrounded by a wall, with a few straw huts outside. The Governor and his immediate following went inside the temple and shut the door; those outside the buildings passed a miserable night enough, a prey to every imaginable horror—the fall of a shield nearly caused a stampede. Inside, the Governor and his friends spent the time in torturing the Brahmins of the temple and in digging up the floor. It was never known exactly what was found, a gold patten worth £50 was all that was ever shown, but as two barrels of matchlock powder were emptied and the barrels passed in, and as afterwards they each required eight slaves in relays to carry them, scandalous tongues were busy. When in the morning they started on their return journey, a Nair, dressed with scrupulous care with all his ornaments, followed by 10 or 12 others, flung himself on the Portuguese ranks. It was the remaining *jangada* with the relatives whom he could collect who thus tried to wipe out by their deaths the stain upon their honour. During their retreat the Portuguese were harassed by the country-people and suffered a loss of thirty killed and 150 wounded, but on the way they sacked another temple, whence was obtained some small amount in silver coins to distribute among the soldiery.

There was at this time another dispute in progress, out of which the peculiar talents of the Governor enabled him to extract more profit even than from sacking temples. Ibrahim Adil Shah (1535—1557) was at this time reigning in Bijapur; he was personally unpopular, and Assad Khan of Belgaum, now old and infirm, was the object of his especial fear and dislike. Assad Khan had never lost sight of Mir Ali, the claimant to the Bijapur throne,[1] who had, since the departure of Sulaiman Pasha, whose assistance he had sought, been living in Guzerat. Assad Khan now induced the Portuguese to send for Mir Ali; the step was an expensive one to arrange, but he kept a liberal disbursing agent, Ruy Gonçalves de Caminha, in Goa. In view of the later discussions, it is interesting to note that Mir Ali came on the personal promise of safety of the Governor. The arrival of Mir Ali in Goa caused the Adil Shahi King to send an agent to the Portuguese and to advance himself at the head of an army against Belgaum, the headquarters of Assad Khan.

Khwaja Shamsu-d-din was a Persian by birth, in the employ of Assad Khan, and when the latter, feeling the effects of age, found his troubles gathering around him, he employed the former to buy a piece of land in Cananor, erect on it a strongly fortified house, and convey there, as opportunity offered, his enormous wealth. In the meantime Mir Ali was kept in honourable captivity in Goa, and the game of intrigue began. Adil Shah's agent opened by pleading the long peace, alliance and even friendship that had bound the Governors of Goa with the Bijapur dynasty.

[1] See *ante* p. 231.

Assad Khan in reply offered two millions in gold. The Adil Shah capped this with an offer of Salsette and Bardes. Assad Khan in whose fief they were, stirred up the local officers to revolt and then pointed out how worthless such a gift was. Martim Afonso de Sousa found it difficult to decide, partly, perhaps, because, in the contemporary slang, neither of the cows had ceased to give milk, partly because he knew that the advice of his council was worthless—each man speaking according to his last bribe. To put Mir Ali in possession of the Bijapur state would have been difficult and expensive; Assad Khan, too, was old and the assistance of native chiefs notoriously unstable. Salsette and Bardes, on the other hand, had long been coveted by the Portuguese and were under any circumstances noteworthy additions to the Goa territory.

The Adil Shah won the day, and about the time of the final decision Assad Khan died, and Belgaum, his capital, was sacked. Under the terms of his arrangement with the Adil Shah, De Sousa should have sent Mir Ali to Malacca; he retained him, however, as a thorn in the side of Bijapur, and the Adil Shah, in revenge, imprisoned a Portuguese envoy and as many Portuguese as he could capture. All the wealth of Assad Khan was in the possession of Shamsu-d-din, and it remained for the Governor to exploit him. He had left Belgaum before the final catastrophe and reached Sangameswar on the Shastri river, north of Goa: but there he found a blockading fleet of the Portuguese. His chief intimate in Goa was Ruy Gonçalves de Caminha, who had been the accredited agent or attorney of Assad Khan. Ruy Gonçalves had been in India since 1525, but had in his 18 years' residence never risen higher than the post he at this time held, of treasurer of Goa, and as such Martim Afonso de Sousa had imprisoned him when he took over charge as Governor, but this was a mere passing cloud. His character by D. João de Castro, who made him for his services at this time Comptroller of Revenue, may be quoted. "He is very "rich—very proud—a good man of business, well thought "of, excellent in flaying factors and merchants, a great "collector of the King's income and careful in expending "it... A man of a bad tongue... ready to libel whom he "chooses... I gave him this post mainly to screw money "out of Shamsu-d-din, whose fast friend he is... Ruy "Gonçalves speaks ill of all and all of him." [1]

Such was the man whose intimacy with Shamsu-d-din brought him into immediate notice; he was employed by the Governor to induce his intimate to visit Goa, and in this he was successful; for, except by sea, Shamsu-d-din had no chance of reaching Cananor, and the road by sea was blocked. In Goa Shamsu-d-din was cajoled or forced into giving £300,000 to the King of Portugal. The second and last instalment of this sum was received by the Governor in person at Cananor in March 1544. Contemporary gossip had it that the Governor received actually over £600,000 from Shamsu-d-din, and kept the balance; that he was well paid there can be no doubt. [2] When the Adil Shah, by the parable of two plates full of betel leaves, the one with very few leaves on it (the amount he had got from Shamsu-d-din), the other with very many (the amount Shamsu-d-din had retained), showed the Governor how he had been deceived—he said, to clear his own character, that he had exacted only £300,000, because Shamsu-d-din had taken the strongest oaths to assure him that all he possessed was £350,000. The King of Portugal also thought, apparently, that the Governor had been moderate, for he

[1] For more of this man's history see p. 295.

[2] Couto, who searched the public accounts, only found a part even of this £300,000 credited. He suggested that a good deal was spent in providing cargo for a certain ship that was lost.

wrote to D. Joâo de Castro on March 6th, 1546, that in this matter the services of Martim Afonso de Sousa had been so excellent that they deserved every recognition. "Still," adds the insatiable King, "it appears to me that more can be got from that Moor, as I hear he has still a very large sum of money." [1]

The services of Martim Afonso de Sousa, which the King considered so worthy of recognition, continued, for, when he found that Shamsu-d-din had in reality more money than he had thought, he spared no effort to get him again into his power, but in vain. These efforts culminated in a double murder. The close ally of Shamsu-d-din in Cananor was Abu Bakar Ali, and it was thought that if this man were secured Shamsu-d-din must of necessity come to terms. Abu Bakar Ali was of a very well-known Cananor family, and his own position stood very high. He was a near relative of that "Mamale" who had roused Albuquerque by calling himself King of the Laccadives. [2] Although Mamale had been rather opposed to that Governor, Bakar Ali had been employed by him; one of his ships had been used at Benasterim, and he himself had been an intermediary in the peace with the Samuri, in 1513. While Albuquerque, however, was in the Red Sea, his services had been most unjustly rewarded by his ill treatment by a subordinate, [3] and he had consequently not much reason to love the Portuguese. His friendship with Shamsu-d-din was his ruin, for when Ruy Gonçalves and everything else failed to draw Shamsu-d-din to Goa, Martim Afonso de Sousa sent a relative, Bastiâo de Sousa Chichorro, to capture Bakar Ali. By appointment Bastiâo de Sousa met him on the Cananor beach, and engaging him in conversation, led him towards

1 Note to Andrade, Vida, p. 434.

2 The Laccadives were often called Mamale Islands by the Portuguese.

3 Castanheda, III. 110.

an ambush. In the scuffle Bakar Ali and his relative Kunji Sufi were killed, and the Portuguese escaped with some wounds and much discredit, to their boats. War broke out between Cananor and the Portuguese.

This was the last effort of Martim Afonso de Sousa, but it is convenient to end here the story of Shamsu-d-din. D. João de Castro made no attempt to rob the man, but engaged with him in an exchange of courtesies, one of the most substantial of which was the grant to him of free passes for his life, for all his ships to the Red Sea and other places. He availed himself of these to become, by 1552, one of the richest merchants on the coast. [1] When Diu was besieged in 1546 he sent the Portuguese a ship-load of supplies; when, in 1559, there was again war between Cananor and the Portuguese he tried to arrange a peace, and when he failed, assisted the latter. He was by this time old and infirm and died in the same year. [2]

In Diu there never had been much peace between the residents of the city and the fortress, and in 1545 war definitely broke out, as the Captain of the fortress pulled down the wall separating the fort from the town, which, under the treaty of peace, the Sultan of Guzerat

[1] Botelho, letter of 1552.

[2] For a very remarkable letter from Martim Afonso de Sousa to someone unnamed, see Fr. Luis de Sousa Coutinho, Annaes de D. João, III., p. 413. In this he says that both the Adil Shah and Mir Ali had so many reasons in their favour that he was compelled to go to masses and prayers to resolve his doubts. As the Adil Shah gave him Salsette and Bardes, £20,000 to help equip the fleet and £6,000 for himself, he decided in his favour. Directly after God killed Assad Khan. Then came a friend who said he could not do better than hand over to him (the Governor) Assad Khan's treasure of £160,000. He sent half to Portugal and kept one-tenth. This moderation clearly astonished himself, for he says—I might have kept the whole and no one would have been the wiser. £20,000 was to go back to the "friend," and the balance would pay some old debts of the King's. On p. 420 of the same volume, however, is an entry that shows that on June 6th, 1546, De Sousa paid in £100,000 to the King, which he had brought home, so the account in the above letter is incorrect.

was entitled to erect. The other events of this term—the religious persecutions, the debasing of the coinage, and the deputation of Simâo Botelho to examine the accounts of the fortresses and the custom-houses, are noticed elsewhere. In August came the news that D. Joâo de Castro was on his way to supersede Martim Afonso de Sousa. De Sousa was unpopular at the time of his government chiefly for his tampering with the subsistence allowance of the soldiers. He was afterwards remembered with some affection, as he usually paid the salary for three-quarters of the year at least. His character can be gathered from his acts. Had they known it, the Indians whom he robbed of their all, might have had some consolation in feeling, that, at least, in the opinion of a modern ecclesiastic, they were being despoiled by one who was a thoroughly religious, good and pious man.[1] His voyage home was prosperous beyond precedent. He left Cochin on Dec. 13th, 1545, and reached Lisbon on June 13th, 1546.

Simâo Botelho.—Next to Afonso Mexia, Simâo Botelho is the most interesting figure among the Comptrollers of Revenue whom the Portuguese employed in the East. He was more of a soldier than Mexia, more of a man of decision of the executive type, and has left more writings behind him. He did not make his mark as did the other, however, as he had not his opportunities. Mexia was sole Comptroller and had to deal with governors who left all in his hands; Botelho was but one of three of equal rank. Both, however, felt alike the royal ingratitude. Mexia's history we have traced. Botelho's honesty did not prevent the King from accusing him of petty frauds, frauds which he disproved with ease, but the mere suspicion left a sting.

[1] Father Coleridge's life of St. Francis Xavier, Vol. I. pp. 110 and 132.

From a statement in his own third letter he appears to have come to India in 1532; in 1536 he was Captain of a small fort near Cranganor, garrisoned to prevent the incursion of the Samuri; and as the captain of a vessel he accompanied Estavâo da Gama to the Red Sea in 1541. The next year he went to Ceylon as factor, where, owing to private quarrels, a strong hand was needed; and in 1543 he was sent by Martim Afonso de Sousa to reform the Malacca custom-house. Duties had been hitherto collected there by a system called by an apparently Malay word, "Bullibuliao", and, owing to the flagrant abuses that had crept in, the commerce of Malacca was almost entirely ruined. Goods coming from any port between the Indus and the Ganges paid 6 p.c. *ad valorem*. From the Ganges to Malacca and thence to China goods paid 25 p.c., and the valuation was made by the Custom House officers, who were careful that it did not err on the side of leniency. The dues thus calculated were paid in kind, the goods taken in payment being similarly valued by the custom-house. Owing to the abuses of this system, merchants preferred the ports of the neighbouring states where they could at least find some moderation. Botelho's orders were to arrange that, in future, all goods should pay 6 per cent; save those from Bengal, which should pay 8 per cent; and those from China imported by the Portuguese, which should pay 10 per cent, although those imported by the Chinese themselves only paid 6 per cent. All food-stuffs were to be free.

In carrying out these orders a very curious incident happened. The Captain of the fortress, Ruy Vaz Pereira, considered that the proposed reforms, if they did not entirely cut away his profits, would at least seriously diminish them, and refused to obey the Governor's instructions. A strongly worded order, however, from the Governor, superseding him if he remained recalcitrant, reduced him to a sullen obedience.

There may have been a reason for this unusual vigour if not for the original order. Martim Afonso de Sousa had a brother, Joâo Rodrigues de Sousa, who was killed at Malacca with Paulo da Gama, brother of Estavâo da Gama, in 1533. Ten years later, when he was governor, Martim Afonso de Sousa sent for his brother's remains to give them a pompous funeral in Goa. Even if his brother's grave had ever been marked, it had been forgotten in the lapse of years, and a good many Javans had been buried around the place. When the Governor's order came, however, some remains were dug up and removed with befitting ecclesiastical pomp. The scoffing remark of Ruy Vaz would certainly be carried to the Governor. "Sing and good luck to you "as much as you like, my padres, but here you are "carrying away the bones of some valiant Javan."[1]

The order of Martim Afonso, though obeyed by Ruy Vaz, was the latter's death-blow, and as he lay sick Simâo Botelho collected the leading officials and read before them a provision of the Governor, by which he was to succeed as Captain whenever and by what ever means the office became vacant. The dying man and the others present acknowledged the validity of this order, and among those who acquiesced was one Alonso Henriques de Sepulveda, then on a China voyage, a brother of the better known Manuel de Sousa Sepulveda. Henriques considered that Botelho was but a mean fellow, and that had the Governor but known that a man of his merit would be in Malacca when the vacancy occurred he would certainly have appointed him. The only step possible for a man of spirit, therefore, was to act as if the Governor had done his duty, and seize the post when it fell vacant.

Ruy Vaz died two days after the council, and in those

[1] Couto, VI. 8. 12.

two days Botelho got some wind of Henriques' scheme. When, therefore, the garrison turned out to bury the dead Captain, Botelho left a trusty Magistrate, Andre Lopes, with 20 men in the keep, and strict orders to admit no one to the fortress. Henriques, as soon as the funeral had started, marched to the fort with 60 men, and finding the gate locked, demanded admittance. Lopes regretted that he was busy making an inventory, with all the boxes open, and that he could admit no one. When those outside tried to batter the door down Lopes rang the alarm bell, and he and his men fell on with their lances. At the sound of the bell Botelho and the garrison snatched up their arms, left the funeral to itself, and ran to the fortress. Henriques thus surrounded had to yield, and was sent back a prisoner to his own ship. Henriques lost heart, was afraid to go to China and afraid to go to India; he went to the Bay of Bengal on a trading voyage, was wrecked, and he and all his crew perished.

In 1545 Botelho was superseded by Garcia de Sa as Captain of Malacca, and appointed one of the three Comptrollers of Revenue. His duty was to make a tour of all the royal fortresses, enquire into their income and expenditure, and see that none of the former was misappropriated. It is to this deputation that we are indebted for his valuable Tombo do Estado da India,[1] that was submitted to the King on October 20th, 1554. He was at Ormuz when Diu was besieged in 1546, and when the season was sufficiently open he went to Diu with reinforcements and with, what was very much better, enough money to pay the soldiers' arrears. He quickly, however, lost the popularity thus acquired. D. Joâo de Castro had proclaimed free plunder for all, but Botelho appropriated

[1] Published in Subsidios.

the prize money to supply the necessities of the Government, the Governor's order, he remarked, was only intended to draw recruits. Four of his letters to the King are extant —a fragment of one of 1547, two of 1548 and one of 1552. He refers to one of 1551 which does not now exist. In his letter of 1552 he speaks of his continued residence in India; he had obtained the royal permission to return, but the Viceroy would not let him go. The end of his service was sad enough. When the new Viceroy, D. Pedro Mascarenhas, reached Goa on September 23rd, 1554, Botelho was ordered to get the treasure-chest on shore; it was removed from the hold and no compensating ballast put in its place. The rest of the cargo made the ship top-heavy, and in a gale it was overset and sank. Botelho felt the disgrace so keenly that he became a Dominican and died in the monastery a few years later.

A few excerpts from his letters will give an idea of what an honest official had to go through, and the conditions of life in those days. At Bassein, in 1548, he found out two men in considerable delinquencies: one, Louis Godinho, was an ordinary thief, who was employed in the custom-house and had been caught there overcharging merchants; the other, Antonio de Saa Pereira, the son of a priest and a nun, who, it was notorious, had killed several men, was a more determined rascal. De Saa had got a grant of land, unculturable through salt, at an annual rent to government of 30*s*. Behind this, and abutting on it, was some good cultivated land that was let out by government at £60 a year. De Saa, trading on his truculent reputation and on the supineness of the officials, included both pieces in his 30*s* grant, until Botelho interfered. The two ruffians then joined, collected twenty of their friends and, all armed, went to Botelho's house, and got up a riot, hoping to tempt the latter out and seize him. Botelho was not to be caught, however, and managed to have them arrested, but from the tone of his letter he was very doubtful whether they would ever be punished.

Another of his experiences was still more strange, and showed the height to which ecclesiastical influence had reached. Diogo Bermudes, a Spaniard, and the vicar of the Dominicans, refused him absolution because he had reformed the Malacca custom-house at the order of one governor and prepared new registers for Bassein at the order of another, neither of which things the priest considered could have been rightly undertaken without the orders of the Pope. Presumably the secular interests of the Dominicans had been touched by Botelho's action, as the latter got absolution from a Franciscan.

Ruy Gonçalves de Caminha, who has already been mentioned in connection with Khwaja Shamsu-d-din, [1] appears in these letters in a bad enough light, in a story in which Botelho himself plays no very heroic part. One Joâo Caeiro died, leaving a boy and a girl by a slave girl, both minors, and a fortune of £4,000 or £5,000. Botelho, with others, was the executor, and as the others renounced, all the work fell on him. The money was left by Caeiro in the hands of Ruy Gonçalves, not at interest, but to be repaid in full when demanded. Ruy Gonçalves had a nephew, a cripple, and a confirmed gambler, and when the boy died and the girl was sole heiress he demanded her in marriage for his nephew. Botelho refused his consent, but Ruy Gonçalves, while Botelho was absent from Goa, took the law into his own hands and married the two forcibly. Botelho dreaded the influence of Gonçalves with the Governor too much to complain except privately to the King.

Among the causes of the decline of the King's revenue

[1] See page 286.

Botelho notices the abuse of the grants of free carriage. A grant made to one officer was sufficient to rouse all others of similar rank to demand similar privileges, until King's ships sailed with nothing but cargo shipped by the holders of free grants. It had reached such a pitch that the King had to buy in India goods from Ormuz and Malacca at a high rate, as his own ships brought none for him to make up his cargoes for Europe. Some of Botelho's instances, too, of the doings of the Captains of fortresses are very strange: One D. Alvaro de Noronha, (son of the Viceroy D. Garcia), Captain of Ormuz, when charged with malpractices, replied that, if his predecessor, a Lima, could make ten thousand pounds out of the place, he, a Noronha, could certainly make more—rivalry in dishonour though not in honour. Another story is told of this same Captain. An active official, Jeronimo Rodriguez, was sent on to Ormuz to prepare for a coming expedition, and on the way he discovered that a certain resident of Ormuz was engaged in that most heinous of offences under the Portuguese code—smuggling pepper. Arrived at Ormuz he ordered this man's arrest, and for this the Captain called him a Jew dog, and had him led in effigy through the town and subjected to every insult.

Beads made on the West Coast of India, at the back of Bombay, were needed for the African trade, and under orders from Portugal no Portuguese was allowed to purchase them. The intention was that the King should buy these beads directly from the producer. The Captains of Bassein and Chaul, however, became rivals in the trade; both fitted out armed bands to go up country to make purchases, and these bands nearly came to blows. The Captain of Bassein won in the struggle, and the King of Portugal had to buy the beads he wanted from him at an enhanced price.

Sixty years later we have another picture of Portuguese

India, drawn by Couto, the historian, in his Soldado Pratico, and it is interesting to compare the two accounts. In the later one the old evils are still present, the only change is a growth in meanness. The Soldado Pratico is the picture of a thoroughly vicious system worked by men more vicious even than itself. The nearest approach to the India it presents is a tropical forest where every animal and every insect, save those parisitical creatures that lead a still more ignoble existence, preys on some animal or some insect weaker than itself; but there is in the Soldado no feature of force or grandeur—the tiger is absent. The book is filled to nauseousness with petty scoundrelisms that a healthy thief would despise.

Couto, writing in the centre of it, pleads for a change of system. He cannot see that no change of system could have eradicated such evils, everything from the top is corrupt. The Governor sends an embassy to a native potentate—he clears his stables of all the screws at the price of the best horses to send with the envoy as a present. He helps his friends to rob by allowing them to buy up old state debts and old salary notes for a song, when the rightful owners are tired of soliciting, and then ordering payment in full. Under a royal order no governor can be sued for any debt; a few days before he starts for Portugal proclamations are made for claims to be brought, but they are only made to allow certificates of his freedom from debt to be given him. The judges from the highest to the lowest are corrupt and sell their orders to him who gives the most; but in doing so they followed apparently a recognised practice, for Falcâo, in reporting to the King of Portugal in 1612, said that he did not give the salaries of judges and magistrates as they varied with the business they did and what they received from the parties.[1] Couto

[1] Falcão, p. 136.

tells us that Captains of fortresses keep armies of dummy soldiers that live only in the pay bills, and Captains of ships follow their lead; while Custom House officers value the goods imported so low, in the hope of a share in the consignment, that even the importers cry shame.

There was nothing new in many of these complaints. D. João de Castro wrote them in full to the King six years before he himself became governor. In 1539 he found that, though the King paid 16,000 men, he could only command 2,000 outside the garrisons of the fortresses. There was in those early days perhaps a little more shame; thus those who bought up soldiers' paynotes were content to buy them at from 15 to 20 per cent below their face value, but the evil was there. Even the judges he complains of for identical practices: all is dead in them, he says, save their hunger.[1]

[1] Letter of D. João de Castro to the King in 1539. Investigador Portuguez, Vol. XVI. p. 269. Same to same, 1546, p. 406.

CHAPTER XIV

D. João de Castro, Governor, 1545-1548—D. João de Castro, Viceroy, 1548—Garcia de Sa, Governor, 1548-1549—Jorge Cabral, Governor, 1549-1550

D. João de Castro.—D. João de Castro, who succeeded Martim Afonso de Sousa, was born on February 27th, 1500, and was the son of D. Alvaro de Castro. In his youth he was the pupil of Dr. Pero Nunes, afterwards Comptroller of Revenue in India; at the age of eighteen—owing to a dispute with his father—he joined the Portuguese Army in Africa. He distinguished himself and returned home in 1527, a marked man. He married his cousin, a daughter of Lionel Coutinho who was killed with D. Ferdinando Coutinho, the Marshal, at Calicut in the time of Albuquerque. During the ten years that he resided in Portugal after his return from Africa, he lived at his country seat in Cintra, where he was visited by the Infante D. Luis, who became warmly attached to him and to whom some of his later writings were addressed. [1]

In 1538 he sailed in the fleet of D. Garcia de Noronha, and on this occasion he refused the Captaincy of Ormuz as beyond his deserts, though he accepted a pension of £450 a year. His log of the voyage of D. Garcia to Diu

[1] The introduction of the orange is attributed to him. The sweet orange was certainly brought by the Portuguese to Europe in 1548. See Hehn, Wanderings of Plants and Animals, p. 338.

contains passages of great value.[1] In 1541 he accompanied D. Estavâo da Gama to Suez, and his log of that voyage is full of interest even at the present day. He gives what we now know to be the true explanation of the rise of the Nile in Egypt;[2] while his dissertation on the origin of the myth of the Satyrs shows the true scientific spirit.[3] He notes the direction of the wind; the deviation of the needle; the presence of birds; the effect of the wind on trees; the signs of rainfall; and rarely fails to give some reasonable explanation of a new place-name. He returned to Europe in 1542, in a ship with many fidalgoes and few sailors; the voyage was noteworthy as the fidalgoes and their servants divided the work of the ship between them, and the passage was an unusually quick one.

He was selected for the post of Governor through the influence of the Infante D. Luis, and against the opinion of the Indian Council; consequently he was sent out with an imperfectly equipped fleet, and three Comptrollers of Revenue to supplement his supposed lack of business capacity. He was a man subject to uncontrollable gusts of passion that denoted an improperly balanced mind.[4] His

[1] His description of the caves of Elephanta is very remarkable. It contains measurements and details rarely found in travellers of that day. This passage should be compared on the spot by a competent observer. There are changes wrought by time.

[2] Roteiro of 1541, p. 64.

[3] Roteiro of 1541, p. 87.

[4] For one instance see Botelho's letters, p. 4. Some correspondence published in the Revista Universal Lisbonense (2 series, Vol. I. p. 89) can only be explained by this defect. These letters between Aleixo de Sousa Chichorro and D. Joâo de Castro are filled with vulgar abuse. The Editor does not say where these letters came from, and rather puts himself out of court by describing Aleixo de Sousa, who had left with Martim Afonso de Sousa, as De Castro's chief subordinate. Correa (IV. page 436) says there was an angry correspondence between the two; Aleixo de Sousa was also specially remembered in the death-bed memorandum dictated by De Castro to Francis Xavier and the other priests, so there was a quarrel which De Castro remembered in charity, and the letters may be genuine.

personal bravery and his personal purity were beyond question, yet he was bombastic beyond even the standard of his age and country. He delighted in imitations of Roman triumphs with their barbarous adjuncts—walls knocked down to admit him—captives trooped to grace his entry, and standards theatrically dragged through the dust. His favourite style of portrait shows his head circled by palm leaves and a palm branch in his hand. [1] Other governors were content to describe themselves in their treaties as "the most magnificent lord," but this was insufficient for de Castro—he is "The Lion of the Sea." [2] The antechamber in Goa, where envoys from native potentates awaited his pleasure, was decorated with representations of dragons, demons and other fictitious monsters, in the hope that the feeling of terror they induced might reduce the envoys to the proper suppleness.

He is unfortunate both in his own biographer and in the histories of his time. His much vaunted life by Andrade is stilted, bombastic and untrustworthy, [3] while the histories of his time have been tampered with. The charge is serious, but can be substantiated. We learn from Couto [4] that Castanheda completed his history in 10 books, but that, at the request of some fidalgoes who were in the second siege of Diu, and who were dissatisfied with the straightforward narrative, the King of Portugal had the last two books

[1] The artist appears to have selected the common "kajur" palm; it is remarkable chiefly for its spikiness.

[2] Tombo, page 39.

[3] It is far more suited to tell the history of that Portuguese ship's captain who, when he heard a soldier asking the cook for an onion, roared at him: "Onion, what the devil do you mean? Our only luxuries here are powder and shot," than that of a man who ever did anything worth remembering. For some judicious remarks on the style of the book and on Andrade's method of dealing with authorities, see the edition of D. Fr. Francisco de S. Luiz, p. 387.

[4] Couto, IV. 5. 1.

destroyed. Couto himself suffered even worse mutilation; his own brother-in-law, a priest, Fr. Adeodato da Trinidade, rewrote the sixth decade that gives the history of D. Joâo de Castro's time. [1] Not only has all faith in the exact truth of the narrative been destroyed, but the literary merits of the history have evaporated.

De Castro's letters have unfortunately never been collected. Those that have been printed are scattered up and down different periodicals; the history of the document is not always given and the spelling is often modernized. Imperfect, however, as they are, they raise our opinion of the man. He was too big to fill his letters with scandalous stories of his subordinates; he was always anxious to press on the King's notice their merits and their good services. Judging from them, he took a sound view of the political aspect of the Portuguese rule in India and saw that its continuance depended on a strong fleet; he looked askance even at the territory attached to Bassein, although it brought in a large income, because its possession involved the danger of intanglements in the internal affairs of continental India. [2] Bassein to him was merely important as a mart for the wood required for ship-building. He saw clearly, too, how the increase in the number of scattered fortresses was weakening the position of the Portuguese in the East.

He left Portugal in the middle of March 1545, and with him sailed his two sons, D. Alvaro and D. Fernandes, and also Rais Sharfu-d-din of Ormuz, who had been in Portugal since 1529. The halt at Mozambique was long enough to enable him to plan a new fortress that was built in his time, [3]

1 Diogo Barbosa Machado *s. v.* Adeodato.

2 Some of his views are weighty,—thus he says that bad men cannot be made good by regulation. The maxim was above the level of his contemporaries, and Portuguese India was wrecked as no one could grasp it.

3 Were Mozambique not fortified, the Turks could seriously incommode the Portuguese by cutting their line of communication at this important point.

and to despatch Lourenço Marquez on that voyage of exploration on the east coast of Africa that has left his name on modern maps. De Castro reached Goa and took over charge on September 1st. His impressions as reflected in his letter to the King were at first favourable;[1] he thought that India was well provided, but his over-hasty expression of opinion had afterwards to be completely withdrawn, for the territory he had to administer had been stripped by his predecessor, and troubles of every kind arising from that predecessor's action had to be faced.

The debased coinage[2] was a grievance real enough to the people of Goa, but it was not difficult to withdraw the light coins, as De Castro did, and issue others of true value. De Sousa looked on the balance of the money he had extracted from Shamsu-d-din as the product of his own industry, and although he left Goa with a promise to credit a considerable sum in the Cochin treasury, his second thoughts told him that this money in hand to present to the King would do more than aught else to make his reception in Portugal pleasant. De Castro had therefore to face his difficulties with an empty treasury.

The murder of Abu Bakar at Cananor and the resulting war were settled with little difficulty; all desired peace at heart, and De Castro's assurance that the whole blame rested on his predecessor was considered sufficient. The dispute with the Adil Shah over Mir Ali was more serious. The original agreement had been to send Mir Ali to Malacca, but this had not been carried out as Martim Afonso de Sousa considered him a useful irritant. When the Adil Shah, however, offered £17,000 to get him into

[1] See Letter of 1545 to King, O Instituto of Coimbra, Vol. II. p. 101; that of 1546 is in the same volume, p. 241.

[2] See p. 70.

his power, De Sousa appears to have lent a ready ear; at all events De Castro found two envoys waiting in Goa to receive Mir Ali. De Castro's action was straightforward and honourable. Mir Ali had come to Goa on the security of the Governor's word and could under no circumstances be given up.[1] War did not immediately break out as a consequence of this refusal, but the relations of the two powers continued very strained and the Portuguese envoy remained a prisoner of the Adil Shah.

In the dispute with the Sultan of Guzerat there was no hope of avoiding war, although there can be no doubt but that De Castro did not realize for some months the gravity of the situation. It was only one of the grievances of the Guzeratis that the Portuguese had pulled down the wall between Diu and the fort which the Sultan had erected under the treaty. Sultan Mahmud III, although too young to personally remember the circumstances of the death of his uncle, Sultan Bahadar, and too much in leading strings to possess much power, had been educated to a desire for revenge and to a hatred of the Portuguese name. On their side the Portuguese, so far from trying to conciliate the Guzeratis, almost went out of their way to exasperate them. In 1545 the custom-house dues of Diu were farmed out to certain Portuguese, and in the agreement with the farmers the Portuguese Government included a clause which embodied what they had always arrogated, but which the Guzeratis had never acknowledged. All trading vessels coming to the Guzerat coast other than those belonging to the Portuguese must first come to Diu to pay customs, and by a refinement of cupidity it was not sufficient that the merchant himself went—his vessel must accompany him. The Captain of Diu was thus enabled to buy what

[1] See correspondence, O Instituto of Coimbra, Vol. I. p. 327.

he pleased of the cargo at his own price. Under this rule, which was enforced by armed vessels, all the ports of Guzerat, save Surat which the Portuguese themselves frequented, were closed. The situation was of course impossible.

When in March 1546 the Captain of Diu, D. Joâo Mascarenhas, was convinced that a siege during the monsoon months was inevitable, the fortress was, through the characteristic improvidence of the Portuguese, almost entirely unprovided with men or material, for in all only 200 men could be mustered where 800 were needed. The carelessness or the good nature of their opponent, Sifr Agha, allowed them to get in a small stock of supplies before the siege began, and a hasty message was sent to the Governor begging earnestly for reinforcements of men and munitions. At Goa, D. Joâo de Castro was beset with difficulties: he had no money, and the fleet had not been repaired and sent to sea for some years.[1] With great personal exertion he equipped six foists from Goa and two from Bassein, and sent them under the command of his son, D. Fernandes, to Diu. War was declared against Guzerat with all the forms of mediæval custom.

The Captain of Diu had in the meantime discovered treason in the fort. One Ruy Freire, a man of Diu, had, while in Surat, been bribed by Sifr Agha to blow up the powder-magazine and admit the Guzerat troops by some low balconies facing the sea. Returned to his home Freire associated with himself a mulatto, one Francisco Rodrigues, and the two had been some days in the fort undiscovered, and had nearly made an opening into the vault of the

[1] In his difficulties D. Joâo de Castro turned to Salim Shah of Delhi and suggested that he should attack Guzerat. The embassy did not meet with a very favourable reception as it brought no present, but Salim Shah was too busy at home to think of Guzerat. See Letter of July 4th, 1546, and reply, O Instituto of Coimbra, Vol. II. p. 47.

powder-magazine, when the Captain got wind of the design from a woman of light character who was married in the fort and had connections with a Turkish soldier in the town; this information was confirmed by that given by an Abyssinian deserter. Mascarenhas met the difficulty with great prudence. An open enquiry would have made the scandal public and weakened his small force by the introduction of general distrust. The two men were sent ostensibly on missions, the one to Goa, the other to Bassein, and not allowed back. On a subsequent occasion Mascarenhas had to face the same difficulty of internal treason. During a general assault a number of the enemy were introduced through the women's quarters, and they were only driven out after a hard fight and with some loss to the Portuguese.

On April 18th, 1546, the Guzerat forces began to collect. Sifr Agha could at first only dispose of some 10,000 fighting men, but he had a very powerful artillery and an unlimited supply of forced labour. The forced labourers were unfortunates who, not fighting themselves, received but scanty food and no pay, and suffered more heavily than any other body of men in a quarrel in which they had nothing to gain or lose by the victory of either side. The water fort was still an important part of the defences; and in this siege, as in the last, the line of fortifications of the main fort facing the city could alone be attacked. This line contained three bastions—St. Thomas nearest the sea, Santiago in the centre, and St. John nearest the channel between the island and the mainland; these bastions were connected by curtains. In the night of April 20th—21st the besiegers raised formidable batteries, and as the water fort prevented a direct attack on the St. John bastion, which was the weak point of the defence,[1] a ship was prepared and filled with com-

[1] Its foundations projected over part of the old fort ditch, which was made ground

bustibles to destroy it, but the Portuguese grappled and fired her. Owing to the failure of this attack on the water fort, the besiegers had to confine their direct attack to the two southern bastions, and batter that of St. John from one side only.

During the first few days in which the batteries were open it was necessary for the Portuguese to economize their scanty supply of powder, and they suffered heavily from the besiegers' fire. On May 18th the reinforcements from Goa and Bassein under D. Fernandes reached them and raised their fighting force to 400 men. Even after this the Portuguese were outmatched in both artillery and musketry fire. The machine most dreaded, however, was a mechanical contrivance for projecting rocks, that demoralized rather than injured the garrison, until relief came through the death of the French renegade who worked it; for while he was skilful enough, it was said, to send 30 rocks in succession into the fort, his successor could only discharge them backward among his own friends so that "they sent the machine to the devil."

In June the besiegers built a high wall opposite the St. Thomas bastion, from the top of which they discovered the whole of the inside of the fort; and when this wall was battered down by the garrison they opened trenches and advanced by covered ways and zigzags to the edge of the ditch to fill it in. For some days the Portuguese carried off by night the earth filled in in the day, using for this purpose an old door in the walls of the fort, leading into the ditch. On June 24th Sifr Agha came in person to examine this door, and while standing looking over a low wall his head was carried off by a cannon ball. The death of the commander of the besieging force gave the Portuguese a respite for a week, until his son, Rumi Khan, was appointed to his place; in the end the Portuguese suffered by the substitution of the son—who was their bitter enemy—for the father, who was but half-hearted in the matter.

While the number and resolution of the besiegers increased the little garrison of the fort diminished daily; sickness, too, broke out among the latter, and hardly 200 men could be mustered to repel attack. By July 4th the first force of the monsoon was spent, and Mascarenhas sent the chaplain of the fort, João Coelho, and two sailors to carry news of the urgent need of reinforcements. By this time D. João de Castro had succeeded in getting some vessels ready and in collecting stores and munitions, and although Mascarenhas' letter only reached him on July 10th, he was able on July 25th, two days before Coelho returned to Diu, to despatch his son, D. Alvaro, with 37 foists. In the meanwhile the difficulties of the little garrison were increasing. The ditch had been filled in and both the St. Thomas and the St. John bastions had been breached, and a "road up which a cart could have been driven" made to the top; assaults on these breaches were of almost daily occurrence.[1] All the medicines were finished; the food had been either used, or spoiled in the magazines, roofless from the enemy's fire; cats and dogs had all been eaten, and it was a feast day for the sick when a crow or an adjutant was shot, feeding on the dead bodies of the slain; rice and coarse sugar were the only supplies left, and the powder was nearly all expended.

On July 27th the enemy's batteries ceased firing, and mining operations began. These operations appear to have taken the Portuguese quite by surprise, and resulted in a terrible disaster. The presence in the garrison of D. Fernandes had not conduced to harmony. There were intriguers enough ready to stir up bad blood by playing the

[1] It was in one of these attacks about July 23rd that the besiegers were admitted to the fort by treachery.

Governor's son off against the Captain. D. Fernandes himself was young and thoughtless, and the mentor provided by his father—that Diogo de Reynoso who had brought Castanhoso from Massowah to Goa in 1544—aggravated instead of smoothing over the difficulty. The St. John bastion stood partly on living rock and partly on made ground, where the ditch of the old fort once was. The besiegers were aware of this defect and laid their mine in the made ground. D. Fernandes had charge of the defence of this bastion, and on August 10th, by a series of feints, he and 70 of the leading men of the garrison were drawn to it to repel a fancied attack. When the besiegers retreated in perfect order and undefeated, Mascarenhas saw that some danger lurked, and ordered the defenders to withdraw from the bastion. D. Fernandes and his men were on the point of obeying when some scornful words of Diogo de Reynoso drew them back; [1] the mine exploded under their feet; D. Fernandes, Diogo de Reynoso and 46 other men were killed and 22 wounded.

The dust of the explosion had not subsided when Joâo Coelho, the chaplain, with his cross, took his stand in the breach and the remnants of the little garrison gathering around the symbol of their religion, were ready to repel the attack. Slaves ran up with beams and stones to build a temporary defence, and that night an inner line cut off the shattered bastion. It is not surprising that the small remnant of the garrison—80 strong and nearly all wounded—begged to be led out to be killed in the open rather than die one by one behind walls. The attacks on the breaches never ceased, and the Muhamedans had by this time got possession of all the outer walls, and were driving the Portuguese back foot by foot. On August 13th the

[1] D. Joâo de Castro reported this in manly words to the King, not trying to exculpate his son's fault.—O Instituto of Coimbra, Vol. II. page 293.

garrison were heartened by the arrival of Antonio Moniz Barreto and a few men who had, at the imminent risk of their lives, crossed in a small boat from Chaul, where D. Alvaro, whose fleet amounted then to 60 vessels, was lying waiting for the weather to moderate to attempt the voyage. After this date small reinforcements began to come in almost daily, and on August 29th D. Alvaro himself arrived, to find the fortress quite open to the besiegers, the walls and bastions heaps of rubbish, and the little garrison defending an inner line of fence.

With the arrival of reinforcements Mascarenhas experienced fresh difficulties. The nerves of the new men were not at the pitch to allow them to listen calmly to the hum of passing bullets and to stand defending walls that at any moment might be blown into the air with themselves. To the raillery of the seasoned garrison they retorted that they were not men to be cooped up behind bricks and mortar, but that they were ready to fight the enemy in the open. Matters went so far that the men, supported by D. Alvaro, mutinied to be led against the enemy, and the Captain was not strong enough to refuse. On the morning of September 1st it rained hard and the wetted matches of the matchlocks were of no use, but in the afternoon the 400 men of the attacking party sallied out, under D. Alvaro and D. Francisco de Menezes, against works at least as strong as those of the fort itself at the commencement of the siege—works too, defended by nearly 20,000 men. Of course the attack failed, and the failure would have been ludicrous if it had not been so disastrous. When D. Francisco de Menezes was killed and it was brought home even to the mutineers that the attack was hopeless, D. Alvaro fled and the men concealed themselves in the long grass at the foot of the enemy's wall until D. Joâo Mascarenhas pricked them out with his pike, then they bolted back in a panic. This disgraceful affair cost the Portuguese 40 killed and seventy wounded, of whom many died.

By this time the besiegers had bridged the channel between the mainland and the island,—a work requiring considerable skill as the tide ran strongly. In the fort—if fort it could still be called—matters remained unchanged. The Guzeratis held the outer line of the fortifications, the Portuguese the houses, and between the two was a wall to which either side advanced at pleasure to take a shot at his enemy. The news that reached the defenders from the outside was not encouraging, for the Turks had occupied Basra and their galleys had been seen at many places on the Arabian coast. The Governor continued to pour in supplies and men, and because the Captain had left his fortress to make the sally of September 1st he sent Vasco da Cunha with special orders to prevent another such occurrence. No attempt even was made to reoccupy the outer line of the fortifications, as all the works there were mined. The Id of the Ramzan fell on October 10th, and by that day there were 1,800 Portuguese in Diu with ample supplies; the festival passed without an attack.

In the meantime D. João de Castro had been collecting reinforcements from all down the coast. On the plain near Goa he erected, from drawings supplied by the Captain, a copy of the enemy's works at Diu, and his soldiers were exercised in sham fights in assaulting them.[1] When all was ready he proceeded north. The first plan had been to hold Diu fort and to harry the Guzerat coast-line until the Sultan was compelled to sue for peace, but this was changed after a personal inspection by D. João de Castro. The fortress was so shattered that it would require all the

[1] Couto, VI. 3, 9.

dry season to repair it, and it was therefore necessary to drive the enemy from before it at once.

The Portuguese could muster in all some 3,500 fighting men to attack the 20,000 men besieging Diu, supported, according to rumour, by the Sultan of Guzerat with 50,000 men in reserve: the odds were certainly enormous. On November 6th, 1546, D. João de Castro appeared before Diu; the enemy was kept amused by feints of landing, and during three successive nights the troops were introduced secretly into the fort, climbing the sea face by rope ladders. Preparations were completed by November 10th; early that morning at the signal of three rockets from the fort, the boats advanced with trumpets sounding, with torches, and forests of lances stacked along the decks, with lighted matches tied to their handles, and over all the Governor's banner displayed. In the boats were only enough sailors to man them; advancing and then retreating, they kept a large part of the Guzerat army on the alert, and until the day dawned the deceit was not discovered. Meanwhile the real attack of the Portuguese in two battles was able to make considerable headway against that part of the enemy that opposed their advance from the fort. D. João Mascarenhas led the van; the Governor in person led the second battle, and before him Antonio de Casal, the Franciscan, carried aloft a crucifix. The men in De Castro's battle hung back, and were only induced to advance by a rumour that the enemy was flying.[1]

The first fight was at the line of batteries; Antonio de Casal with his cross scaled the wall. A bullet broke one of its arms—"Look," cried the brave monk, "what the infidel dogs have done to the signal of your faith. Die

[1] De Castro led them—he did not merely order them to attack. He says they showed considerable reluctance to advance, only 25 accompanied him. O Instituto of Coimbra, Vol. III. p. 34: De Castro's general letter of 1546.

for Christ!" With a rush the line of batteries was carried before the troops who had been drawn off by the feint of the boats could return. When these fresh troops reinforced the enemy there was a renewal of the fight, but the Portuguese would take no denial, and with one sustained effort the Muhamedans were forced back. So sudden was the final sweep of fugitives that several Portuguese were carried away in the stream, pinned and impotent of harm. As Rumi Khan was never seen alive again he is believed to have been among the 3,000 of the enemy killed: 600 were taken prisoners. The Portuguese acknowledged a loss of 100 killed and 400 wounded; of these latter, as there was no proper supply of medicines, many died. The dead were burned, but so many corpses had been buried in the ruins, that, after the siege, a terrible sickness swept away 1,500 Portuguese and many natives of the country.

There was no delay in rebuilding the fort. The new outer walls were drawn to include the former ditch, and as the inner walls were also rebuilt there was a double line of fortifications. Work went on night and day, and the Governor had to disobey the direct commands of the King of Portugal and assist fidalgoes to keep open table for those under their orders. The Governor had no money to pay the many who only clamoured for what was justly due; as a last resource he sent to borrow from the municipality of Goa, and failing any other pledge of repayment, sent them some hairs from his beard.[1] The Goa municipality returned the pledge and £6,000,[2] but as

[1] See p. 168 for a similar story of Albuquerque.

[2] The reply of the Goa municipality on sending the money is printed on p. 460 of the Lisbon Academy edition of Andrade's Vida. It recapitulates their grievances. The sum collected was 20,146 pardâos and one tanga, of five tangas to the pardâo. In view of the recent persecution of the Hindus it details that 9,200 and odd pardâos had been lent by them. It presses for repayment,—the case of D. Garcia de Noronha's loan had not been forgotten.

a rich ship was soon after captured the debt was not long unliquidated. Owing to the impossibility of getting any fidalgo to undertake the onerous charge of the captaincy of Diu,[1] D. Joâo Mascarenhas had to stay on after his term was completed. When the works were far enough advanced to be defensible the Governor returned to Goa, and on April 21st, 1547, made that triumphal entry into the town that led the Queen of Portugal to say of him that he had fought like a Christian and triumphed like a heathen.[2]

The rest of the Governor's term is a monotonous history of struggles for money to pay the troops, of petty successes and of hollow triumphs. The Adil Shah had taken advantage of the Governor's absence at Diu to overrun the territories of Salsette and Bardes, which he had given to the Portuguese on the condition that they deported Mir Ali, whom, on the contrary, they had kept in Goa. The leader he employed was that Gonçalo Vaz Coutinho, now a renegade, who had broken out of Goa goal in 1540. This incursion was only supported by a force of 700 men, and D. Joâo de Castro easily defeated it in October with his 6,000 troops; this petty success was the occasion of another triumphal entry into Goa city, and the hostilities with the Adil Shah smouldered on. They came to no conclusion during De Castro's lifetime.

The effects of the war with Guzerat were felt wherever the Portuguese trade in the East extended. Guzerat cloths were the articles of barter most commonly employed in Bassein, Goa, Ormuz and Malacca, and the diminution in the custom-house receipts from those places began to be

[1] Some of the persons mentioned in De Castro's last wishes were included, as he feared the King might forget their really meritorious services and only remember that they had refused to go to Diu.

[2] See Corea, IV. 587, for a very detailed account of this procession. The tablet commemorating it still exists in Goa.—Fonseca, p. 227.

seriously felt by the Portuguese government.[1] Impecunious though he was, D. Joâo de Castro considered himself compelled to make a vigorous attack on Sultan Mahmud in the hope of bringing him to his knees, and in November 1547 he went north with 1,500 men; but his conduct in thus personally taking the command of an expedition of raiders was severely criticized by many of his leading fidalgoes, who considered that such "birding" as they called it, could more decently be undertaken by younger men. At Bassein he found himself forestalled by the nephew of the Captain of that place, who had already sacked his objective, Broach. D. Alvaro was next detached to plunder Surat, held by Kara Hussain, the son-in-law of Sifr Agha; the chicken-hearted D. Alvaro was, however, afraid to attack the town, although, as it was afterwards discovered, the place was entirely unprepared for defence.

When news came that Sultan Mahmud had, on hearing of the approach of D. Joâo de Castro, marched with his army and was encamped near Broach, the Governor, who had been gasconading in the then approved manner, by forging spits on which to roast his opponent, sailed for that place, but when the enemy showed himself in great strength the Portuguese declined an engagement and retreated.[2] The story of the harrying of towns already plundered, and of the nameless cruelties practised on defenceless men and women, need not be detailed.[3] The Governor did not dare to go to Diu where the complaints of the soldiers that

1 Albuquerque saw the necessity for Guzerat cloths, and therefore kept peace with the country.—Cartas, p. 51.

2 Couto in his VI. 5. 7 gives a curious picture of the Portuguese army on this occasion; its head, the Governor, was full of indecision and ready to accept the advice of the last speaker.

3 Correa tells us that they found little but the old cooking-pots, and in one place two whale ribs which the Governor carried back with him to Goa and erected across a street, where they lasted for ten years.

they received no pay were too true to be faced by an impecunious governor eager to reward good service and unable now even to meet just demands. The Governor of India, he tells the King, has not even the five loaves and the two small fishes to divide among 5,000 applicants, "nor are their merits such that our Lord should work a miracle for them." [1]

After a hasty visit to Goa at the end of the year the Governor again sailed northward, with an easier mind as a way of meeting a part of his difficulties had been found. Luis Falcâo had been Captain of Ormuz and had left that fortress wealthy, but with unusually heavy charges of misconduct hanging over his head. Hoping that, if he advanced some of the arrears of the soldiers' pay, a more favourable view of his delinquencies would be taken, he offered himself for the Captaincy of Diu and his offer was accepted; his advance of one quarter's arrears was a temporary alleviation. The soldiers could, however, get no more pay from the Governor; he would not transfer them as he could get none to fill their places; while the savagery of the Portuguese themselves had reduced Diu to a solitude; no ship ever came into the deserted harbour. Luiz Falcâo was, in this same year, killed while sitting in his room in the fortress, and it was not discovered who fired the fatal shot. [2]

By 1547 the town of Aden had wearied of the Turkish rule established by Sulaiman, the eunuch, in 1538; and a neighbouring Arab chieftain, Ali bin Sulaiman, with little difficulty expelled the small Turkish garrison. Fearing that the Turks would return in overwhelming numbers, Ali applied to the Portuguese, and the Captain of Ormuz, who

[1] O Instituto of Coimbra, Vol. III. p. 87.

[2] A mulatto confessed on his death-bed some years after, that he had fired the shot. In a crowded garrison there must have been several who knew the secret.

received the message, sent D. Payo de Noronha, a near relative both of the Viceroy D. Garcia de Noronha and of the Governor D. João de Castro, with a small force to his help. When D. Payo reached Aden he was well received, and it was agreed that while Ali bin Sulaiman marched out to attack the Turks, D. Payo should remain in charge both of the city and of the former's children. The first night of his stay, however, he was so alarmed at the noises he heard in the town, which he took to mean that treason was intended, that he never slept on shore again. When Ali was defeated and killed and the Turks came to besiege Aden, D. Payo de Noronha slipped away in the night.[1]

Meanwhile, when the Governor heard of the original message from Aden, he prepared a fleet to take advantage of the opening. He had no money, and rather than embark without their arrears of pay the Bassein garrison mutinied and marched with fife and drum to the lodgings where he lay ill. The revolt was quieted with soft words, and no one was better or worse for the mutiny except the unfortunate drummer, whose hands were cut off. With some help from the fidalgoes D. Alvaro and 300 men were at length sent to Aden, but they reached there six days after the Turks had reoccupied it and D. Payo had left. As D. Alvaro had not force enough to attack the Turks he returned to Shahr, where, near the town, there was a small fort of sun-dried bricks, held by 35 Arabs, who offered to surrender. Some victims were necessary: the miserable mud fort was

[1] His pusillanimity was a scorn among the Portuguese, and some years after, a certain fidalgo, passing his door, saw a little girl weeping bitterly. She told him D. Payo's servants had taken her hen and would neither return it nor pay for it. "Keep quiet, little girl," said the fidalgo; "do not worry yourself. If they had taken Aden they would restore it, but a hen—never." He, however, after his return to Portugal, was rewarded with the Captaincy of Cananor for life, and sailed for India in 1558. In Cananor he again imperilled his country's interests, and brought on a war that lasted until his recall in 1565.

attacked, and with a great expenditure of powder and with the loss of 40 Portuguese killed, the garrison was put to the sword. The trophies of the fight consisted of an old man and an old woman, whom the Arabs had sent out from the fort to arrange their surrender and whom the Portuguese had not killed, and with these to grace his entry D. Alvaro had his triumph in Goa in April 1548; but the failure of the expedition was the Governor's death-blow.[1]

Since the death of his son, D. Fernandes, troubles had gathered fast round D. João de Castro. He left Bassein in April, 1548, ill with fever, and in Goa, so far from shaking off the sickness, he grew rapidly worse. When he could not any longer attend to business, he made over his duties to a council of the Captain of Goa, the Bishop, the Chancellor and Ruy Gonçalves de Caminha, one of the Comptrollers of Revenue. On May 23rd came a quick sailing ship from Portugal with the news that, as a recompense for his services at Diu, D. João de Castro had been created Viceroy with a three years' extension of his term. The dying man was past both joy and sorrow, and on June 5th the end came. He died of a disease, says Faria y Sousa, that now kills no man, for even diseases die—it was grief for the miserable state India was reduced to without any means of redressing it.[2] When the successions were opened it was found that the new Governor was Garcia de Sa.

[1] It is said that the Bishop of Goa, D. João d'Albuquerque, had a priest in whose wit he delighted. The following dialogue between them—even if it never took place—at least expressed the general sentiment. Says the Bishop: "What is that which from bitter became sweet—from large, small—and from small, large?" Said the priest: "That which from bitter became sweet were the almonds with which the Governor was bombarded when he returned from Diu. From large became small—the capture of Broach, because D. Jorge de Menezes took it. From small became large—the capture of Shahr, because the Governor's son took it." Couto, VI. 6, 6.

[2] Y matole un genero de enfermedad que oy no mata algun hombre como succedio mil vezes en la antiquedad porque se vea que tambien las enfermdades

Garcia de Sa.—Garcia de Sa had come out originally to India with Diogo Lopes de Sequeira in 1518, and had been Captain both of Malacca and of Bassein, but it was noted, as an example of rare disinterestedness, that in all his service he had accumulated only £10,000. He had distinguished himself during the first rebuilding of Diu fort, and had subsequently been the victim of a gross royal outrage that passed even the wide bounds within which those outrages were condoned. There came an order while he was Captain of Bassein, to confiscate all his property and send him a prisoner in irons to Portugal. On enquiry it turned out that he had, for the general convenience, caused some small copper coins to be struck while at Malacca, and that this had been represented by scandalmongers and accepted by the royal wisdom as an infringement of the royal prerogative. His friends in India stood by him and the order was never carried out. His love of coining had, however, not left him in consequence of this misfortune, for, during the short time he was governor, he brought out a new gold piece, the San Thomé, which was equivalent to about one pound sterling; and although the coin met with some opposition at first, it was found to be convenient, and was current for many years. He owed his nomination to the strong recommendations of D. Joâo de Castro.

Garcia de Sa was over 70 years of age: he had married on her death-bed a woman, a native of the country, by whom he had had two daughters, who were married while he was governor. Both were famous for their beauty, and one, D. Leonor, for her misfortunes. The latter married Manuel de Sousa Sepulveda and perished with him in that shipwreck which is one of the most pathetic incidents of the

mueren. Esta era un penetrante sentimiento del miserable estado en que via la India sin ver algun camino de reparar la.—Faria y Sousa, Tom. II. pt. 2, chap. 7.

Indo-Portuguese history of the time. The Governor's long experience in the Indian administration supplied the place of bodily activity, and he devoted his attention to the routine work of his office. The change of rulers proved fortunate for the Portuguese in their relations with other powers. The Adil Shah sent his envoy, Muatabar Khan, to Goa, and on August 28th, 1548, a peace very favourable to them was concluded.[1] They got all they wanted, including the cession of Salsette and Bardes, and the return of their imprisoned envoy, and in exchange had only to promise that before allowing Mir Ali to leave Goa they would give notice to the Adil Shah. The peace with Guzerat was signed in January 1549, and the terms of the former treaty were re-enacted, except that no wall was to be built between the city and the town.

In the ships of 1548 there had come out a number of men called soldiers who were little fitted to raise the reputation of their nation in the East. None had received any pay on their voyage out, and they could claim none for a year after their arrival. With no means of their own, therefore, and no power to earn their living, they were driven to beg in bands in the streets. The Governor did what he could; he had four tables, both for dinner and supper; and he fed 200 at each meal; but the famished wretches fought at his very tables for the food, and on one occasion there was a riot in which swords were drawn.

The Raja of Tanur, a subordinate of the Samuri, had for many years been trying to throw off his suzerain's yoke. He began in 1531, when he sold the site of the Chaliyam fort to Nuno da Cunha for £300. He had apparently not reaped all the result he hoped from this step, and his next was to express a desire to become a Christian, which at

[1] Botelho Tombo, p. 11.

least showed that he was sufficiently advanced to read the signs of the times. This subject had been first mooted in 1545, during the term of D. Joâo de Castro, but he was suspicious, as the Raja expressed his desire for the conversion to be kept secret, and he sent Diogo de Borba to Chaliyam to discover what the real intention of the Raja was; on the priest's report that the conversion was only a pretext to get some help in his quarrel with the Samuri over some territory, the matter was not proceeded with. Having failed with one governor was no bar to succeeding with the next, and the fresh attempt of the Raja was more fortunate. Antonio Gomez, [1] the Jesuit, was sent to teach him the true doctrine. The Raja left his capital secretly, came to Goa, was received there with royal honours and was admitted with great pomp into the Roman Catholic Church. His zeal was fervent, and he ordered his subjects to become Christians under pain of being turned out of the Kingdom; twenty days were allowed for the great change. It was well, perhaps, they did not obey, for his own conversion was not lasting. Even on his way to Goa he had retained all the social habits of a high-caste Hindu, and in the following year, at the summons of the Samuri, he collected his troops and appeared in the field against his friends the Portuguese. In the rains of 1549 Garcia de Sa had a return of an old malady, and died on July 6th, 1549. The new governor was Jorge Cabral.

Jorge Cabral.—Jorge Cabral had been in India since 1525, and, like his predecessor, had been captain of both the fortresses of Malacca and Bassein. He had married and brought out to India a Portuguese lady, and was the first governor who had his wife with him in Goa. It was

[1] For the history of this man, the Life and Letters of St. Francis Xavier may be consulted; see especially Vol. II. pp. 55 and 398.

owing, in fact, to her influence that he accepted the post, as his own inclination was to retain the solid advantages of the Bassein captaincy in preference to the more problematical ones of the governorship, which might be lost in a month by the arrival of D. Joâo de Castro's successor.

Correa, who had seen all the governors of India except Almeida, considered that Cabral was the best man of business of all; but judging from the letters of Botelho, he seems to have been an official of the type then common, though it is true that the acts of which he was guilty were not so much for his own benefit as for that of his wife and her relatives. Cabral himself had to contend with the same difficulties as the other governors who had been promoted by the successions; the fidalgoes refused to follow with any enthusiasm a man who was merely one of themselves. The interest of the earlier months of his term centred in the preparations to meet the Turkish galleys that rumour said were gathering in the Red Sea, and it was not until August 1550 that definite news came that, although these preparations had been in progress, they were for a time definitely stopped.

The interest of the end of Cabral's term lies in the acute phase which the chronic rivalry between the Samuri and the Raia of Cochin had reached. The earlier governors had with great wisdom secured the adhesion of the small southern Malabar chiefs, in whose country pepper grew, or through whose country it reached the sea, by small annual payments. Five chiefs, for instance, received £72 a year, and one £42.[1] The policy of these payments

[1] Botelho Tombo, p. 25, gives their names as follows: £72 each, (1) Pepper King, (2) King of Porcat (Porakkat), (3) King of Dianpur (Udiampura), (4) Lambeea of Perun, (5) Manguate Caimal; and £42 a year, Manguate Casta da Lua.

was shown when the Samuri wished to extend his influence over the south of Malabar by the ceremony at Eddapalli, but after, however, this intention had been frustrated, Martim Afonso de Sousa, who was in command of the forces acting at Cochin, retrenched these allowances.

Disputes between the Raja of Cochin and the other southern Malabar States began as early as 1541, and although the latter professed their devotion to the Portuguese, the Portuguese had to support their old ally of Cochin against them. The chief who most unreservedly joined the Samuri was called by them indifferently the Pepper King, or the Arel of Bardela. Bardela is an island south of Cochin, and appears in modern maps as Warradhula. Had the Captain of Cochin, Francisco da Silva, been a diplomat the dispute could have been easily settled in the rains of 1550, for the Raja of Cochin was very averse to war, and the Arel offered to refer the dispute to the arbitration of the captain himself. Da Silva, however, refused anything except complete submission, and as this was not accepted he landed. Technically, perhaps, the troops of the Arel were defeated, as the Arel was killed and his palace burned; but, on the other hand, Da Silva himself was killed. The followers of the dead Arel devoted themselves to avenging their chief and caused terrible destruction even in Cochin town itself, while the other Malabar chieftains definitely joined the Samuri.

On receipt of the news of the Arel's death the Samuri collected his forces and marched south. He was headed off by the Captain of Cranganor and a small force at the great Trichur lake, but he evaded him by a detour under the Ghats. On his arrival among the southern Malabar States, 18 chiefs joined him, raising his forces to a nominal total of 140,000 men. Of these about 40,000 occupied

Warradhula, and the remainder stayed on the mainland. Manuel de Sousa Sepulveda, in command of the Portuguese forces, took advantage of this faulty disposition to cut the army in two with his fleet. The Governor followed with a large force to attack the island, but just as he was ready his army melted away. The new Viceroy who was to oust Jorge Cabral had arrived at Cochin, and the fidalgoes deserted the latter to worship at the rising sun of D. Afonso de Noronha. No further fighting took place, and for some years the disturbed state of the country prevented the Portuguese getting their annual supply of pepper. In November D. Afonso de Noronha took over charge of India. An event had occurred in Cochin during the term of Jorge Cabral, which may be partly attributed to the ecclesiastical influence to which he was very subservient. There was a temple near that town particularly venerated by the Raja, and hearing that it contained a large amount of treasure, Cabral had arranged to rob it; he desisted at the earnest request of the Raja, but shortly after he left, the crime was committed by his subordinate, and from this time the Raja of Cochin also was estranged from the Portuguese.

With the conclusion of the terms of Garcia de Sa and Jorge Cabral, who carried on the duties after the death of D. Joâo de Castro, this history has reached the point destined for its conclusion. D. Joâo de Castro was the last man with any pretensions to superiority who held office in the early days of the Portuguese connection with India, and the names of his successors for many generations, some indolent, some corrupt, some both, and all superstitious, are but the mile-stones that mark the progress along the dismal path of degeneration. The symptoms of decay are, it is true, plainly discernible from the date of Albuquerque's death, but amid the disappearance of both public and private morality the Portuguese race retained for some years a vigour which enabled it to triumph over the weaker peoples of the East. The task of an historian of the "The Rise of the Portuguese Power in India" has been concluded when the date on which even that vigour vanished, has been reached.

APPENDIX

MALACCA—THE MOLUCCAS—CHINA

Malacca.—For many years after Albuquerque captured Malacca its history was one of continual unrest; he had left the country unsubdued, and the conduct of the Portuguese who remained in the fort he built helped to keep alive the feeling of hatred with which they were regarded. After the decapitation of Utimute Raja his party was still powerful, and his son-in-law, whom the Portuguese called Patequatir, became its leader. The son of the ex-Raja of Malacca, too, had a considerable following, and Laksamana, his admiral, who was absent when Albuquerque conquered the town, returned with his fleet to his assistance. The Portuguese had only 253 men fit for duty and held their own with difficulty until the arrival of reinforcements enabled them to carry the war into the enemy's camp. In the end Patequatir was driven to Java, and the son of the ex-Raja[1] and the Laksamana left the immediate neighbourhood of Malacca and stockaded themselves strongly in the island of Bintam, whence they could deal shrewd blows by address as well as by strength. A dependant of the Raja of Bintam, a Bengal Muhamedan, appeared in Malacca as a fugitive from Bintam, wormed himself into the confidence of the officials by his eagerness to trade, and seizing an opportunity when the garrison was supine, all but gained possession of the fort.

[1] This man is for clearness called the Raja of Bintam in this Appendix.

A blow still more bitter followed. Albuquerque had appointed a Hindu, Ninachetty, to the post of Bendara or native governor of the town; the appointment was in every way unsuitable as the man could, from his nationality and religion, be only popular with a very small number the townspeople. The friction at length became unbearable, and he poisoned himself. The then Captain, Jorge d'Albuquerque, a near relative of the great Governor, made a most suitable appointment—that of the son-in-law of the Raja of Bintam, and therefore a Muhamedan—to the vacant post, and for a short time prosperity was restored to Malacca. The success of the new governor was his ruin, for his father-in-law, the Raja of Bintam, spread the report that he was his partizan and only biding his time to destroy the Portuguese. The device was shallow, but successful, and the new governor, condemned by the Portuguese, expiated on the scaffold his efforts in their interest. Such a flagrant injustice was the death-blow to the reviving prosperity—the returning merchants fled from the accursed town, and the fort again suffered all the horrors of famine.

Jorge d'Albuquerque endeavoured to atone for his error by favouring the hitherto proscribed Malays and restoring to them their property. Among those who under these circumstances returned were a number of so-called royal slaves, both indoor and outdoor, whose position under the native rulers was rather privileged than onerous. For a time these slaves were well treated, but Jorge de Brito who succeeded as Captain, threw all into confusion by dividing up both classes among the Portuguese residents as their private slaves. He also opened an enquiry at which anyone could pay off an old grudge by producing two witnesses to prove that his enemy was a slave, while another enquiry reopened all the titles on which property was held. To add to the confusion there was, on De

Brito's death, a dispute as to the succession to the Captaincy; one claimant imprisoned the other, and the Raja of Bintam took advantage of the general uproar to stockade himself on the Muar river, at the very gates of Malacca.

Hearing of these events, Lopo Soares deputed his nephew, D. Aleixo de Menezes, to the relief of the fort, which he reached on June 18th, 1517, to find it nearly at its last effort. The Raja had cut off its supplies, the nominal Captain was on his death-bed, and the factions into which the Portuguese were divided only awaited his death to again fly at each other's throats. Beyond relieving the immediate necessities of the place, D. Aleixo did little. Everyone agreed that the Raja of Bintam ought to be driven from the Muar river, but as to details they disagreed. Don Aleixo could not leave his fleet, the Captain of the fort could not leave his fort, so in December D. Aleixo returned to India.

Through the greater part of 1519 famine pressed the town sorely, but better times were approaching. Antonio Correa [1] who had been saved from the massacre at Calicut in 1500, had left India on a voyage to open up trade with Pegu. He swore his treaty of peace with the king of that country on an old song book, partly because it was the most imposing-looking volume he had, and partly because, as he cynically remarked, neither side intended to keep the treaty longer than was necessary. He left Pegu for Malacca in June 1520, and on July 15th, with a force of 150 Portuguese and 250 natives, he stormed the Raja's stronghold, to which the advance—retarded by numerous stockades—lay up a river so narrow that the trees met overhead. The Raja had again to take refuge in Bintam.

On April 25th, 1521, Jorge d'Albuquerque left Cochin for a second term as Captain of Malacca. He was headstrong

[1] For his subsequent service see p. 193.

and incompetent: the stronghold on Bintam had never been reconnoitred, yet Albuquerque led his large force to attack it and was of course defeated. As a consequence, the Raja of Bintam again established himself on the Muar river, and an attempt to dislodge him in April 1523 was defeated with a loss of 65 Portuguese killed. Isolated ships of the Portuguese were from time to time captured, and in 1524 one was taken less than a mile from the fort and every Portuguese in her slain. As a result, the 80 men in the fort were closely invested by their persistent enemy, led by a renegade Portuguese.

At the time of the first capture of Malacca the chief powers in the north of Sumatra were Pasai and Pedir. In the time that had elapsed since that date Achin had risen at their expense. The fort which the Portuguese built at Pasai in 1521 was lost with its stores and artillery almost immediately on its completion, and in the same year an event occurred which gave a definite bent, hostile to the Portuguese, to the Achinese policy. The brothers Jorge de Brito and Antonio de Brito[1] touched at Achin on their outward voyage to the Moluccas, and found there some shipwrecked Portuguese under a leader, João de Borba. These men had been most kindly treated by the Achinese, and they repaid it by telling the De Britos of a temple some miles inland worth the sacking. Jorge de Brito started with 200 men to plunder it, but he was attacked and killed with 70 of his men.

While things were going so badly at Malacca, and when, in fact, just half the little garrison of 80 men had been killed in a sudden attack, came the news that Achin had definitely joined Bintam against them. In spite of some reinforcements, the new Captain, Pero Mascarenhas, was not

[1] They were not related to the Jorge de Brito who died as Captain of Malacca.

at first more successful than his predecessors. When, however, news came that he had by the successions been appointed governor he collected all the forces he could muster, and on October 23rd started to attack Bintam. The information as to the stronghold was this time complete; it lay 12 miles up a winding creek, navigable only at high water and defended by stockades that allowed only the passage of one boat at a time. The position was carried after 12 days' continuous fighting, and the death of the Raja soon after deprived the Portuguese of a determined enemy. His son, the Raja of Ujantana, on the mainland, carried on the feud for a few years longer and Achin remained irreconcilable, still for some years Malacca had some rest.

By 1533 the Raja of Ujantana had formed alliances with Pahang and some other Malay States, and this alliance Paulo da Gama set himself by dint of sheer hard fighting to dissolve. In the following year Paulo was relieved of the Captaincy by his brother Estavâo da Gama, and 8 days later was killed in a disastrous skirmish with the Ujantana flotilla. The skilful arrangements of Estavâo da Gama, however, detached Ujantana from the alliance, and for some years, except for the Achin war, Malacca had peace.

In 1535 occurred the famous defence of his ship by Francisco de Barros. He and Henrique Mendez, each in his ship, were returning to Malacca from a cruise; they were at anchor when the enemy's fleet of 24 double-banked row-boats with 2,500 men was sighted. De Barros, as his mainsail and part of his crew were on shore, could not leave, but Mendez got under way, and the first fighting, which commenced about 3 in the afternoon, fell on his ship. When, however, the Captain received a poisoned blow-pipe dart in his beard, he was laid out in his cabin as dying and his vessel bore up and left her comrade. De Barros had 16 men to defend his ship, and by eleven that night only three of them were left alive; the survivors still fought on, and the enemy, not daring to board again, lay round, firing sullenly. When Mendez found that he was not dead he returned, and at his coming the enemy decamped.

The Moluccas.—In November 1511, after he had occupied Malacca, Albuquerque sent 3 ships to explore the route to the Moluccas or Spice Islands, Antonio d'Abreu was the Commander, and Francisco Serrâo, the friend of Magalhaens, was the next senior officer.[1] D'Abreu only got as far as Amboina. Serrâo was wrecked on an uninhabited and rarely visited island, where soon after a native boat fortunately arrived; he and his companions lay in ambush near the landing-place, got between the new-comers and their boat, and compelled them to accept their terms, which included taking them to the Spice Islands. In the constant wars between Tidor and Ternate, Serrâo and his companions fought on the side of the latter and acquired a reputation that ensured them a cordial welcome on that island. The Portuguese expedition of 1514 reached the Moluccas, but though his companions returned to Europe, Serrâo remained, sending by the returning ships full accounts of the islands to his friend Magalhaens.

When he received these letters Magalhaens had already left Portugal for Spain, and knowing that the Spaniards had had for some years doubts as to the exact position of the line of demarcation laid down by the Pope, he was able

[1] Albuquerque's letter of August 20th, 1512, Cartas, p. 68, gives the composition of the fleet. At the end of Barbosa's Description of East Africa and Malabar, published by the Hakluyt Society, is a translation from the Spanish of an unverified paper professing to give the narrative of Serrâo's voyage of 1512 to the Moluccas in a carvel *which he stole in Malacca*. This narrative is inaccurate, and in it, apparently, his later adventures have become confused. Serrâo commanded the St. Catherine, and Simâo Afonso the carvel. The Moluccas are Ternate, Tidor, Mortir, Makian and Bachian.

to give them valuable information as to the resources of the Spice Islands. From some orders issued to the first Portuguese viceroy, Francisco d'Almeida, on April 6th, 1506,[1] it appears that at that early date the Spaniards were considering whether even Malacca were not within their boundary. Having been forestalled there, they were the more ready to appoint Magalhaens to the command of that expedition to the Moluccas which was to immortalize his name by the first circumnavigation of the world. At the end of October 1521 the remnants of this expedition whose commander had been killed, reached Tidor from the East; Serrâo had died at Ternate but a short time before their arrival, about the same date that his friend Magalhaens was killed. The Spaniards, leaving a few representatives behind, sailed again in December.

These Spaniards were still in Tidor when Antonio de Brito reached Ternate on June 24th, 1522, where the Portuguese began at once to build a fort that was only completed at the cost of much sickness and suffering. The rivalry between the Spaniards and the Portuguese added fuel to the chronic war between Ternate and Tidor, and De Brito made matters still worse by offering a piece of cloth for the head of every Tidor islander brought in. A peace between the two islands was concluded in 1524, but the Portuguese considered it contrary to their interests; they poisoned the King of Tidor, and in the confusion burned his capital. When therefore a fresh expedition which had left Spain in 1525 reached Tidor they were received with open arms. The Spaniards, 300 in number, fortified themselves, and in December 1526 repulsed an attack of the Portuguese.

On August 22nd, 1526, a new Portuguese commander,

[1] An. Mar. e Col., Series 4, p. 112.

D. Jorge de Menezes, who had distinguished himself in the action in which Diogo Fernandes de Beja was killed, left Malacca. He took a new route to the Moluccas by the north of Borneo, in which island he touched at the capital of a Malay State, Brunei.[1] Menezes desired to make friends with the chief, and after his arrival at the Moluccas he sent a messenger with presents, among which was a piece of tapestry with life-sized figures representing the marriage of the Prince of Wales, afterwards Henry VIII, with Catherine of Aragon. The chief, seeing this in his room, believed that the figures were enchanted and that they would come to life at night and kill him to secure the Brunei State; the tapestry was removed and the messenger expelled. To return to De Menezes' voyage—after leaving Brunei he spent some time on the New Guinea coast, the first visit of the Portuguese to that island, and reached the Moluccas at the end of May 1527. D. Jorge de Menezes received charge of the Ternate fort without much difficulty from his predecessor, D. Garcia de Henriques, but directly after the two fell out over some carpenters whom both wanted. D. Jorge put the other in irons, and when D. Garcia was released he in turn put D. Jorge in irons, spiked the fort guns, and got clear off with the men and ships he wanted. A speedy boat reached Banda before he did, and enlisted the help of some Portuguese; when D. Garcia arrived there there was some fighting, one of his ships was taken, but he escaped with the others. He met with a hostile reception everywhere, and while he was waiting in doubt outside Cochin, his ships were sunk in a storm and he lost everything. He returned to Portugal a pauper and a prisoner.

As the number of Spaniards in Tidor was reduced by

[1] Hence the present name of the island.

disease to 40 they were no match for the force De Menezes could bring against them. About the end of 1528 they capitulated: some were sent to India, and the rest were deported to a neighbouring island[1] on the promise not to return to the Moluccas. Relieved from the fear of external enemies, D. Jorge could indulge unrestrained in his more brutal passions. The King of Ternate was poisoned, and his successor, a youth, was kept a close prisoner lest he should form a nucleus for resistance. One morning a China pig, much valued by its owner, the Captain, was found killed, and suspecting a near relative of the imprisoned king, a man of great religious reputation, De Menezes threw him into prison. A revolt of the whole population was only prevented by a release of the prisoner, but as he left, his face was smeared with bacon fat by the Captain's servant.[2] The news of this outrage spread at once over the island, and all intercourse with the garrison ceased. The condition of the Portuguese grew rapidly worse; owing to their ferocity no one would trade with them, and they had no money to buy supplies; while raiding parties treated the island as conquered territory and met with resistance. The ruffian De Menezes seized three headmen of a village where some Portuguese had been well beaten, cut off the hands of two and sent them back mutilated to the village. The fate of the third was worse; with his hands tied behind him he was thrown out alive to be worried to death by two savage dogs. Shortly after the regent, to whom the Portuguese owed everything, turned against them, was captured and beheaded, and the inhabitants left the island in a body. In February 1532 De Menezes was sent a prisoner to Portugal, when banishment

[1] Camafo is given as the name.

[2] A complaint to De Jorge produced the brutal jest that he should certainly punish his servant fer spoiling a good piece of bacon.

to the Brazils was all the punishment he received. His successor, Gonçalo Pereira, had reached Ternate in October of the previous year, and soon found himself in fresh troubles, though he showed his desire to be just by releasing the unfortunate king.

It was only the baser sort of Portuguese who wandered as far as the Moluccas, and they were not attracted by their pay, irregularly received. There was no trade, save that in cloves, by which they could enrich themselves, and the constant attempts to make this a royal monopoly were steadily resisted, the more so as it was known that it was not the king who would be benefited by such a monopoly, but some snugly berthed official who never risked his neck. Pereira was ruined by this question. Not content with issuing the royal proclamation, he seized the stores of cloves in private houses, and burnt publicly all weights and weighing machines, save one at the house of the King of Ternate and another at the Portuguese factory. The order enraged equally the natives who were debarred from benefiting by competition, and the Portuguese who were deprived of their livelihood. Owing to a conspiracy headed by Artur Lopes, chaplain of the fort, the captain was murdered on May 17th, 1532, and no one could be found to investigate the murder or even bury the body.

The mutineers made one Vicente d'Afonseca captain, but his new dignity was full of perils; he constantly wore a coat of mail, he never spoke to anyone except with his eyes fixed on him and his hand on his sword, and he never received anything, except from his own servants, save with his left hand, to leave his sword arm free. In October 1533 he was released from this position by the arrival of a new captain, Tristâo d'Ataide, but he was never punished for his participation in the mutiny. Ataide could only emulate—he could not surpass—the exploits of his predecessors. He affected to believe that the king was in a conspiracy to murder him, and got up a sham dispute between two Portuguese, whom he imprisoned. At his suggestion the king and his mother were induced to come to the fort to beg for mercy for the Portuguese, and when they came they were captured. A bastard was next raised to the throne, to the despair of his mother, who committed suicide on receipt of the dreadful news of his elevation. The king whom the Captain had imprisoned was sent to Goa, which he reached in 1536; there he became a Christian, was declared innocent and sent back to Ternate in 1545, but he died on the way, leaving by will his distracted island to the King of Portugal. An appeal of the royal family of Ternate to those of the neighbouring islands for help, brought the pitiless reply that they were suffering no more than they deserved for their crime in first welcoming the Portuguese to those seas. A general league of all the neighbouring tribes was, however, formed against the intruders, and the excitement was such that the recently converted Christians abandoned Christianity and reverted to the religion of their ancestors.

On October 25th, 1536, Antonio Galvâo, the last surviving son of Duarte Galvâo who died in the Red Sea in 1517, reached Ternate,[1] and his administration forms the one bright spot in the gloomy history of the connection of the Portuguese with the Moluccas. He was so far outwitted by the cunning of his predecessor that the latter carried away with him a large part of his garrison. He lost a portion of the remainder by his fidelity in obeying the King's order. One Joâo Mascarenhas came with a permit to load cloves, and, to get the help of the Captain, Galvâo was given a

[1] For his conduct on his outward voyage see Castanheda, Bk. 8, ch. 64. The same author's account of his administration of the Moluccas is almost idyllic, Bk. 8, c. 199.

share in the venture. Galvão at once refused to avail himself of this grant, but enforced the rest of the royal order. Mascarenhas was all but killed by the enraged Portuguese and had to remain in concealment on board his ship, and the stowing of the cargo was only effected by the personal exertions of Galvão. When this was complete, Galvão, hearing that a number of the Portuguese had determined to leave Ternate in Mascarenhas' vessel, sent a magistrate with his rod to warn the latter not to take away the garrison with him. Mascarenhas, thinking the man was coming to arrest him, kept him at a distance with matchlock bullets. The harassed official broke his rod, the order was not delivered, and Galvão lost a good part of his force.

In spite of the desertions, Galvão broke up the league of the natives against the Portuguese by dint of sheer hard fighting;[1] he then won over his defeated opponents by his justice. He used indifferently whatever weapon came to his hands. One expedition was led by a priest, Fernão Vinaigre, who, after defeating the enemy with carnal weapons, converted him with spiritual. One of his most popular acts was allowing the King of Ternate to marry, for no King had received this permission since the Portuguese had come to the country. Mindanao had been discovered in 1536, and an expedition which Galvão sent out under Francisco de Castro added materially to the knowledge of the Philippines. Galvão returned to Portugal poor because he would not enrich himself at the expense of the King, and died in neglect, after passing his last seventeen years in an almshouse, leaving only his debts and his voluminous writings behind him.[2] It was said of

[1] When it was necessary to sound for an anchorage close under a fort of the enemy, Galvão personally undertook the work rather than make over the perilous duty to a subordinate.

[2] A translation of one of his books, called Discoveries of the World, was published by the Hakluyt Society in 1863.

him that he was never made haughty by his success in the Moluccas, or soured by his neglect in Portugal.

The only other event of much importance in the Spice Islands was the arrival of another Spanish expedition, under the command of Ruy Lopes de Villa Lobas, in 1542, which suffered terribly from hunger and disease. The troops sent from India on receipt of the news of their arrival reached Ternate in November 1545. The Spaniards could not resist the superior force, and surrendered on the promise that they should be sent to India. Their Captain died shortly after.

China.—The Portuguese were from early days determined to discover China. In the sailing orders of Diogo Lopes de Sequiera, dated February 13th, 1508,[1] he is directed to enquire all about the "Chins," whether they were Christians and whether they were a powerful people. Sequiera seems to have seen their ships at Malacca, but Albuquerque was the first brought actually much into contact with them. He was able to do them some slight service, and in return they lent their boats to help land the Portuguese for the attack on Malacca, and when they left took an envoy, Duarte Fernandes, to Siam, whither they were bound. At the first meeting then all went well, and the first voyage also, of which we have any record, was equally successful. Fernâo Pires d'Andrade first left Malacca on August 12th, 1516, but the season was too far advanced and he had to return and make a fresh start in June 1517. He reached the mouth of the Canton river with 8 ships on August 15th, but, delayed on one pretext or another, did not reach the city until September. He carried a messenger to the Emperor of China, one Thomé Pires, an apothecary by

[1] An. Mar. e Col., Series 4. p. 479.

trade, who had been sent to India to collect drugs. It was more than two years, however, before Thomé Pires could get permission to make the journey to Pekin. Fernâo Pires left on his return with a very rich cargo in September 1518: his stay had not, owing to his discretion, been marked by any unpleasant incident. This expedition did not penetrate much further than Canton; one of the ships sailed to explore the Lew Chews, but failing to make good her passage, returned to the mainland at Fuhkien, where her traffic was as successful as that of her sister ships in Canton.

In August 1519 Simâo d'Andrade, brother of Fernâo Pires, made another voyage to Canton. He found Thomé Pires still awaiting permission to travel to Pekin,—a permission which arrived finally in January 1520. Simâo d'Andrade was a pompous braggart, he built a small fort and erected a gallows, and used the latter to hang one of his sailors—all acts which scandalized the Chinese feelings of sovereignty. He tried to prevent any ships of other nations getting cargo before his own, and he and his officers outraged the Chinese by freely buying boys and girls who, as it turned out, had been kidnapped. To crown all, on the death of the Emperor of China, Simâo refused to leave the port when ordered. Several Portuguese were killed in the streets of Canton, and although at the end of June 1521 they were successful in a naval skirmish, they had to leave on September 8th, 1521, fighting their way out to sea. Matters were left hopelessly embroiled, and every vessel reaching Chinese shores with a Portuguese on board was confiscated.

These events reacted on the unfortunate Thomé Pires. He reached Pekin, after a year's journey, in January 1521, but his reception was not encouraging. The news of the capture of Malacca, over which, through Siam, the

Chinese claimed some shadowy influence, and of the earlier proceedings of Simâo d'Andrade at Canton, had preceded him.[1] He was treated as a spy and refused even the privilege granted to other envoys, who were allowed to kneel and bow five times to the wall of the palace behind which the Emperor was said to be living. He was sent back to Canton with orders that he was to be imprisoned until Malacca was restored, and there after a few years he died.

The profits of the China voyage were, however, so great that the temptations to make it were irresistible. The Portuguese vessels were accustomed to lie off the coast near Fuhkien, and the barter was conducted at sea. In 1542 three Portuguese started from Siam on this voyage. They were caught in a typhoon off the Chinese coast and blown out of their reckonings. After several days they found themselves in an unknown country, where they were kindly treated and allowed to trade. This was the first visit to Japan made by Europeans.[2]

[1] His letters from the King of Portugal, as translated into Chinese, contained a request to the Emperor to grant the Kings of the Franks his seal, that is, make him his vassal.

[2] The history of the intercourse of the Portuguese with China and Japan increases in interest after the date chosen for the termination of this work.

INDEX

INDEX

A

B

C

D

E

F

G

H

I

J

K

L

M

Q

R

S

T

U

V

W

X

Y

Z

THE RISE OF PORTUGUESE POWER IN INDIA.

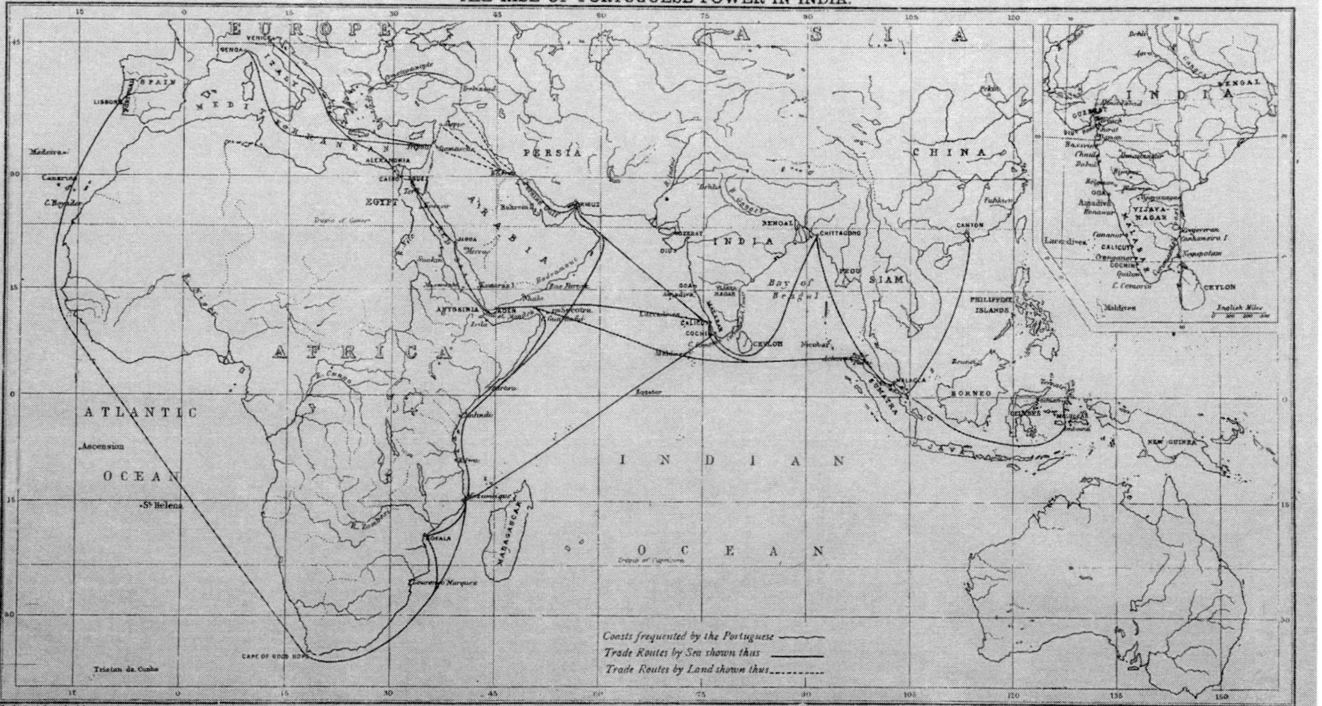